D0099165

Poor Economics

Poor Economics

A Radical Rethinking of the Way to Fight Global Poverty

ABHIJIT V. BANERJEE
AND ESTHER DUFLO

PUBLICAFFAIRS
New York

Published in the United States by PublicAffairs™, a Member of the Perseus Books Group.
All rights reserved.

Printed in the United States of America.

PublicAffairs books are available at special discounts for bulk purchases in the U.S. by corporations, institutions, and other organizations. For more information, please contact the Special Markets Department at the Perseus Books Group, 2300 Chestnut Street, Suite 200, Philadelphia, PA 19103, call (800) 810–4145, ext. 5000, or e-mail special.markets@perseusbooks.com.

Book Design by Jeff Williams

Library of Congress Cataloging-in-Publication Data
Banerjee, Abhijit V.
Poor economics : a radical rethinking of the way to fight global poverty / Abhijit V. Banerjee, Esther Duflo.
    p. cm.
    Includes index.
    Summary: "Billions of government dollars, and thousands of charitable organizations and NGOs, are dedicated to helping the world's poor. But much of the work they do is based on assumptions that are untested generalizations at best, flat out harmful misperceptions at worst. Banerjee and Duflo have pioneered the use of randomized control trials in development economics. Work based on these principles, supervised by the Poverty Action Lab at MIT, is being carried out in dozens of countries. Their work transforms certain presumptions: that microfinance is a cure-all, that schooling equals learning, that poverty at the level of 99 cents a day is just a more extreme version of the experience any of us have when our income falls uncomfortably low. Throughout, the authors emphasize that life for the poor is simply not like life for everyone else: it is a much more perilous adventure, denied many of the cushions and advantages that are routinely provided to the more affluent" —Provided by publisher.
    ISBN 978-1-58648-798-0 (hardback)
    1. Economic assistance—Developing countries. 2. Poverty—Prevention. I. Duflo, Esther, 1972- II. Title.

HC59.7.B323 2011
339.4'6091724—dc22

                                             2010050938

First Edition

10 9 8 7 6 5 4 3 2

Contents

For our mothers,
Nirmala Banerjee and
Violaine Duflo

Foreword

Esther was six when she read in a comic book on Mother Teresa that the city then called Calcutta was so crowded that each person had only 10 square feet to live in. She had a vision of a vast checkerboard of a city, with 3 feet by 3 feet marked out on the ground, each with a human pawn, as it were, huddled into it. She wondered what she could do about it.

When she finally visited Calcutta, she was twenty-four and a graduate student at MIT. Looking out of the taxi on her way to the city, she felt vaguely disappointed; everywhere she looked, there was empty space—trees, patches of grass, empty sidewalks. Where was all the misery so vividly depicted in the comic book? Where had all the people gone?

At six, Abhijit knew where the poor lived. They lived in little ramshackle houses behind his home in Calcutta. Their children always seemed to have lots of time to play, and they could beat him at any sport: When he went down to play marbles with them, the marbles would always end up in the pockets of their ragged shorts. He was jealous.

This urge to reduce the poor to a set of clichés has been with us for as long as there has been poverty: The poor appear, in social theory as much as in literature, by turns lazy or enterprising, noble or thievish, angry or passive, helpless or self-sufficient. It is no surprise that the policy stances that correspond to these views of the poor also tend to be captured in simple formulas: "Free markets for the poor," "Make human rights substantial," "Deal with conflict first," "Give more money to the poorest," "Foreign aid kills development," and the like. These ideas all have important elements of truth, but they rarely have much space for average poor women or men, with their hopes and doubts, limitations and aspirations, beliefs and confusion. If the poor appear at all, it is usually as the dramatis personae of some uplifting anecdote or tragic episode, to be admired or pitied, but not as a source of knowledge, not as people to be consulted about what they think or want or do.

All too often, the economics of poverty gets mistaken for poor economics: Because the poor possess very little, it is assumed that there is nothing interesting about their economic existence. Unfortunately, this misunderstanding severely undermines the fight against global poverty: Simple problems beget simple solutions. The field of anti-poverty policy is littered with the detritus of instant miracles that proved less than miraculous. To progress, we have to abandon the habit of reducing the poor to cartoon characters and take the time to really understand their lives, in all their complexity and richness. For the past fifteen years, we have tried to do just that.

We are academics, and like most academics we formulate theories and stare at data. But the nature of the work we do has meant that we have also spent months, spread over many years, on the ground working with NGO (nongovernmental organization) activists and government bureaucrats, health workers and microlenders. This has taken us to the back alleys and villages where the poor live, asking questions, looking for data. This book would not have been written but for the kindness of the people we met there. We were always treated as guests even though, more often than not, we had just walked in. Our questions were answered with patience, even when they made little sense; many stories were shared with us.[1]

Back in our offices, remembering these stories and analyzing the data, we were both fascinated and confused, struggling to fit what we were hearing and seeing into the simple models that (often Western or Western-trained) professional development economists and policy makers have traditionally used to think about the lives of the poor. More often than not, the weight of the evidence forced us to reassess or even abandon the theories that we brought with us. But we tried not to do so before we understood exactly why they were failing and how to adapt them to better describe the world. This book comes out of that interchange; it represents our attempt to knit together a coherent story of how poor people live their lives.

Our focus is on the world's poorest. The average poverty line in the fifty countries where most of the poor live is 16 Indian rupees per person per day.[2] People who live on less than that are considered to be poor by the government of their own countries. At the current exchange rate, 16 rupees corresponds to 36 U.S. cents. But because prices are lower in most developing countries, if the poor actually bought the things they do at U.S. prices, they would need to spend more— 99 cents. So to imagine the lives of the poor, you have to imagine having to live in Miami or Modesto with 99 cents per day for almost all your everyday needs (excluding housing). It is not easy—in India, for example, the equivalent amount would buy you fifteen smallish bananas, or about 3 pounds of low-quality rice. Can one live on that? And yet, around the world, in 2005, 865 million people (13 percent of the world's population) did.

What is striking is that even people who are that poor are just like the rest of us in almost every way. We have the same desires and weaknesses; the poor are no less rational than anyone else—quite the contrary. Precisely because they have so little, we often find them putting much careful thought into their choices: They have to be sophisticated economists just to survive. Yet our lives are as different as liquor and liquorice. And this has a lot to do with aspects of our own lives that we take for granted and hardly think about.

Living on 99 cents a day means you have limited access to information—newspapers, television, and books all cost money—and so you often just don't know certain facts that the rest of the world takes as given, like, for example, that vaccines can stop your child from getting measles. It means living in a world whose institutions are not built for someone like you. Most of the poor do not have a salary, let alone a retirement plan that deducts automatically from it. It means making decisions about things that come with a lot of small print when you cannot even properly read the large print. What does someone who cannot read make of a health insurance product that doesn't cover a lot of unpronounceable diseases? It means going to vote when your entire experience of the political system is a lot of promises, not delivered; and not having anywhere safe to keep your money, because what the bank manager can make from your little savings won't cover his cost of handling it. And so on.

All this implies that making the most of their talent and securing their family's future take that much more skill, willpower, and commitment for the poor. And conversely, the small costs, the small barriers, and the small mistakes that most of us do not think twice about loom large in their lives.

It is not easy to escape from poverty, but a sense of possibility and a little bit of well-targeted help (a piece of information, a little nudge) can sometimes have surprisingly large effects. On the other hand, misplaced expectations, the lack of faith where it is needed, and seemingly minor hurdles can be devastating. A push on the right lever can make a huge difference, but it is often difficult to know where that lever is. Above all, it is clear that no single lever will solve every problem.

Poor Economics is a book about the very rich economics that emerges from understanding the economic lives of the poor. It is a book about the kinds of theories that help us make sense of both what the poor are able to achieve, and where and for what reason they need a push. Each chapter in this book describes a search to discover what these sticking points are, and how they can be overcome. We open with the essential aspects of people's family lives: what they buy; what they do about their children's schooling, their own health, or that of their children or parents; how many children they choose to have; and so on. Then we go on to describe how markets and institutions work for the poor: Can they borrow, save, insure themselves against the risks they face? What do governments do for them, and when do they fail them? Throughout, the book returns to the same basic questions. Are there ways for the poor to improve their lives, and what is preventing them from being able to do these things? Is it more the cost of getting started, or is it easy to get started but harder to continue? What makes it costly? Do people sense the nature of the benefits? If not, what makes it hard for them to learn them?

Poor Economics is ultimately about what the lives and choices of the poor tell us about how to fight global poverty. It helps us understand, for example, why microfinance is useful without being the miracle some hoped it would be; why the poor often end up with health care that does them more harm than good; why children of the poor can go to school year after year and not learn anything; why the poor don't want health insurance. And it reveals why so many magic bullets of yesterday have ended up as today's failed ideas. The book also tells a lot about where hope lies: why token subsidies might have more than token effects; how to better market insurance; why less may be more in education; why good jobs matter for growth. Above all, it makes clear why hope is vital and knowledge critical, why we have to keep on trying even when the challenge looks overwhelming. Success isn't always as far away as it looks.

1

Think Again, Again

E very year, 9 million children die before their fifth birthday.[1] A woman in sub-Saharan Africa has a one-in-thirty chance of dying while giving birth—in the developed world, the chance is one in 5,600. There are at least twenty-five countries, most of them in sub-Saharan Africa, where the average person is expected to live no more than fifty-five years. In India alone, more than 50 million school-going children cannot read a very simple text.[2]

This is the kind of paragraph that might make you want to shut this book and, ideally, forget about this whole business of world poverty: The problem seems too big, too intractable. Our goal with this book is to persuade you not to.

A recent experiment at the University of Pennsylvania illustrates well how easily we can feel overwhelmed by the magnitude of the problem.[3] Researchers gave students $5 to fill out a short survey. They then showed them a flyer and asked them to make a donation to Save the Children, one of the world's leading charities. There were two different flyers. Some (randomly selected) students were shown this:

Food shortages in Malawi are affecting more than 3 million children;
In Zambia, severe rainfall deficits have resulted in a 42% drop in maize

production from 2000. As a result, an estimated 3 million Zambians face hunger; Four million Angolans—one third of the population— have been forced to flee their homes; More than 11 million people in Ethiopia need immediate food assistance.

Other students were shown a flyer featuring a picture of a young girl and these words:

Rokia, a 7-year-old girl from Mali, Africa, is desperately poor and faces a threat of severe hunger or even starvation. Her life will be changed for the better as a result of your financial gift. With your support, and the support of other caring sponsors, Save the Children will work with Rokia's family and other members of the community to help feed her, provide her with education, as well as basic medical care and hygiene education.

The first flyer raised an average of $1.16 from each student. The second flyer, in which the plight of millions became the plight of one, raised $2.83. The students, it seems, were willing to take some responsibility for helping Rokia, but when faced with the scale of the global problem, they felt discouraged.

Some other students, also chosen at random, were shown the same two flyers after being told that people are more likely to donate money to an identifiable victim than when presented with general information. Those shown the first flyer, for Zambia, Angola, and Mali, gave more or less what that flyer had raised without the warning—$1.26. Those shown the second flyer, for Rokia, after this warning gave only $1.36, less than half of what their colleagues had committed without it. Encouraging students to think again prompted them to be less generous to Rokia, but not more generous to everyone else in Mali.

The students' reaction is typical of how most of us feel when we are confronted with problems like poverty. Our first instinct is to be generous, especially when facing an imperiled seven-year-old girl. But, like the Penn students, our second thought is often that there is really no point: Our contribution would be a drop in the bucket, and the bucket probably leaks. This book is an invitation to think again, *again*: to turn away from the feeling that the fight against poverty is too overwhelming, and to start to think of the challenge as a set of concrete problems that, once properly identified and understood, can be solved one at a time.

Unfortunately, this is not how the debates on poverty are usually framed. Instead of discussing how best to fight diarrhea or dengue, many of the most vocal experts tend to be fixated on the "big questions": What is the ultimate cause of poverty? How much faith should we place in free markets? Is democracy good for the poor? Does foreign aid have a role to play? And so on.

Jeffrey Sachs, adviser to the United Nations, director of the Earth Institute at Columbia University in New York City, and one such expert, has an answer to all these questions: Poor countries are poor because they are hot, infertile, malaria infested, often landlocked; this makes it hard for them to be productive without an initial large investment to help them deal with these endemic problems. But they cannot pay for the investments precisely because they are poor—they are in what economists call a "poverty trap." Until something is done about these problems, neither free markets nor democracy will do very much for them. This is why foreign aid is key: It can kick-start a virtuous cycle by helping poor countries invest in these critical areas and make them more productive. The resulting higher incomes will generate further investments; the beneficial spiral will continue. In his bestselling 2005 book, *The End of Poverty*,[4] Sachs argues that if the rich world had committed $195 billion in foreign aid per year between 2005 and 2025, poverty could have been entirely eliminated by the end of this period.

But then there are others, equally vocal, who believe that all of Sachs's answers are wrong. William Easterly, who battles Sachs from New York University at the other end of Manhattan, has become one of the most influential anti-aid public figures, following the publication of two books, *The Elusive Quest for Growth* and *The White Man's Burden*.[5] Dambisa Moyo, an economist who previously worked at Goldman Sachs and at the World Bank, has joined her voice to Easterly's with her recent book, *Dead Aid*.[6] Both argue that aid does more bad than good: It prevents people from searching for their own solutions, while corrupting and undermining local institutions and creating a self-perpetuating lobby of aid agencies. The best bet for poor countries is to rely on one simple idea: When markets are free and the incentives are right, people can find ways to solve their problems. They do not need handouts, from foreigners or from their own governments. In this sense, the aid pessimists are actually quite optimistic about the way the world works. According to Easterly, there are no such things as poverty traps.

Whom should we believe? Those who tell us that aid can solve the problem? Or those who say that it makes things worse? The debate cannot be solved in the abstract: We need evidence. But unfortunately, the kind of data usually used to answer the big questions does not inspire confidence. There is never a shortage of compelling anecdotes, and it is always possible to find at least one to support any position. Rwanda, for example, received a lot of aid money in the years immediately after the genocide, and prospered. Now that the economy is thriving, President Paul Kagame has started to wean the country off aid. Should we count Rwanda as an example of the good that aid can do (as Sachs suggests), or as a poster child for self-reliance (as Moyo presents it)? Or both?

Because individual examples like Rwanda cannot be pinned down, most researchers trying to answer the big philosophical questions prefer multicountry comparisons. For example, the data on a couple of hundred countries in the world show that those that received more aid did not grow faster than the rest. This is often interpreted as evidence that aid does not work, but in fact, it could also mean the opposite. Perhaps the aid helped them avoid a major disaster, and things would have been much worse without it. We simply do not know; we are just speculating on a grand scale.

But if there is really no evidence for or against aid, what are we supposed to do—give up on the poor? Fortunately, we don't need to be quite so defeatist. There are in fact answers—indeed, this whole book is in the form of an extended answer—it is just that they are not the kind of sweeping answers that Sachs and Easterly favor. This book will not tell you whether aid is good or bad, but it will say whether particular instances of aid did some good or not. We cannot pronounce on the efficacy of democracy, but we do have something to say about whether democracy could be made more effective in rural Indonesia by changing the way it is organized on the ground and so on.

In any case, it is not clear that answering some of these big questions, like whether foreign aid works, is as important as we are sometimes led to believe. Aid looms large for those in London, Paris, or Washington, DC, who are passionate about helping the poor (and those less passionate, who resent paying for it). But in truth, aid is only a very small part of the money that is spent on the poor every year. Most programs targeted at the world's poor are funded out of their country's own resources. India, for example, receives essentially no aid. In 2004–2005, it spent half a trillion rupees ($31 billion USD PPP)[7] just on primary-education programs for the poor. Even in Africa, where foreign aid has a much more important role, it represented only 5.7 percent of total government budgets in 2003 (12 percent if we exclude Nigeria and South Africa, two big countries that receive very little aid).[8]

More important, the endless debates about the rights and wrongs of aid often obscure what really matters: not so much where the money comes from, but where it goes. This is a matter of choosing the right kind of project to fund—should it be food for the indigent, pensions for the elderly, or clinics for the ailing?—and then figuring out how best to run it. Clinics, for example, can be run and staffed in many different ways.

No one in the aid debate really disagrees with the basic premise that we should help the poor when we can. This is no surprise. The philosopher Peter Singer has written about the moral imperative to save the lives of those we don't know. He observes that most people would willingly sacrifice a $1,000 suit to rescue a child seen drowning in a pond[9] and argues that there should be no difference between that drowning child and the 9 million children who, every year, die before their fifth birthday. Many people would also agree with Amartya Sen, the economist-philosopher and Nobel Prize Laureate, that poverty leads to an intolerable waste of talent. As he puts it, poverty is not just a lack of money; it is not having the capability to realize one's full potential as a human being.[10] A poor girl from Africa will probably go to school for at most a few years even if she is brilliant, and most likely won't get the nutrition to be the world-class athlete she might have been, or the funds to start a business if she has a great idea.

It is true that this wasted life probably does not directly affect people in the developed world, but it is not impossible that it might: She might end up as an HIV-positive prostitute who infects a traveling American who then brings the disease home, or she might develop a strain of antibiotic-resistant TB that will eventually find its way to Europe. Had she gone to school, she might have turned out to be the person who invented the cure for Alzheimer's. Or perhaps, like Dai Manju, a Chinese teenager who got to go to school because of a clerical error at a bank, she would end up as a business tycoon employing thousands of others (Nicholas Kristof and Sheryl WuDunn tell her story in their book *Half the Sky*).[11] And even if she doesn't, what could justify not giving her a chance?

The main disagreement shows up when we turn to the question, "Do we know of effective ways to help the poor?" Implicit in Singer's argument for helping others is the idea that you know how to do it: The moral imperative to ruin your suit is much less compelling if you do not know how to swim. This is why, in *The Life You Can Save*, Singer takes the trouble to offer his readers a list of concrete examples of things that they should support, regularly updated on his Web site.[12] Kristof and WuDunn do the same. The point is simple: Talking about the problems of the world without talking about some accessible solutions is the way to paralysis rather than progress.

This is why it is really helpful to think in terms of concrete problems which can have specific answers, rather than foreign assistance in general: "aid" rather than "Aid." To take an example, according to the World Health Organization (WHO), malaria caused almost 1 million deaths in 2008, mostly among African children.[13] One thing we know is that sleeping under insecticide-treated bed nets can help save many of these lives. Studies have shown that in areas where malaria infection is common, sleeping under an insecticide-treated bed net reduces the incidence of malaria by half.[14] What, then, is the *best* way to make sure that children sleep under bed nets?

For approximately $10, you can deliver an insecticide-treated net to a family and teach the household how to use it. Should the government or an NGO give parents free bed nets, or ask them to buy their own, perhaps at a subsidized price? Or should we let them buy it in the market at full price? These questions can be answered, but the answers are by no means obvious. Yet many "experts" take strong positions on them that have little to do with evidence.

Because malaria is contagious, if Mary sleeps under a bed net, John is less likely to get malaria—if at least half the population sleeps under a net, then even those who do not have much less risk of getting infected.[15] The problem is that fewer than one-fourth of kids at risk sleep under a net:[16] It looks like the $10 cost is too much for many families in Mali or Kenya. Given the benefits both to the user and others in the neighborhood, selling the nets at a discount or even giving them away would seem to be a good idea. Indeed, free bed-net distribution is one thing that Jeffrey Sachs advocates. Easterly and Moyo object, arguing that people will not value (and hence will not use) the nets if they get them for free. And even if they do, they may become used to handouts and refuse to buy more nets in the future, when they are not free, or refuse to buy other things that they need unless these are also subsidized. This could wreck well-functioning markets. Moyo tells the story of how a bed-net supplier was ruined by a free bed-net distribution program. When free distribution stopped, there was no one to supply bed nets at any price.

To shed light on this debate, we need to answer three questions. First, if people must pay full price (or at least a significant fraction of the price) for a bed net, will they prefer to go without? Second, if bed nets are given to them free or at some subsidized price, will people use them, or will they be wasted? Third, after getting the net at subsidized price once, will they become more or less willing to pay for the next one if the subsidies are reduced in the future?

To answer these questions, we would need to observe the behavior of comparable groups of people facing different levels of subsidy. The key word here is "comparable." People who pay for bed nets and people who get them for free are usually not going to be alike: It is possible that those who paid for their nets will be richer and better educated, and have a better understanding of why they need a bed net; those who got them for free might have been chosen by an NGO precisely because they were poor. But there could also be the opposite pattern: Those who got them for free are the well connected, whereas the poor and isolated had to pay full price. Either way, we cannot draw any conclusion from the way they used their net.

For this reason, the cleanest way to answer such questions is to mimic the randomized trials that are used in medicine to evaluate the effectiveness of new drugs. Pascaline Dupas, of the University of California at Los Angeles, carried out such an experiment in Kenya, and others followed suit with similar experiments in Uganda and Madagascar.[17] In Dupas's experiment, individuals were randomly selected to receive different levels of subsidy to purchase bed nets. By comparing the behavior of randomly selected equivalent groups that were offered a net at different prices, she was able to answer all three of our questions, at least in the context in which the experiment was carried out.

In Chapter 3 of this book, we will have a lot to say about what she found. Although open questions remain (the experiments do not yet tell us about whether the distribution of subsidized imported bed nets hurt local producers, for example), these findings did a lot to move this debate and influenced both the discourse and the direction of policy.

The shift from broad general questions to much narrower ones has another advantage. When we learn about whether poor people are willing to pay money for bed nets, and whether they use them if they get them for free, we learn about much more than the best way to distribute bed nets: We start to understand how poor people make decisions. For example, what stands in the way of more widespread bed net adoption? It could be a lack of information about their benefits, or the fact that poor people cannot afford them. It could also be that the poor are so absorbed by the problems of the present that they don't have the mental space to worry about the future, or there could be something entirely different going on. Answering these questions, we get to understand what, if anything, is special about the poor: Do they just live like everyone else, except with less money, or is there something fundamentally different about life under extreme poverty? And if it is something special, is it something that could keep the poor trapped in poverty?

TRAPPED IN POVERTY?

It is no accident that Sachs and Easterly have radically opposite views on whether bed nets should be sold or given away. The positions that most rich-country experts take on issues related to development aid or poverty tend to be colored by their specific worldviews even when there seem to be, as with the price of the bed nets, concrete questions that should have precise answers. To caricature ever so slightly, on the left of the political spectrum, Jeff Sachs (along with the UN, the World Health Organization, and a good part of the aid establishment) wants to spend more on aid, and generally believes that things (fertilizer, bed nets, computers in school, and so on) should be given away and that poor people should be enticed to do what we (or Sachs, or the UN) think is good for them: For example, children should be given meals at school to encourage their parents to send them to school regularly. On the right, Easterly, along with Moyo, the American Enterprise Institute, and many others, oppose aid, not only because it corrupts governments but also because at a more basic level, they believe that we should respect people's freedom—if they don't want something, there is no point in forcing it upon them: If children do not want to go to school it must be because there is no point in getting educated.

These positions are not just knee-jerk ideological reactions. Sachs and Easterly are both economists, and their differences, to a large extent, stem from a different answer to an economic question: Is it possible to get trapped in poverty? Sachs, we know, believes that some countries, because of geography or bad luck, are trapped in poverty: They are poor because they are poor. They have the potential to become rich but they need to be dislodged from where they are stuck and set on the way to prosperity, hence Sachs's emphasis on one big push. Easterly, by contrast, points out that many countries that used to be poor are now rich, and vice versa. If the condition of poverty is not permanent, he argues, then the idea of a poverty trap that inexorably ensnares poor countries is bogus.

The same question could also be asked about individuals. Can people be trapped in poverty? If this were the case, a onetime infusion of aid could make a huge difference to a person's life, setting her on a new trajectory. This is the underlying philosophy behind Jeffrey Sachs's Millennium Villages Project. The villagers in the fortunate villages get free fertilizer, school meals, working health clinics, computers in their school, and much more. Total cost: half a million dollars a year per village. The hope, according to the project's Web site, is that "Millennium Village economies can transition over a period from subsistence farming to self-sustaining commercial activity."[18]

On a video they produced for MTV, Jeffrey Sachs and actress Angelina Jolie visited Sauri, in Kenya, one of the oldest millennium villages. There they met Kennedy, a young farmer. He was given free fertilizer, and as a result, the harvest from his field was twenty times what it had been in previous years. With the savings from that harvest, the video concluded, he would be able to support himself forever. The implicit argument was that Kennedy was in a poverty trap in which he could not afford fertilizer: The gift of fertilizer freed him. It was the only way he could escape from the trap.

But, skeptics could object that if fertilizer is really so profitable, why could Kennedy not have bought just a little bit of it and put it on the most suitable part of his field? This would have raised the yield, and with the extra money generated, he could have bought more fertilizer the following year, and so on. Little by little, he would have become rich enough to be able to put fertilizer on his entire field.

So is Kennedy trapped in poverty, or is he not?

The answer depends on whether the strategy is feasible: Buy just a little to start with, make a little extra money, and then reinvest the proceeds, to make even more money, and repeat. But maybe fertilizer is not easy to buy in small quantities. Or perhaps it takes several tries before you can get it to work. Or there are problems with reinvesting the gains. One could think of many reasons why a farmer might find it difficult to get started on his own.

We will postpone trying to get to the heart of Kennedy's story until Chapter 8. But this discussion helps us see a general principle. There will be a poverty trap whenever the scope for *growing income or wealth at a very fast rate* is limited for those who have too little to invest, but expands dramatically for those who can invest a bit more. On the other hand, if the potential for fast growth is high among the poor, and then tapers off as one gets richer, there is no poverty trap.

Economists love simple (some would say simplistic) theories, and they like to represent them in diagrams. We are no exception: There are two diagrams shown below that we think are helpful illustrations of this debate about the nature of poverty. The most important thing to remember from them is the shape of the curves: We will return to these shapes a number of times in the book.

For those who believe in poverty traps, the world looks like Figure 1. Your income today influences what your income will be in the future (the future could be tomorrow, next month, or even the next generation): What you have today determines how much you eat, how much you have to spend on medicine or on the education of your children, whether or not you can buy fertilizer or improved seeds for your farm, and all this determines what you will have tomorrow.

The shape of the curve is key: It is very flat at the beginning, and then rises rapidly, before flattening out again. We will call it, with some apologies to the English alphabet, the *S-shape curve*.

The S-shape of this curve is the source of the poverty trap. On the diagonal line, income today is equal to income tomorrow. For the very poor who are in the *poverty trap zone*, income in the future is lower than income today: The curve is below the diagonal line. This means that over time, those in this zone become poorer and poorer, and they will eventually end up trapped in poverty, at point N. The arrows starting at point A1 represent a possible trajectory: from A1, move to A2, and then A3, and so forth. For those who start outside of the poverty trap zone, income tomorrow is higher than income today: Over time they become richer and richer, at least up to a point. This more cheerful destiny is represented by the arrow starting at point B1, moving to B2 and B3, and so forth.

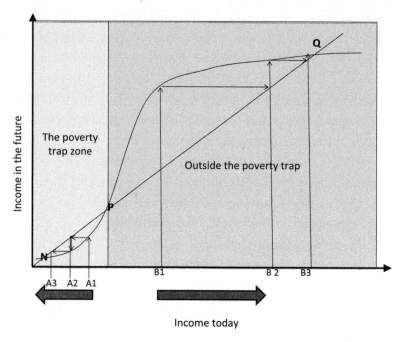

Figure 1: The S-Shape Curve and the Poverty Trap

Many economists (a majority, perhaps) believe, however, that the world usually looks more like Figure 2.

Figure 2 looks a bit like the right-hand side of Figure 1, but without the flat left side. The curve goes up fastest at the beginning, then slower and slower. There is no poverty trap in this world: Because the poorest people earn more than the income they started with, they become richer over time, until eventually their incomes stop growing (the arrows going from A1 to A2 to A3 depict a possible trajectory). This income may not be very high, but the point is that there is relatively little we need or can do to help the poor. A onetime gift in this world (say, giving someone enough income that, instead of starting with A1 today, he or she start with A2) will not boost anyone's income permanently. At best, it can just help them move up a little bit faster, but it cannot change where they are eventually headed.

So which of these diagrams best represents the world of Kennedy, the young Kenyan farmer? To know the answer to this question we need

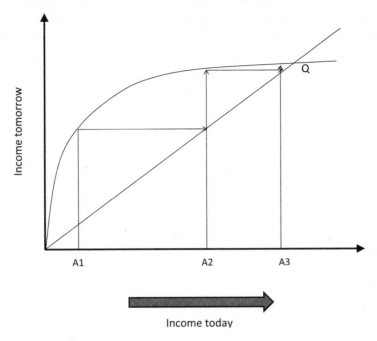

Figure 2: The Inverted L-Shape: No Poverty Trap

to find out a set of simple facts, such as: Can one buy fertilizer in small quantities? Is there something that makes it hard to save between planting seasons, so that even if Kennedy can make money in one season, he cannot turn it into further investment? The most important message from the theory embedded in the simple diagrams is thus that theory is not enough: To really answer the question of whether there are poverty traps, we need to know whether the real world is better represented by one graph, or by the other. And we need to make this assessment case by case: If our story is based on fertilizer, we need to know some facts about the market for fertilizer. If it is about savings, we need to know how the poor save. If the issue is nutrition and health, then we need to study those. The lack of a grand universal answer might sound vaguely disappointing, but in fact it is exactly what a policy maker should want to know—not that there are a million ways that the poor are trapped but that there are a few key factors that create the trap, and that alleviating those particular problems could set them free and point them toward a virtuous cycle of increasing wealth and investment.

This radical shift in perspective, away from the universal answers, required us to step out of the office and look more carefully at the world. In doing so, we were following a long tradition of development economists who have emphasized the importance of collecting the right data to be able to say anything useful about the world. However, we had two advantages over the previous generations: First, there are now high-quality data from a number of poor countries that were not available before. Second, we have a new, powerful tool: randomized control trials (RCTs), which give researchers, working with a local partner, a chance to implement large-scale experiments designed to test their theories. In an RCT, as in the studies on bed nets, individuals or communities are randomly assigned to different "treatments"—different programs or different versions of the same program. Since the individuals assigned to different treatments are exactly comparable (because they were chosen at random), any difference between them is the effect of the treatment.

A single experiment does not provide a final answer on whether a program would universally "work." But we can conduct a series of experiments, differing in either the kind of location in which they are conducted or the exact intervention being tested (or both). Together, this allows us to both verify the robustness of our conclusions (Does what works in Kenya also work in Madagascar?) and narrow the set of possible theories that can explain the data (What is stopping Kennedy? Is it the price of fertilizer or the difficulty of saving money?). The new theory can help us design interventions and new experiments, and help us make sense of previous results that may have been puzzling before. Progressively, we obtain a fuller picture of how the poor really live their lives, where they need help, and where they don't.

In 2003, we founded the Poverty Action Lab (which later became the Abdul Latif Jameel Poverty Action Lab, or J-PAL) to encourage and support other researchers, governments, and nongovernmental organizations to work together on this new way of doing economics, and to help diffuse what they have learned among policy makers. The response has been overwhelming. By 2010, J-PAL researchers had completed or were engaged in over 240 experiments in forty countries around the world, and very large numbers of organizations, researchers, and policy makers have embraced the idea of randomized trials.

The response to J-PAL's work suggests that there are many who share our basic premise—that it is possible to make very significant progress against the biggest problem in the world through the accumulation of a set of small steps, each well thought out, carefully tested, and judiciously implemented. This might seem self-evident, but as we will argue throughout the book, it is not how policy usually gets made. The practice of development policy, as well as the accompanying debates, seems to be premised on the impossibility of relying on evidence: Verifiable evidence is a chimera, at best a distant fantasy, at worst a distraction. "We have to get on with the work, while you indulge yourselves in the pursuit of evidence," is what hardheaded policy makers and their even harder-headed advisers often told us when we started down this path. Even today, there are many who hold this view. But there are also many people who have always felt disempowered by this unreasoned urgency. They feel, as we do, that the best anyone can do is to understand deeply the specific problems that afflict the poor and to try to identify the most effective ways to intervene. In some instances, no doubt, the best option will be to do nothing, but there is no general rule here, just as there is no general principle that spending money always works. It is the body of knowledge that grows out of each specific answer and the understanding that goes into those answers that give us the best shot at, one day, ending poverty.

This book builds on that body of knowledge. A lot of the material that we will talk about comes from RCTs conducted by us and others, but we also make use of many other types of evidence: qualitative and quantitative descriptions of how the poor live, investigations of how specific institutions function, and a variety of evidence on which policies have worked and which have not. In the companion Web site for the book, www.pooreconomics.com, we provide links to all the studies we cite, photographic essays that illustrate each chapter, and extracts and charts from a data set on key aspects of the lives of those who live on less than 99 cents per person per day in eighteen countries, which we will refer to many times in the book.

The studies we use have in common a high level of scientific rigor, openness to accepting the verdict of the data, and a focus on specific, concrete questions of relevance to the lives of the poor. One of the questions that we will use these data to answer is when and where we should worry about poverty traps; we will find them in some areas, but not in others. In order to design effective policy, it is crucial that we get answers to such questions right. We will see many instances in the chapters that follow where the wrong policy was chosen, not out of bad intentions or corruption, but simply because the policy makers had the wrong model of the world in mind: They thought there was a poverty trap somewhere and there was none, or they were ignoring another one that was right in front of them.

The message of this book, however, goes well beyond poverty traps. As we will see, ideology, ignorance, and inertia—the three Is—on the part of the expert, the aid worker, or the local policy maker, often explain why policies fail and why aid does not have the effect it should. It is possible to make the world a better place—probably not tomorrow, but in some future that is within our reach—but we cannot get there with lazy thinking. We hope to persuade you that our patient, step-by-step approach is not only a more effective way to fight poverty, but also one that makes the world a more interesting place.

PART I

Private Lives

2

A Billion Hungry People?

For many of us in the West, poverty is almost synonymous with hunger. Other than major natural catastrophes such as the Boxing Day tsunami in 2004 or the Haiti earthquake in 2010, no single event affecting the world's poor has captured the public imagination and prompted collective generosity as much as the Ethiopian famine of the early 1980s and the resulting "We Are the World" concert in March 1985. More recently, the announcement by the UN Food and Agriculture Organization (FAO) in June 2009 that more than a billion people are suffering from hunger[1] grabbed the headlines, in a way that the World Bank's estimates of the number of people living under a dollar a day never did.

This association of poverty and hunger is institutionalized in the UN's first Millennium Development Goal (MDG), which is "to reduce poverty and hunger." Indeed, poverty lines in many countries were originally set to capture the notion of poverty based on hunger—the budget needed to buy a certain number of calories, plus some other indispensable purchases (such as housing). A "poor" person was essentially defined as someone without enough to eat.

It is no surprise, therefore, that a large part of governments' effort to help the poor is posited on the idea that the poor desperately need food, and that quantity is what matters. Food subsidies are ubiquitous in the Middle East: Egypt spent $3.8 billion in food subsidies in 2008–2009 (2 percent of the GDP).[2] Indonesia has the Rakshin Program, which distributes subsidized rice. Many states in India have a similar program: In Orissa, for example, the poor are entitled to 55 pounds of rice a month at about 4 rupees per pound, less than 20 percent of the market price. Currently, the Indian parliament is debating instituting a Right to Food Act, which would allow people to sue the government if they are starving.

The delivery of food aid on a massive scale is a logistical nightmare. In India, it is estimated that more than one-half of the wheat and over one-third of the rice get "lost" along the way, including a good fraction that gets eaten by rats.[3] If governments insist on such policy despite the waste, it is not only because hunger and poverty are assumed to go hand in hand: The inability of the poor to feed themselves properly is also one of the most frequently cited root causes of a poverty trap. The intuition is powerful: The poor cannot afford to eat enough; this makes them less productive and keeps them poor.

Pak Solhin, who lives in a small village in the province of Bandung, Indonesia, once explained to us exactly how such a poverty trap worked.

His parents used to have a bit of land, but they also had thirteen children and had to build so many houses for each of them and their families that there was no land left for cultivation. Pak Solhin had been working as a casual agricultural worker, which paid up to 10,000 rupiah per day ($2 USD PPP) for work in the fields. However, a recent hike in fertilizer and fuel prices had forced farmers to economize. According to Pak Solhin, the local farmers decided not to cut wages but to stop hiring workers instead. Pak Solhin became unemployed most of the time: In the two months before we met him in 2008, he had not found a single day of agricultural labor. Younger people in this situation could normally find work as construction workers. But, as he explained, he was too weak for the most physical work, too inexperienced for more skilled labor, and at forty, too old to be an apprentice: No one would hire him.

As a result, Pak Solhin's family—he and his wife, and their three children—were forced to take some drastic steps to survive. His wife left for Jakarta, approximately 80 miles away, where, through a friend, she found a job as a maid. But she did not earn enough to feed the children. The oldest son, a good student, dropped out of school at twelve and started as an apprentice on a construction site. The two younger children were sent to live with their grandparents. Pak Solhin himself survived on about 9 pounds of subsidized rice he got every week from the government and on fish that he caught from the edge of a lake (he could not swim). His brother fed him once in a while. In the week before we last spoke with him, he had had two meals a day for four days, and just one for the other three.

Pak Solhin appeared to be out of options, and he clearly attributed his problem to food (or, more precisely, the lack of it). It was his opinion that the landowning peasants had decided to fire their workers instead of cutting wages because they thought that with the recent rapid increases in food prices, a cut in wages would push workers into starvation, which would make them useless in the field. This is how Pak Solhin explained to himself the fact that he was unemployed. Although he was evidently willing to work, lack of food made him weak and listless, and depression was sapping his will to do something to solve his problem.

The idea of a nutrition-based poverty trap, which Pak Solhin explained to us, is very old. Its first formal statement in economics dates from 1958.[4]

The idea is simple. The human body needs a certain number of calories just to survive. So when someone is very poor, all the food he or she can afford is barely enough to allow for going through the motions of living and perhaps earning the meager income that the individual originally used to buy that food. This is the situation Pak Solhin saw himself in when we met him: The food he got was barely enough for him to have the strength to catch some fish from the bank.

As people get richer, they can buy more food. Once the basic metabolic needs of the body are taken care of, all that extra food goes into building strength, allowing people to produce much more than they need to eat merely to stay alive.

This simple biological mechanism creates an S-shaped relationship between income today and income tomorrow, very much as in Figure 1 in the previous chapter: The very poor earn less than they need to be able to do significant work, but those who have enough to eat can do serious agricultural work. This creates a poverty trap: The poor get poorer, and the rich get richer and eat even better, and get stronger and even richer, and the gap keeps increasing.

Although Pak Solhin's logical explanation of how someone might get trapped in starvation was impeccable, there was something vaguely troubling about his narrative. We met him not in war-infested Sudan or in a flooded area of Bangladesh, but in a village in prosperous Java, where, even after the increase in food prices in 2007–2008, there was clearly plenty of food available, and a basic meal did not cost much. He was clearly not eating enough when we met him, but he was eating enough to survive; why would it not pay someone to offer him the extra bit of nutrition that would make him productive in return for a full day's work? More generally, although a hunger-based poverty trap is certainly a logical possibility, how relevant is it in practice, for most poor people today?

ARE THERE REALLY A BILLION HUNGRY PEOPLE?

One hidden assumption in our description of the poverty trap is that the poor eat as much as they can. And indeed, it would be the obvious implication of an S-shaped curve based on a basic physiological mechanism: If there was any chance that by eating a bit more, the poor could start doing meaningful work and get out of the poverty trap zone, then they should eat as much as possible.

Yet, this is not what we see. Most people living with less than 99 cents a day do not seem to act as if they are starving. If they were, surely they would put every available penny into buying more calories. But they do not. In our eighteen-country data set on the lives of the poor, food represents from 36 to 79 percent of consumption among the rural extremely poor, and 53 to 74 percent among their urban counterparts.[5]

It is not because all the rest is spent on other necessities: In Udaipur, for example, we find that the typical poor household could spend up to 30 percent more on food than it actually does if it completely cut expenditures on alcohol, tobacco, and festivals. The poor seem to have many choices, and they don't elect to spend as much as they can on food.

This is evident from looking at how poor people spend any extra money that they happen upon. Although they clearly have some un-avoidable expenses (they need clothes, medicines, and so forth) to take care of first, if their livelihoods depended on getting extra calories, one would imagine that when a little bit more spendable money is avail-able, it would all go into food. The food budget should go up propor-tionally faster than total spending (since both go up by the same amount, and food is only a part of the total budget, it increases by a bigger proportion). However, this does not seem to be the case. In the Indian state of Maharashtra, in 1983 (much before India's recent suc-cesses—a majority of households then lived on 99 cents per person per day or less), even for the very poorest group, a 1 percent increase in overall expenditure translated into about a 0.67 percent increase in the total food expenditure.[6] Remarkably, the relationship was not very dif-ferent for the poorest individuals in the sample (who earned about 50 cents per day per person) and the richest (who earned around $3 per day per person). The Maharashtra case is pretty typical of the relation-ship between income and food expenditures the world over: Even among the very poor, food expenditures increase much less than one for one with the budget.

Equally remarkable, even the money that people spend on food is not spent to maximize the intake of calories or micronutrients. When very poor people get a chance to spend a little bit more on food, they don't put everything into getting more calories. Instead, they buy bet-ter-tasting, *more expensive* calories. For the poorest group in Maharash-tra in 1983, out of every additional rupee spent on food when income rose, about half went into purchasing more calories, but the rest went into more expensive calories. In terms of calories per rupee, the millets (*jowar* and *bajra*) were clearly the best buy. Yet only about two-thirds of the total spending on grains was on these grains, while another 30 percent was spent on rice and wheat, which cost on average about twice as much per calorie. In addition, the poor spent almost 5 percent of their total budget on sugar, which is both more expensive than grains as a source of calories and bereft of other nutritional value.

Robert Jensen and Nolan Miller found a particularly striking example of the "flight to quality" in food consumption.[7] In two regions of China, they offered randomly selected poor households a large subsidy on the price of the basic staple (wheat noodles in one region, rice in the other). We usually expect that when the price of something goes down, people buy more of it. The opposite happened. Households that received subsidies for rice or wheat consumed *less* of those two items and ate more shrimp and meat, even though their staples now cost less. Remarkably, overall, the caloric intake of those who received the subsidy did not increase (and may even have decreased), despite the fact that their purchasing power had increased. Neither did the nutritional content improve in any other sense. The likely explanation is that because the staple formed such a large part of the household budget, the subsidies had made them richer: If the consumption of the staple is associated with being poor (say, because it is cheap but not particularly tasty), feeling richer might actually have made them consume *less* of it. Once again, this suggests that at least among these very poor urban households, getting more calories was not a priority: Getting better-tasting ones was.[8]

What is happening to nutrition in India today is another puzzle. The standard media story about it is about the rapid rise of obesity and diabetes as the urban upper-middle classes get richer. However, Angus Deaton and Jean Dreze have shown that the real story of nutrition in India over the last quarter century is not that Indians are becoming fatter: It is that *they are in fact eating less and less.*[9] Despite rapid economic growth, there has been a sustained decline in per capita calorie consumption; moreover, the consumption of all other nutrients except fat also appears to have declined among all groups, even the poorest. Today, more than three-fourths of the population live in households whose per capita calorie consumption is less than 2,100 calories in urban areas and 2,400 in rural areas—numbers that are often cited as "minimum requirements" in India for individuals engaged in manual labor. It is still the case that richer people eat more than poorer people. But at all levels of income, the share of the budget devoted to food has declined. Moreover, the composition of the food basket has changed, so that the same amount of money is now spent on more expensive edibles.

The change is not driven by declining incomes; by all accounts, real incomes are increasing. Yet, though Indians are richer, they eat so much less at each level of income that they eat less on average today than they used to. Nor is it because of rising food prices—between the early 1980s and 2005, food prices declined relative to the prices of other things, both in rural and urban India. Although food prices have increased again since 2005, the decline in calorie consumption happened precisely when the price of food was going down.

So the poor, even those whom the Food and Agriculture Organization would classify as hungry on the basis of what they eat, do not seem to want to eat much more even when they can. Indeed, they seem to be eating less. What could be going on?

The natural place to start to unravel the mystery is to assume that the poor must know what they are doing. After all, they are the ones who eat and work. If they could indeed be tremendously more productive, and earn much more by eating more, then they probably would when they had the chance. So could it be that eating more doesn't actually make us particularly more productive, and as a result, there is no nutrition-based poverty trap?

One reason the poverty trap might not exist is that most people have enough to eat.

At least in terms of food availability, today we live in a world that is capable of feeding every person that lives on the planet. On the occasion of the World Food Summit in 1996, the FAO estimated that world food production in that year was enough to provide at least 2,700 calories per person per day.[10] This is the result of centuries of innovation in food supply, thanks no doubt to great innovations in agricultural science, but attributable also to more mundane factors such as the adoption of the potato into the diet after the Spanish discovered it in Peru in the sixteenth century and imported it to Europe. One study finds that potatoes may have been responsible for 12 percent of the global increase in population between 1700 and 1900.[11]

Starvation exists in today's world, but only as a result of the way the food gets shared among us. There is no absolute scarcity. It is true that if I eat a lot more than I need or, more plausibly, turn more of the corn into biofuels so that I can heat my pool, then there will be less for everybody else.[12] But, despite this, it seems that most people, even most very poor people, earn enough money to be able to afford an adequate diet, simply because calories tend to be quite cheap, except in extreme situations. Using price data from the Philippines, we calculated the cost of the cheapest diet sufficient to give 2,400 calories, including 10 percent calories from protein and 15 percent calories from fat. It would cost only 21 cents at PPP, very affordable even for someone living on 99 cents a day. The catch is, it would involve eating only bananas and eggs. . . . But it seems that so long as people are prepared to eat bananas and eggs when they need to, we should find very few people stuck on the left part of the S-shaped curve, where they cannot earn enough to be functional.

This is consistent with evidence from Indian surveys in which people were asked whether they had enough to eat (i.e., whether "everyone in the household got two square meals a day" or whether everyone eats "enough food every day"). The percentage of people who consider that they do not have enough food has dropped dramatically over time: from 17 percent in 1983 to 2 percent in 2004. So, perhaps people eat less because they are less hungry.

And perhaps they are really less hungry, despite eating fewer calories. It could be that because of improvements in water and sanitation, they are leaking fewer calories in bouts of diarrhea and other ailments. Or maybe they are less hungry because of the decline of heavy physical work—with the availability of drinking water in the village, women do not need to carry heavy loads for long distances; improvements in transportation have reduced the need to travel on foot; in even the poorest village, flour is now milled by the village miller using a motorized mill, instead of women grinding it by hand. Using the average calorie requirements calculated by the Indian Council of Medical Research for people engaged in heavy, moderate, or light activity, Deaton and Dreze note that the decline in calorie consumption over the last twenty-five years could be entirely explained by a modest decrease in the number of people engaged in physically heavy work for a large part of the day.

If most people are at the point where they are not starving, it is possible that the productivity gains from consuming more calories are relatively modest for them. It would then be understandable if people chose to do something else with their money, or move away from eggs and bananas toward a more exciting diet. Many years ago, John Strauss was looking for a clear case to demonstrate the role of calories in productivity. He settled on self-employed farmers in Sierra Leone, because they really have to work hard.[13] He found that the productivity of a worker on a farm increased at most by 4 percent when his calorie intake increased by 10 percent. Thus, even if people doubled their food consumption, their income would only increase by 40 percent. Furthermore, the shape of the relationship between calories and productivity was not an S-shape, but an inverted L-shape, as in Figure 2 in the previous chapter: The largest gains are obtained at low levels of food consumption. There is no steep jump in income once people start eating enough. This suggests that the very poor benefit more from eating extra calories than the less poor. This is precisely the type of situation where we would not see a poverty trap. So it is not because they don't eat enough that most people stay poor.

This is not to say that the logic of the hunger-based poverty trap is flawed. The idea that better nutrition would propel someone on the path to prosperity was almost surely very important at some point in history, and it may still be important in some circumstances today. The Nobel Prize Laureate and economic historian Robert Fogel calculated that in Europe during the Renaissance and the Middle Ages, food production did not provide enough calories to sustain a full working population. This could explain why there were large numbers of beggars—they were literally incapable of any work.[14] The pressure of just getting enough food to survive seems to have driven some people to take rather extreme steps: There was an epidemic of "witch" killing in Europe during the "little ice age" (from the mid-sixteenth century to 1800), when crop failures were common and fish was less abundant.

Witches were most likely to be single women, particularly widows. The logic of the S-shape suggests that when resources are tight, it makes "economic sense" to sacrifice some people, so that the rest have enough food to be able to work and earn enough to survive.[15]

Evidence that poor families might occasionally be forced to make such horrific choices is not hard to find even in more recent times. During droughts in India in the 1960s, little girls in landless households were much more likely to die than boys, but boys' and girls' death rates were not very different when there was normal rainfall.[16] Reminiscent of the witch hunt of the little ice age, Tanzania experiences a rash of "witch" killings whenever there is a drought—a convenient way to get rid of an unproductive mouth to feed at times where resources are very tight.[17] Families, it seems, suddenly discover that an older woman living with them (usually a grandmother) is a witch, after which she gets chased away or killed by others in the village.

So it is not that the lack of food could not be a problem or isn't a problem from time to time, but the world we live in today is for the most part too rich for it to be a big part of the story of the persistence of poverty. This is of course different during natural or man-made disasters, or in famines that kill and weaken millions. As Amartya Sen has shown, however, most recent famines have been caused not by lack of food availability but by institutional failures that led to poor distribution of the available food, or even hoarding and storage in the face of starvation elsewhere.[18]

Should we let it rest here, then? Can we assume that the poor, though they may be eating little, do eat as much as they need to?

ARE THE POOR REALLY
EATING WELL, AND EATING ENOUGH?

It is hard to avoid the feeling that the story does not add up. Can it be true that the poorest individuals in India are cutting back on food because they don't need the calories, given that they live in families that consume around 1,400 calories per capita per day to start with? After all, 1,200 calories is the famous semi-starvation diet, recommended for those who want rapid weight loss; 1,400 does not seem too far from there. According to the Centers for Disease Control, the average American male consumed 2,475 calories per day in 2000.[19]

It is true that the poorest in India are also smaller, and if one is small enough, one doesn't need as many calories. But doesn't that just push the question back one level? Why are the poorest in India so small? Indeed, why are all South Asians so scrawny? The standard way to measure nourishment status is by the Body Mass Index (BMI), which is essentially a way to scale weight by height (i.e., adjusting for the fact that taller people are going to be heavier). The international cutoff for being malnourished is a BMI of 18.5, with 18.5 to 25 being the normal range, and people beyond 25 considered obese. By this measure, 33 percent of men and 36 percent of women in India were undernourished in 2004–2005, down from 49 percent for both in 1989. Among the eighty-three countries that have demographic and health survey data, only Eritrea has more undernourished adult women.[20] Indian women, along with Nepalese and Bangladeshi women, are also among the shortest in the world.[21]

Is this something to be concerned about? Could this be something purely genetic about South Asians, like dark eyes or black hair, but irrelevant for their success in the world? After all, even the children of South Asian immigrants in the United Kingdom or the United States are smaller than Caucasian or black children. It turns out, however, that two generations of living in the West without intermarriage with other communities is enough to make the grandchildren of South Asian immigrants more or less the same height as other ethnicities. So although genetic makeup is certainly important at the individual level, the genetic differences in height between populations are believed to be minimal. If the children of first-generation mothers are still small, it is partly because women who were themselves malnourished in childhood tend to have smaller children.

Therefore, if South Asians are small, it is probably because they, and their parents, did not get as much nourishment as their counterparts in other countries. And indeed, everything suggests that children are very badly nourished in India. The usual measure of how well a child has been fed through the childhood years is height, compared to the international average height for that age. By this measure, the numbers for

India from the National Family Health Survey (NFHS 3) are devastating. Roughly half the children under five are stunted, which means that they are far below the norm. One-fourth of them are severely stunted, representing extreme nutritional deprivation. The children are also extraordinarily underweight *given their height:* About one in five children under three is wasted, which means they fall below the international definition of severe malnourishment. What makes these facts more striking is that the stunting and wasting rates in sub-Saharan Africa, undoubtedly the poorest area of the world, are only about half those in India.

But once again, should we care? Is being small a problem, in and of itself? Well, there are the Olympic Games. India, a country with a billion inhabitants, has won an average of 0.92 medals per Olympics, over the course of twenty-two Olympic Games, putting it just below Trinidad and Tobago, at 0.93. To put these numbers in perspective, China has won 386 medals in eight games, at an average of 48.3, and there are seventy-nine countries that average better than India. Yet India has ten times as many people as all but six of those countries.

Of course India is poor, but not as poor as it used to be, and not nearly as poor as Cameroon, Ethiopia, Ghana, Haiti, Kenya, Mozambique, Nigeria, Tanzania, and Uganda, each of which, per head, has more than ten times India's medal count. Indeed, no country that has fewer medals per Olympics than India is even one-tenth of its size, with two notable exceptions—Pakistan and Bangladesh. Bangladesh, in particular, is the only country of over 100 million people that has never won an Olympic medal. The next largest such country is Nepal.

There is clearly a pattern. One could perhaps blame the South Asian obsession with cricket—that colonial cousin of baseball that baffles most Americans—but if cricket is absorbing all the sporting talent of one-fourth of the world's population, the results are really not that impressive. South Asians have never had the dominance over cricket that Australia, England, and even the tiny West Indies had in their heydays, despite their intense fealty to the sport and their massive size advantage—Bangladesh, for example, is bigger than England, South Africa, Australia, New Zealand, and the West Indies put together. Given that child malnutrition is one other area where South Asia really stands out, it seems plausible that these two facts—wasted children and Olympian failure—have something to do with each other.

The Olympics are not the only place where height plays a role. In poor countries and rich countries alike, taller people do earn more. It has long been debated whether this is because height really matters for productivity—it could be discrimination against shorter people, for example. But a recent paper by Anne Case and Chris Paxson made some progress in nailing down what explains this relationship. They show that in the United Kingdom and the United States, the effect of height is entirely accounted for by differences in IQ: When we compare people who have the same IQ, there is no relationship between height and earning.[22] They interpret their findings as showing that what matters is good nutrition in early childhood: On average, adults who have been well nourished as children are both taller and smarter. And it is because they are smarter that they earn more. Of course, there are many not-so-tall people who are very bright (because they have reached the height they were meant to reach), but overall, tall people do better in life, because they are visibly more likely to have reached their genetic potential (both in height and in intelligence).

The study, when reported by Reuters under the not-so-subtle headline "Taller People Are Smarter—Study," created a firestorm. Case and Paxson were deluged by hostile e-mails. "Shame on you!" scolded one man (4 feet 9 inches). "I find your hypothesis insulting, prejudicial, inflammatory and bigoted," said another (5 feet 6 inches). "You have loaded a gun and pointed it at the vertically challenged man's head" (no height given).[23]

But in fact, there is a lot of evidence for the general view that childhood malnutrition directly affects the ability of adults to function successfully in the world. In Kenya, children who were given deworming pills in school for two years went to school longer and earned, as young adults, 20 percent more than children in comparable schools who received deworming for just one year: Worms contribute to anemia and general malnutrition, essentially because they compete with the child for nutrients.[24] A review study by some of the best experts on nutrition leaves little doubt that proper nutrition in childhood has far-reaching implications. They conclude: "Undernourished children are

— 31 —

more likely to become short adults, to have lower educational achievement, and to give birth to smaller infants. Undernutrition is also associated with lower economic status in adulthood."[25]

The impact of undernutrition on future life chances starts before birth. In 1995, the *British Medical Journal* coined the term "Barker Hypothesis" to refer to Dr. David Barker's theory that conditions in utero have long-term impact on a child's life chances.[26] There is considerable support for the Barker Hypothesis: To cite just one example, in Tanzania, children who were born to mothers who received sufficient amounts of iodine during pregnancy (because of an intermittent government program of distributing iodine capsules to would-be mothers) completed between one-third and one-half year more schooling, compared to their younger and older siblings who were in utero when the mother was not getting these capsules.[27] Although half a year of education might seem a small gain, it is a substantial increase, given that most of these children will complete only four or five years of schooling. In fact, based on their estimates, the study concludes that if every mother were to take iodine capsules, there would be a 7.5 percent increase in the total educational attainment of children in Central and Southern Africa. This, in turn, could affect the child's productivity throughout his or her life.

Although we saw that the impact of just increasing calories on productivity may not be very large per se, there are some ways to improve nutrition even for adults that will much more than pay for themselves. The one that we know most about is iron to treat anemia. In many Asian countries, including India and Indonesia, anemia is a major health problem. Six percent of men and 38 percent of women in Indonesia are anemic. The corresponding numbers in India are 24 percent and 56 percent. Anemia is associated with low aerobic capacity, general weakness and lethargy, and in some cases (especially for pregnant women) it can be life-threatening.

The Work and Iron Status Evaluation (WISE) study in Indonesia provided randomly chosen men and women in rural Indonesia with regular iron supplementation for several months, while the comparison group received a placebo.[28] The study found that the iron supplements made the men able to work harder, and the resulting increase in their income was many times the cost of a yearly supply of iron-fortified fish sauce. A year's supply of the fish sauce cost $7 USD PPP, and for a self-employed male, the yearly gain in earnings was $46 USD PPP—an excellent investment.

The puzzle is that people do not seem to want more food, and yet more food and especially more judiciously purchased food would probably make them, and almost certainly their children, significantly more successful in life. The key investments that would achieve this are not expensive. Most mothers could surely afford iodized salt, which is now standard in many parts of the world, or one dose of iodine every two years (at 51 cents per dose). In Kenya, when International Child Support, the NGO that was running the deworming program, asked the parents in some schools to pay a few cents for deworming their children, almost all of them refused, which deprived their children of hundreds of dollars of extra earning over their lifetime.[29] As for food, households could easily get a lot more calories and other nutrients by spending less on expensive grains (like rice and wheat), sugar, and processed foods, and more on leafy vegetables and coarse grains.

WHY DO THE POOR EAT SO LITTLE?

Who Knew?

Why did anemic Indonesian workers not buy iron-fortified fish sauce on their own? One answer is that it is not clear that the additional pro-ductivity translates into higher earnings if employers do not know that a well-nourished worker is more productive. Employers may not real-ize that their employees are more productive now because they have eaten more, or better. The Indonesian study found a significant increase in earnings *only* among self-employed workers. If the employers pay everyone the same flat wage, there would be no reason to eat more to get stronger. In the Philippines, a study found that workers who worked both for a piece rate and for a flat wage ate 25 percent more food on days they worked for piece rate (where effort mattered, since the more they worked, the more they got paid).

This does not explain why all pregnant women in India aren't using only iodine-fortified salt, which is now available for purchase in every village. A possibility is that people may not realize the value of feeding themselves and their children better. The importance of micronutrients was not fully understood, even by scientists, until relatively recently. Although micronutrients are cheap and can sometimes lead to a large increase in lifetime income, it is necessary to know exactly what to eat (or what pills to take). Not everyone has the information, even in the United States.

Moreover, people tend to be suspicious of outsiders who tell them that they should change their diet, probably because they like what they eat. When rice prices went up sharply in 1966–1967, the chief minister of West Bengal suggested that eating less rice and more vegetables would be both good for people's health and easier on their budget. This set off a flurry of protests, and the chief minister was greeted by protesters with garlands of vegetables wherever he went. Yet he was probably right. Understanding the importance of popular support, Antoine Parmentier, an eighteenth-century French pharmacist who was an early fan of the potato, clearly anticipating resistance, offered the public a set of recipes he had invented using potatoes, including the classic dish Hachis Parmentier (essentially what the British call shepherd's pie, a layered casserole composed of ground meat with a covering of mashed potatoes). He thereby set off a trajectory that ultimately led, through many twists and turns, to the invention of "freedom fries."

Also, it is not very easy to learn about the value of many of these nutrients based on personal experience. Iodine might make your children smarter, but the difference is not huge (though a number of small differences may add up to something big) and in most cases you will not find out either way for many years. Iron, even if it makes people stronger, does not suddenly turn you into a superhero: The $40 extra a year the self-employed man earned may not even have been apparent to him, given the many ups and downs of his weekly income.

Consequently, it is no surprise that the poor choose their foods not mainly for their cheap prices and nutritional values, but for how good they taste. George Orwell, in his masterful description of the life of poor British workers in *The Road to Wigan Pier*, observes:

The basis of their diet, therefore, is white bread and Margarine, corned beef, sugared tea, and potato—an appalling diet. Would it not be better if they spent more money on wholesome things like oranges and wholemeal bread, or if they even, like the reader of the *New States-man,* saved on fuel and ate their carrots raw? Yes it would, but the point is, no human being would ever do such a thing. The ordinary human being would sooner starve than live on brown bread and raw carrots. And the peculiar evil is this, that the less money you have the less you are inclined to spend it on wholesome food. A millionaire may enjoy breakfasting off orange juice and Ryvita biscuits; an unemployed man does not. . . . When you are unemployed, you don't *want* to eat dull wholesome food. You want to eat something a little *tasty*. There is always some cheap pleasant thing to tempt you.[30]

More Important Than Food

The poor often resist the wonderful plans we think up for them be-cause they do not share our faith that those plans work, or work as well as we claim. This is one of the running themes in this book. Another explanation for their eating habits is that other things are more impor-tant in the lives of the poor than food.

It has been widely documented that poor people in the developing world spend large amounts on weddings, dowries, and christenings, probably in part as a result of the compulsion not to lose face. The cost of weddings in India is well-known, but there are also less cheerful oc-casions when the family is compelled to throw a lavish party. In South Africa, social norms on how much to spend on funerals were set at a time when most deaths occurred in old age or in infancy.[31] Tradition called for infants to be buried very simply but for elders to have elabo-rate funerals, paid for with money the deceased had accumulated over a lifetime. As a result of the HIV/AIDS epidemic, many prime-age adults started dying without having accumulated burial savings, but their families felt compelled to honor the norm for adults. A family that had just lost one of its main potential earners might have to spend something like 3,400 rand (around $825 USD PPP), or 40 percent of the household annual per capita income, for the funeral party. After such a funeral, the family clearly has less to spend, and more family members tend to complain about "lack of food," even when the deceased was not earning before he died, which suggests that funeral costs are responsible. The more expensive the funeral, the more depressed the adults are one year later, and the more likely it is that children have dropped out of school.

Not surprisingly, both the king of Swaziland and the South African Council of Churches (SACC) have tried to regulate funeral expenditures. In 2002, the king simply banned lavish funerals[32] and announced that if a family was found to have slaughtered a cow for their funeral, they would have to give one cow to the chief's herd. The SACC, rather more soberly, called for a regulation of the funeral industry, which, they felt, was putting pressure on families to spend more than they could afford.

The decision to spend money on things other than food may not be due entirely to social pressure. We asked Oucha Mbarbk, a man we met in a remote village in Morocco, what he would do if he had more money. He said he would buy more food. Then we asked him what he would do if he had even more money. He said he would buy better-tasting food. We were starting to feel very bad for him and his family, when we noticed a television, a parabolic antenna, and a DVD player in the room where we were sitting. We asked him why he had bought all these things if he felt the family did not have enough to eat. He laughed, and said, "Oh, but television is more important than food!"

After spending some time in that Moroccan village, it was easy to see why he thought that. Life can be quite boring in a village. There is no movie theater, no concert hall, no place to sit and watch interesting strangers go by. And not a lot of work, either. Oucha and two of his neighbors, who were with him during the interview, had worked about seventy days in agriculture and about thirty days in construction that year. For the rest of the year, they took care of their cattle and waited for jobs to materialize. This left plenty of time to watch television. These three men all lived in small houses without water or sanitation. They struggled to find work, and to give their children a good education. But they all had a television, a parabolic antenna, a DVD player, and a cell phone.

Generally, it is clear that things that make life less boring are a priority for the poor. This may be a television, or a little bit of something special to eat—or just a cup of sugary tea. Even Pak Solhin had a television, although it was not working when we visited him. Festivals may be seen in this light as well. Where televisions or radios are not available, it is easy to see why the poor often seek out the distraction of a special family celebration of some kind, a religious observance, or a daughter's wedding. In our eighteen-country data set, it is clear that the poor spend more on festivals when they are less likely to have a radio or a television. In Udaipur, India, where almost no one has a television, the extremely poor spend 14 percent of their budget on festivals (which includes both lay and religious occasions). By contrast, in Nicaragua, where 56 percent of rural poor households have a radio and 21 percent own a television, very few households report spending anything on festivals.[33]

The basic human need for a pleasant life might explain why food spending has been declining in India. Today, television signals reach into remote areas, and there are more things to buy, even in remote villages. Cell phones work almost everywhere, and talk time is extremely cheap by global standards. This would also explain why countries with a large domestic economy, where a lot of consumer goods are available cheaply, like India and Mexico, tend to be the countries where food spending is the lowest. Every village in India has at least one small shop, usually more, with shampoo sold in individual sachets, cigarettes by the stick, very cheap combs, pens, toys, or candies, whereas in a country like Papua New Guinea, where the share of food in the household budget is above 70 percent (it is 50 percent in India), there may be fewer things available to the poor. Orwell captured this phenomenon as well in *The Road to Wigan Pier* when he described how poor families managed to survive the depression.

> Instead of raging against their destiny, they have made things tolerable by reducing their standards. But they don't necessarily reduce their

standards by cutting out luxuries and concentrating on necessities; more often it is the other way around—the more natural way, if you come to think of it—hence the fact that in a decade of unparalleled depression, the consumption of all cheap luxuries has increased.[34]

These "indulgences" are not the impulsive purchases of people who are not thinking hard about what they are doing. They are carefully thought out, and reflect strong compulsions, whether internally driven or externally imposed. Oucha Mbarbk did not buy his TV on credit—he saved up over many months to scrape enough money together, just as the mother in India starts saving for her eight-year-old daughter's wedding some ten years or more into the future, by buying a small piece of jewelry here and a stainless steel bucket there.

We are often inclined to see the world of the poor as a land of missed opportunities and to wonder why they don't put these purchases on hold and invest in what would really make their lives better. The poor, on the other hand, may well be more skeptical about supposed opportunities and the possibility of any radical change in their lives. They often behave as if they think that any change that is significant enough to be worth sacrificing for will simply take too long. This could explain why they focus on the here and now, on living their lives as pleasantly as possible, celebrating when occasion demands it.

SO IS THERE REALLY
A NUTRITION-BASED POVERTY TRAP?

We opened this chapter with Pak Solhin, and his view that he was caught in a nutrition-based poverty trap. At the most literal level, the main problem in his case was probably not a lack of calories. The Rakshin Program was providing him with some free rice, and between that and the help his brother was giving him, he would probably have been physically able to work in the field or on a construction site. Our reading of the evidence suggests that most adults, even the very poor, are outside of the nutrition poverty trap zone: They can easily eat as much as they need to be physically productive.

This was probably the case with Pak Solhin. This not to say that he was not trapped. But his problem may have come from the fact that his job had vanished, and he was too old to be taken as an apprentice on a construction site. His situation was almost surely made worse by the fact that he was depressed, which made it difficult for him to do anything at all.

The fact that the basic mechanics of a nutrition-based poverty trap do not seem to be at work for adults does not mean that nutrition is not a problem for the poor. But the problem may be less the quantity of food than its quality, and in particular the shortage of micronutrients. The benefits of good nutrition may be particularly strong for two sets of people who do not decide what they eat: unborn babies and young children. In fact, there may well be an S-shaped relationship between their parent's income and the eventual income of these children, caused by childhood nutrition. That is because a child who got the proper nutrients in utero or during early childhood will earn more money *every year of his or her life:* This adds up to large benefits over a lifetime. For example, the study of the long-term effect of deworming children in Kenya, mentioned above, concluded that being dewormed for two years instead of one (and hence being better nourished for two years instead of one) would lead to a lifetime income gain of $3,269 USD PPP. Small differences in investments in childhood nutrition (in Kenya, deworming costs $1.36 USD PPP per year; in India, a packet of iodized salt sells for $0.62 USD PPP; in Indonesia, fortified fish sauce costs $7 USD PPP per year) make a huge difference later on. This suggests that governments and international institutions need to completely rethink food policy. Although this may be bad news for American farmers, the solution is not to simply supply more food grains, which is what most food security programs are currently designed to do. The poor like subsidized grains, but as we discussed earlier, giving them more does little to persuade them to eat better, especially since the main problem is not calories, but other nutrients. It also is probably not enough just to provide the poor with more money, and even rising incomes will probably not lead to better nutrition in the short run. As we saw in India, the poor do not eat any more or any better when their income goes up; there are too many other pressures and desires competing with food.

In contrast, the social returns of directly investing in children and pregnant mother nutrition are tremendous. This can be done by giving away fortified foods to pregnant mothers and parents of small children, by treating children for worms in preschool or at school, by providing them with meals rich in micronutrients, or even by giving parents incentives to consume nutritional supplements. All of this is already being done in some countries. The government of Kenya is now systematically deworming children in school. In Colombia, micronutrient packets are sprinkled on kids' meals in preschool. In Mexico, social welfare payments come with free nutritional supplements for the family. Developing ways to pack *foods that people like to eat* with additional nutrients, and coming up with new strains of nutritious and tasty crops that can be grown in a wider range of environments, need to become priorities for food technology, on an equal footing with raising productivity. We do see some instances of this across the world, pushed by organizations such as the Micronutrient Initiative and HarvestPlus: A variety of orange sweet potatoes (richer in beta carotene than the native yam) suitable for Africa was recently introduced in Uganda and Mozambique.[35] A new salt, fortified both with iron and iodine, is now approved for use in several countries, including India. But there are all too many instances where food policy remains hung up on the idea that all the poor need is cheap grain.

3

Low-Hanging Fruit
for Better (Global) Health?

Health is an area of great promise but also great frustration.
There seems to be plenty of "low-hanging fruit" available,
from vaccines to bed nets, that could save lives at a minimal
cost, but all too few people make use of such preventive technologies.
Government health workers, who are in charge of delivering basic
health-care services in most countries, are often blamed for this failure,
not entirely unfairly, as we will see. They, on the other hand, insist that
plucking these low-hanging fruits is much harder than it seems.

In winter 2005 in the beautiful town of Udaipur in western India,
we had an animated discussion with a group of government nurses.
They were very upset with us because we were involved in a project
that aimed to get them to come to work more often. At some point in
the proceedings, one of them got so exasperated that she decided to be
blunt: The job was essentially pointless anyway, she announced. When a
child came to them with diarrhea, all they could offer the mother was
a packet of oral rehydration solution (or ORS, a mixture of salt, sugar,
potassium chloride, and an antacid to be mixed with water and drunk
by the child). But most mothers didn't believe that ORS could do any
good. They wanted what they thought was the right treatment—an

antibiotic or an intravenous drip. Once a mother was sent away from the health center with just a packet of ORS, the nurses told us, she never came back. Every year, they saw scores of children die from diarrhea, but they felt utterly powerless.

Of the 9 million children who die before their fifth birthdays each year, the vast majority are poor children from South Asia and sub-Saharan Africa, and roughly one in five dies of diarrhea. Efforts are under way to develop and distribute a vaccine against rotavirus, the virus responsible for many (though not all) of the cases of diarrhea. But three "miracle drugs" could already save most of these children: chlorine bleach, for purifying water; and salt and sugar, the key ingredients of the rehydration solution ORS. A mere $100 spent on chlorine packaged for household use can prevent thirty-two cases of diarrhea.[1] Dehydration is the main proxy cause of death from diarrhea, and ORS, which is close to being free, is a wonderfully effective way to prevent it.

Yet neither chlorine nor ORS is used very much. In Zambia, thanks to the efforts of Population Service International (PSI), a large organization that markets it at subsidized prices worldwide, chlorine is cheap and widely available. At the cost of 800 kwachas ($0.18 USD PPP), a family of six can buy enough bleach to purify its water supply, avoiding waterborne diarrhea. But only 10 percent of families use it.[2] In India, according to the United Nations Children's Fund (UNICEF), only one-third of children under five who had diarrhea were given ORS.[3] Why are some 1.5 million children dying every year of diarrhea, a disease that could often be avoided in the first place, and could often be treated with boiled water, sugar, and salt?

Bleach and ORS are not unique examples. There is other relatively "low-hanging fruit" with promise to improve health and save many lives. These are cheap and simple technologies that, if properly utilized, would save much in resources (in terms of extra days worked, less antibiotics used, stronger bodies, and so on). They could pay for themselves, in addition to saving lives. But too many of these fruits are left unpicked. It is not that people don't care about their health. They do, and they devote considerable resources to it. They just seem to spend money elsewhere: on antibiotics that are not always necessary, on surgery that comes too late to help. Why does it have to be this way?

THE HEALTH TRAP

In a village in Indonesia we met Ibu Emptat, the wife of a basket weaver. A few years before our first meeting (in summer 2008), her husband was having trouble with his vision and could no longer work. She had no choice but to borrow money from the local moneylender—100,000 rupiah ($18.75 USD PPP) to pay for medicine so that her husband could work again, and 300,000 rupiah ($56 USD PPP) for food for the period when her husband was recovering and could not work (three of her seven children were still living with them). They had to pay 10 percent per month in interest on the loan. However, they fell behind on their interest payments and by the time we met, her debt had ballooned to 1 million rupiah ($187 USD PPP); the moneylender was threatening to take everything they had. To make matters worse, one of her younger sons had recently been diagnosed with severe asthma. Because the family was already mired in debt, she couldn't afford the medicine needed to treat his condition. He sat with us throughout our visit, coughing every few minutes; he was no longer able to attend school regularly. The family seemed to be caught in a classic poverty trap—the father's illness made them poor, which is why the child stayed sick, and because he was too sick to get a proper education, poverty loomed in his future.

Health certainly has the potential to be a source of a number of different traps. For example, workers living in an insalubrious environment may miss many workdays; children may be sick often and unable to do well in school; mothers who give birth there may have sickly babies. Each of these channels is potentially a mechanism for current misfortunes to turn into future poverty.

The good news is that if something like this is what is going on, we may only need one push, one generation that gets to grow up and work in a healthy environment, to set the trap loose. This is Jeffrey Sachs's view, for example. As he sees it, a large proportion of the world's poorest people, and indeed entire countries, are stuck in a health-based poverty trap. Malaria is his favorite example: Countries in which a large fraction of the population is exposed to malaria are much poorer (on average, countries like Côte d'Ivoire or Zambia, where 50 percent or more of the population is exposed to malaria, have per capita incomes that are one-third of those in the countries where no one today gets malaria).[4] And being so much poorer makes it harder for them to take steps to prevent malaria, which in turns keeps them poor. But this also means, according to Sachs, that public health investments aimed at controlling malaria (such as the distribution of bed nets to keep the mosquitoes at bay during the night) in these countries could have very high returns: People would be sick less often and able to work harder, and the resulting income gains would easily cover the costs of these interventions and more. To put it in terms of the S-shaped curve in Chapter 1, African countries where malaria is endemic are stuck in the left part of the curve, where their malaria-weakened labor force is too unproductive and hence too poor to be able to pay for malaria eradication. But if someone did them the favor of financing malaria eradication, they would end up on the right part of the curve, on the road to prosperity. The same argument could be made about other diseases that are prevalent in poor countries. This is the core of the optimistic message of Sachs's book *The End of Poverty.*

Skeptics have been quick to point out that it is not clear whether malaria-infested countries are poor because of malaria, as Sachs assumes, or perhaps their inability to eradicate malaria is an indicator of the fact that they are poorly governed. If it is the latter, then the mere eradication of malaria may achieve very little, as long as governance remains weak.

Whose story—the activists' or the skeptics'—does the evidence support? Successful campaigns to eradicate malaria have been studied in a number of different countries. Each of these studies compares high-malaria-prevalence regions in the country with low-prevalence regions and checks what happens to children born in these areas before and after the campaign. They all find that life outcomes (such as education or earnings) of children born after the campaign in areas where malaria was once prevalent catch up with those of children born in low-incidence areas. This strongly suggests that eradicating malaria indeed results in a reduction in long-term poverty, although the effects are not nearly as large as those suggested by Jeffrey Sachs: One study on malaria eradication in the U.S. South (which had malaria until 1951)[5] and several countries in Latin America[6] suggests that *a child who grew up malaria-free earns 50 percent more per year, for his entire adult life*, compared to a child who got the disease. Qualitatively similar results were found in India,[7] Paraguay, and Sri Lanka, although the magnitude of the gain varies from country to country.[8]

This result suggests that the financial return to investing in malaria prevention can be fantastically high. A long-lasting insecticide-treated bed net costs at most $14 USD PPP in Kenya, and lasts about five years. Assume conservatively that a child in Kenya sleeping under a treated net has 30 percent less risk of being infected with malaria between birth and age two, compared to a child who doesn't. In Kenya, an adult makes on average $590 USD PPP a year. Thus, if malaria indeed reduces earnings in Kenya by 50 percent, a $14 investment will increase incomes by $295 for the 30 percent of the population that would have gotten malaria without the net. The average return is $88 every year over the child's entire adult work life—enough for a parent to buy a lifetime supply of bed nets for all his or her children, with a chunk of change left over.

There are other examples of highly effective health investments. Access to clean water and sanitation is one of them. Overall, in 2008, according to estimates by WHO and UNICEF, approximately 13 percent of the world's population lacked access to improved water sources (typically meaning a tap or a well) and about one-fourth did not have access to water that is safe to drink.[9] And many of these people are the very poor. In our eighteen-country data set, access to tap water at home among the rural extremely poor varied from less than 1 percent (in rural Rajasthan and Uttar Pradesh in India) to 36.8 percent (in Guatemala). The numbers tend to be much better for richer households, though they vary a lot from country to country (from less than 3.2 percent in Papua New Guinea to 80 percent in Brazil, for the rural middle class). They are higher in urban areas, both for the poor and the middle class. Decent sanitation facilities are even rarer among the poor—42 percent of the world's population live without a toilet at home.

Most experts agree that access to piped water and sanitation can have a dramatic impact on health. A study concluded that the introduction of piped water, better sanitation, and chlorination of water sources was responsible for something like three-fourths of the decline in infant mortality between 1900 and 1946 and nearly half the overall reduction in mortality over the same period.[10] Moreover, repeated bouts of diarrhea during childhood permanently impair both physical and cognitive development. It is estimated that by piping uncontaminated, chlorinated water to households, it is possible to reduce diarrhea by up to 95 percent.[11] Poor water quality and pools of stagnant water are also a cause of other major illnesses, including malaria, schistosomiasis, and trachoma,[12] any of which can kill children or make them less productive adults.

Nevertheless, the conventional wisdom is that today, at $20 per household per month, providing piped water and sanitation is too expensive for the budget of most developing countries.[13] The experience of Gram Vikas, an NGO that works in Orissa, India, shows, however, that it is possible to do it much more cheaply. Its CEO, Joe Madiath, a man with a self-deprecating sense of humor who attends the annual meeting of the world's rich and powerful at the World Economic Forum in Davos, Switzerland, in outfits made from homespun cotton, is used to doing things differently. Madiath's career as an activist started early: He was twelve when he first got into trouble—for organizing the labor on the plantation that his father owned. He came to Orissa in the early 1970s with a group of left-wing students to help out after a devastating cyclone. After the immediate relief work was over, he decided to stay and see if he could find some more permanent ways to help the poor Oriya villagers. He eventually settled on water and sanitation. What attracted him to the issue was that it was simultaneously a daily challenge and an opportunity to initiate long-term social change. He explained to us that in Orissa, water and sanitation are social issues. Madiath insists that every single household in the villages where Gram Vikas operates should be connected to the same water mains: Water is piped to each house, which contains a toilet, a tap, and a bathing room, all connected to the same system. For the high-caste households, this means sharing water with low-caste households, which, for many in Orissa, was unacceptable when first proposed. It takes the NGO a while to get the agreement of the whole village and some villages eventually refuse, but it has always stuck to the principle that it would not start its work in a village until everyone there agreed to participate. When agreement is finally reached, it is often the first time that some of the upper-caste households participate in a project that involves the rest of the community.

Once a village agrees to work with Gram Vikas, the building work starts and continues for one to two years. Only after every single house has received its tap and toilet is the system turned on. In the meantime, Gram Vikas collects data every month on who has gone to the health center to get treated for malaria or diarrhea. We can thus directly observe what happens in a village as soon as the water starts flowing. The effects are remarkable: Almost overnight, and for years into the future, the number of severe diarrhea cases falls by one-half, and the number of malaria cases falls by one-third. The monthly cost of the system for each household, including maintenance, is 190 rupees, or $4 per household (in current USD), only 20 percent of what is conventionally assumed to be the cost of such a system.

There are even cheaper ways to avert diarrhea, such as adding chlorine to water. Other very inexpensive medical or public health technologies with proven effectiveness include ORS, getting children immunized, deworming drugs, exclusive breast-feeding until six months, and some routine antenatal procedures such as a tetanus shot for the would-be mother. Vitamin B against night blindness, iron pills and iron-fortified flour against anemia, and so on are other examples of low-hanging fruit.

The existence of these technologies is the source of both Jeffrey Sachs's optimism and his impatience. As he sees it, there are health-based poverty traps, but there are also ladders we can give to the poor to help them escape from these traps. If the poor cannot afford these ladders, the rest of the world should help them out. This is what Gram Vikas does in Orissa, by helping to organize the villages, and by subsidizing the cost of the water systems. A few years ago, Joe Madiath told us he felt he had to turn down funding from the Bill & Melinda Gates Foundation when the grant officer insisted that the villagers should pay the full cost of what they were getting (fortunately, the foundation subsequently changed its view on this question). He argued that villagers simply cannot afford 190 rupees per month, even though it is true that the health benefits are potentially worth far more—Gram Vikas only asks villagers to pay enough money into a village fund to be able to keep the system in good repair and be able to add new households as the village grows. The rest the NGO raises from donors all over the world. In Sachs's view, this is how things should be.

WHY AREN'T THESE TECHNOLOGIES USED MORE?

Underutilized Miracles

There is one wrinkle with Sachs's theory that poor people are stuck in a health-based poverty trap and that money can get them out of it. Some of these technologies are so cheap that everyone, even the very poor, should be able to afford them. Breast-feeding, for example, costs nothing at all. And yet fewer than 40 percent of the world's infants are breast-fed exclusively for six months, as the WHO recommends.[14] Another good example is water: Piping water to homes (combined with sewerage) costs 190 rupees per month, or 2,280 rupees per year, as we saw, which in terms of purchasing power is equivalent to about 300,000 Zambian kwachas. It is likely that poor villagers in Zambia cannot afford that much. But for less than 2 percent of that, a Zambian family of six can buy enough chlorine bleach to purify their entire drinking water intake for the year: A bottle of Chlorin (a brand of chlorine distributed by PSI) costs 800 kwachas ($0.18 USD PPP) and lasts a month. This can reduce diarrhea in young children by up to 48 percent.[15] People in Zambia know about the benefits of chlorine. Indeed, when asked to name something that cleans drinking water, 98 percent mention Chlorin. Although Zambia is a very poor country, 800 kwachas for a bottle that lasts a month is really not a lot of money—the average family spends 4,800 kwachas ($1.10 USD PPP) per week just on cooking oil. Yet only 10 percent of the population actually uses bleach to treat their water. When, as part of an experiment, some households were offered a discount voucher that would entitle them to a bottle of Chlorin for 700 kwachas ($0.16 USD PPP), only about 50 percent wanted to buy it.[16] This fraction went up sharply when the price was lowered to 300 kwachas ($0.07 USD PPP), but remarkably, even at this reduced price one-fourth of the people did not buy the product.

Demand is similarly low for bed nets. In Kenya, Jessica Cohen and Pascaline Dupas set up an NGO called TAMTAM (Together Against Malaria), to distribute free mosquito nets in prenatal clinics in Kenya.[17] At some point, PSI started distributing subsidized, but not free, nets in the same clinics. Cohen and Dupas wanted to find out whether their organization was still needed. They set up a simple test: They offered nets at various prices in different clinics, chosen at random. The price varied from free in some places to the (still subsidized) price charged by PSI in others. Much as in the case of Chlorin, they found that the purchase of nets was indeed very sensitive to the price. Almost everybody took a free net home. But the demand for nets fell to very close to zero at the PSI price (about $0.75 USD PPP). When Dupas replicated the experiment in different market towns but gave people the time to go home and collect cash (rather than having to buy on the spot), more people bought at the PSI price, but demand still went up by several times when the price was brought down toward zero.[18]

Even more troubling is the related fact that the demand for bed nets, though very sensitive to price, is not very sensitive to income. To get on the right part of the S-shaped curve and start a virtuous circle where improved health and increased income reinforce each other, the increase in income coming from one person avoiding malaria should be enough to make it very likely that his or her children buy a net and avoid malaria as well. We argued above that buying bed nets to reduce the risk of getting malaria has the potential to raise annual incomes by a substantial 15 percent on average. However, even though a 15 percent increase in income is far more than the cost of a bed net, people who are 15 percent richer are only 5 percent more likely to buy a net than others.[19] In other words, far from virtually ensuring that the next generation sleeps under a net, distributing free bed nets once would only increase the number of children in the next generation sleeping under a net from 47 percent to 52 percent. That is not nearly enough to eradicate malaria.

What the lack of demand underscores is perhaps the fundamental difficulty of the problem of health: The ladders to get out of the poverty trap exist but are not always in the right place, and people do not seem to know how to step onto them or even want to do so.

The Desire for Better Health

Since they do not seem to be willing to sacrifice much money or time to get clean water, bed nets, or for that matter, deworming pills or fortified flour, despite their potentially large health benefits, does that mean the poor do not care about health? The evidence suggests the opposite. When asked whether there was a period of a month in the recent past when they felt "worried, tense, or anxious," roughly one-fourth of the poor in both rural Udaipur and urban South Africa said yes.[20] This is much higher than what we see in the United States. And the most frequent source of such stress (44 percent of the time in Udaipur) is their own health or that of their close relatives. In many of the countries in our eighteen-country data set, the poor spend a considerable amount of their own money on health care. The average extremely poor household spends up to 5 percent of its monthly budget on health in rural India, and 3 percent to 4 percent in Pakistan, Panama, and Nicaragua. In most countries, more than one-fourth of the households had made at least one visit to a health practitioner in the previous month. The poor also spend large amounts of money on single health events: Among the poor families in Udaipur, 8 percent of the households recorded total expenditures on health of more than 5,000 rupees ($228 USD PPP) in the previous month, ten times the monthly budget per capita for the average family, and some households (the top 1 percent spenders) spent up to twenty-six times the average monthly budget per capita. When faced with a serious health issue, poor households cut spending, sell assets, or borrow, like Ibu Emptat, often at very high rates: In Udaipur, every third household we interviewed was currently repaying a loan taken out to pay for health care. A substantial proportion of those loans are from moneylenders, at rates that can be very high: The standard interest rate is 3 percent per month (42 percent per year).

Money for Nothing

The issue is therefore not how much the poor spend on health, but what the money is spent on, which is often expensive cures rather than cheap prevention. To make health care less expensive, many developing countries officially have a triage system to ensure that affordable (often free) basic curative services are available to the poor relatively close to their homes. The nearest center typically does not have a doctor, but the person there is trained to treat simple conditions and detect more serious ones, in which case the person is sent up to the next level. There are countries where this system is under severe strain for lack of manpower, but in many countries, like India, the facilities do exist, and the positions are filled. Even in Udaipur District, which is particularly remote and sparsely populated, a family needs to walk only a mile and a half to find a subcenter staffed with a trained nurse. Yet we have collected data that suggest that this system is not working. The poor mostly shun the free public health-care system. The average adult we interviewed in an extremely poor household saw a health-care provider once every two months. Of these visits, less than one-fourth were to a public facility.[21] More than one-half were to private facilities. The remainder were to *bhopas*—traditional healers who primarily offer exorcism from evil spirits.

The poor in Udaipur seem to select the doubly expensive plan: cure, rather than prevention, and cure from private doctors rather than from the trained nurses and doctors the government provides for free. That might make sense if the private doctors were better qualified, but this does not seem to be the case: Just over half of the private "doctors" have a medical college degree (this includes unconventional degrees like BAMS [Bachelor of Ayurvedic Medical Science] and BUMS [Bachelor of Unani Medical Science]), and one-third have no college education whatsoever. When we look at the people who "help the doctor," most of whom also see patients, the picture becomes even bleaker: Two-thirds have no formal qualification in medicine at all.[22]

In the local parlance, unqualified doctors like these are referred to as "Bengali doctors," because one of the earliest medical colleges in India was in Bengal and doctors from Bengal fanned across northern India looking for places to practice medicine. That tradition has continued— people continue to show up in a village with little more than a stetho- scope and a bag of standard medications and set up as Bengali doctors, irrespective of whether they are from Bengal or not. We interviewed one who explained how he became a doctor: "I graduated from high school and couldn't find a job, which is when I decided to set up as a doctor." He very graciously showed us his high school diploma. His qualifications were in geography, psychology, and Sanskrit, the ancient Indian language. Bengali doctors are not only a rural phenomenon. In the slums of Delhi, a study found that only 34 percent of the "doctors" had a formal medical degree.[23]

Of course, not having a degree is not necessarily synonymous with being incompetent: These doctors could very well have learned to treat easy cases and to refer the rest to a real hospital. Another of the Bengali doctors we talked to (who really was from Bengal) was very clear that he knew his limits—he gave out paracetamols (like Tylenol) and anti- malarials, perhaps some antibiotics when the disease looked like it might respond to it. If it looked like a difficult case, he referred patients to the Primary Health Center (PHC) or to a private hospital.

However, this kind of self-awareness is unfortunately not universal. In urban Delhi, Jishnu Das and Jeff Hammer, two World Bank economists, set out to find what doctors actually know.[24] They started with a sample of doctors of all kinds (public and private, qualified and unqual- ified) and presented each of them with five health-related "vignettes." For example, a hypothetical child patient arrives with symptoms of di- arrhea: The recommended medical practice is for the doctor to first ask enough questions to figure out whether the child has been running a high fever or vomiting, and if the answer is no, so that more serious conditions are ruled out, to prescribe ORS. Another vignette involves a pregnant woman arriving with the visible symptoms of preeclampsia, a potentially fatal condition that requires immediate referral to a hospital.

The doctors' answers and the questions they chose to ask were compared to the "ideal" questions and responses to form an index of each doctor's competence. The average competence in the sample was remarkably low. Even the very best doctors (the top twenty out of 100) asked fewer than half the questions they should have, and the worst (the bottom twenty) asked only one-sixth of those questions. Moreover, the large majority of these doctors would have recommended a course of action that, based on the assessment of an expert panel of doctors, was more likely to do harm than good. The unqualified private doctors were by far the worst, particularly those who worked in poor neighborhoods. The best were the qualified private doctors. The public doctors were somewhere in the middle.

There was also a clear pattern in the errors: Doctors tended to underdiagnose and overmedicate. In our health survey in Udaipur, we found that a patient was given a shot in 66 percent of the visits to a private facility and a drip in 12 percent of the visits. A test is performed in only 3 percent of the visits. The usual form of treatment for diarrhea, fever, or vomiting is to prescribe antibiotics or steroids, or both, usually injected.[25]

This is not only unnecessary in most cases, but potentially dangerous. First, there is the issue of sterilizing needles: Some friends of ours used to run a primary school in a small village on the outskirts of Delhi, where there was a doctor of unknown credentials but with a flourishing practice. Outside his dispensary was a huge drum that was always kept filled with water, with a little tap attached to it. After every patient left, the doctor would come outside and make a show of washing his needle with water from the drum. This was his way of signaling that he was being careful. We do not know whether he actually infected anyone with his syringe, but doctors in Udaipur talk about a particular doctor who infected an entire village with Hepatitis B by reusing the same unsterilized needle.

The misuse of antibiotics increases the likelihood of the emergence of drug-resistant strains of bacteria.[26] This is particularly true if, as many of these doctors are wont to do to save their patients money, the advised course is shorter than the standard regimen. Across the developing world, we are seeing a rise in antibiotic resistance. Similarly, incorrect dosage and poor patient compliance explain the emergence, in several African countries, of strains of malaria parasites that are resistant to mainstream medications, which has the makings of a public health disaster.[27] In the case of steroids, the damage from overuse is even more insidious. Any researchers of age forty or older who have surveyed the poor in countries like India can recall an occasion when they were surprised to discover that someone they thought was much older than they were was in fact significantly younger. Premature aging can result from many causes, but steroid use is definitely one of them—and it is not just that affected individuals look older, they also die sooner. Yet because the immediate effect of the medicine is to make the patient feel rapidly better and she is not told what might happen later, she goes home happy.

What is going on here? Why do the poor sometimes reject inexpensive effective sanitation—the cheap and easy way to dramatically improve people's health—in favor of spending a lot of money on things that don't help and might actually hurt?

Are Governments to Blame?

A part of the answer is that a lot of the cheap gains are in prevention, and prevention has traditionally been the area where the government is the main player. The trouble is that governments have a way of making easy things much less easy than they should be. The high absenteeism rates and low motivation among government health providers are certainly two reasons we don't see more preventive care being delivered.

Government health centers are often closed when they are supposed to be open. In India, the local health posts are supposed to be open six days a week, six hours a day. But in Udaipur, we visited over 100 facilities once a week at some random time during working hours for a year. We found them closed 56 percent of the time. And in only 12 percent of the cases was this because the nurse was on duty somewhere else near the center. The rest of the time, she was simply absent. This rate of absence is similar elsewhere. In 2002–2003, the World Bank conducted a World Absenteeism Survey in Bangladesh, Ecuador, India, Indonesia, Peru, and Uganda and found that the average absentee rate of health workers (doctors and nurses) was 35 percent (it was 43 percent in India).[28] In Udaipur, we found that these absences are also unpredictable, which makes it even harder for the poor to rely on these facilities. Private facilities offer the assurance that the doctor will be there. If he isn't, he won't get paid, whereas the absent government employee on a salary will.

Furthermore, even when government doctors and nurses are around, they do not treat their patients particularly well. Working with the same group of doctors who had responded to the vignette questions, one member of Das and Hammer's research team sat with each provider for a whole day. For each patient, the researcher recorded details about the visit, including the number of questions the doctor asked concerning the history of the problem, the examinations performed, medicines prescribed or given, and (for the private sector) prices charged. The overall sense we get from their study about health care in India, both public and private, is frightening. Das and Hammer describe it as the 3-3-3 rule: The median interaction lasts *three minutes;* the provider asks *three questions* and occasionally performs some examinations. The patient is then provided with *three medicines* (providers usually dispense medicine directly rather than writing prescriptions). Referrals are rare (fewer than 7 percent of the time); patients are given instructions only about half the time and only about one-third of doctors offer any guidance regarding follow-up. As if this is not bad enough, things are much worse in the public sector than in the private sector. Public providers spend about two minutes per patient on average. They ask fewer questions, and in most cases don't touch the patient at all. Mostly, they just ask the patient for a diagnosis and then treat the patient's self-diagnosis. Similar findings were discovered in several countries.[29]

So perhaps the answer is relatively simple: People avoid the public health system because it does not work well. This could also explain why other services that are provided through the government system, like immunizations and antenatal checks for prospective mothers, are underused.

But we know that this cannot be the whole story. Bed nets are not exclusively distributed by the government; neither is Chlorin for purifying water. And even when government nurses do come to work, the number of patients demanding their services does not go up. There was a period of about six months when a collaborative effort by Seva Mandir, a local NGO, and the district authorities was effective in sharply reducing absenteeism—the probability of finding someone in the health center went up from a dismal 40 percent to over 60 percent. But that had no effect on the number of clients who came to the facilities.[30]

In another Seva Mandir initiative, the NGO organized monthly immunization camps in the same set of villages. This was in reaction to abysmally low immunization rates in the area: less than 5 percent of the children had been receiving the basic package of immunizations (as defined by WHO and UNICEF) before the NGO got involved. Given the very broad consensus that immunization saves lives (2 to 3 million people are estimated to die from vaccine-preventable diseases every year) and the low cost (for the villagers, it is free), this seems like something that would be a priority for every parent. The low immunization rates, it was widely held, must have been the result of the delinquency of the nurses. Mothers would just get tired of walking all the way there with a young child and not finding the nurse.

To solve this problem, in 2003, Seva Mandir decided to start its own camps, which were widely advertised, held monthly on the same date, and as our data confirm, took place with clocklike regularity. This led to some increase in the immunization rate: In the camp villages, on average 77 percent of children received at least one shot. But the problem was in completing the course. Overall, from the 6 percent in a set of control villages, full immunization rates increased to 17 percent in the camp villages. But even with high-quality, privately provided free immunization services, available right at the parents' doorsteps, eight out of ten children remained without full immunization.

We must therefore accept the possibility that if people do not go to the public health centers, it is also in part because they are not particularly interested in receiving the services they offer, including immunizations. Why do poor people demand so much (bad) health care, but show such indifference toward these preventive services, and more generally toward all the wonderful, cheap gains that the medical profession has invented for them?

UNDERSTANDING HEALTH-SEEKING BEHAVIOR

Does Free Mean Worthless?

If people do not take advantage of cheap preventive technologies to improve their health, could it be precisely because the cheap technologies are cheap?

This is not as implausible as it might seem. Plain vanilla economic rationality dictates that the cost, once paid or "sunk," should not have any effect on usage, but there are many who claim that as is often the case, economic rationality gets it wrong. In fact, there is a "psychological sunk cost" effect—people are more likely to make use of something they have paid a lot for. In addition, people may judge quality by price: Things may be judged to be valueless precisely because they are cheap.

All of these possibilities are important because health is one place where even free market economists have traditionally supported subsidies and, as a result, most of these cheap gains are made available at below-market prices. The logic is simple: A bed net protects not only the child who sleeps under it, but also other kids who are not getting malaria from that child. A nurse who treats diarrhea with ORS rather than antibiotics prevents the spread of drug resistance. The immunized child who avoids mumps helps protect his or her classmates as well. If making these technologies cheaper ensures that more people use them, everyone else will gain, too.

On the other hand, if people are subject to a sunk-cost effect, for example, these subsidies can backfire—usage will be low *because* the price is so low. In *The White Man's Burden,*[31] William Easterly seems to suggest that this is what is going on. He points to examples of subsidized bed nets being used as wedding veils. Others talk about toilets being used as flowerpots or, more graphically, condoms being used as balloons.

However, there are now a number of careful experiments that suggest that such anecdotes are oversold. Several studies that have tested whether people use things less because they got them for free found no evidence of such behavior. Recall Cohen and Dupas's TAMTAM experiments, which found that people are much more likely to buy bed nets when they are very cheap or free. Do these subsidized bed nets actually get used? To figure this out, a few weeks after the initial experiment, TAMTAM sent field officers to the homes of people who had purchased nets at the various subsidized prices. They found that between 60 percent and 70 percent of women who had acquired a net were indeed using it. In another experiment, over time usage went up to about 90 percent. Furthermore, they found no difference in usage rates among those who had paid for them and those who had not. The same kinds of results, which rule out the possibility that subsidies are to blame for low usage, have now been found in other settings.

But if subsidies are not the cause, what is?

Faith?

Abhijit grew up in a family that came from two different ends of India. His mother was from Mumbai, and in her family no meal could be considered complete without the unleavened breads called *chapatis* and *bhakris*, made from wheat and millets. His father was from Bengal, where people eat rice with pretty much every meal. The two regions also have very different views about how to treat fevers. Every Maharashtrian mother knows that rice aids in a fast recovery. In Bengal, on the other hand, rice is forbidden: When a Bengali wants to say that someone has recovered from a fever, he says that "he was allowed rice today." When a puzzled six-year-old Abhijit asked his Bengali aunt about this apparent contradiction, she said that it had to do with faith.

Faith, or to use the more secular equivalents, a combination of beliefs and theories, is clearly a very important part of how we all navigate the health system. How else do we know that the medicine that we were prescribed will make the rash better and that we shouldn't apply leeches instead? In all likelihood, none of us has observed a randomized trial where some people with, say, pneumonia were given antibiotics and others were offered leeches. Indeed, we do not even have any direct evidence that such a trial ever took place. What assures us is a belief in the way drugs get certified by the Food and Drug Administration (FDA) or its equivalent. We feel that an antibiotic would not be on the market if it had not gone through some kind of trial and, sometimes wrongly, given the financial incentives to manipulate medical trials, we trust the FDA to make sure the studies are reliable and the antibiotic is safe and effective.

The point is not at all to imply that our decision to trust doctors' prescriptions is wrong, but rather to underscore the fact that a lot of beliefs and theories for which we have little or no direct evidence contribute to that trust. Whenever this trust erodes for some reason in rich countries, we witness backlashes against conventionally accepted best practices. Despite the continuous reassurance by high-powered medical panels that vaccines are safe, there are a number of people in the United States and the United Kingdom, for example, who refuse to immunize their children against measles because of a supposed link with autism. The number of measles cases is growing in the United States, even as it is declining everywhere else.[32] Consider the circumstances of average citizens of a poor country. If people in the West, with all of the insights of the best scientists in the world at their disposal, find it hard to base their choices on hard evidence, how hard must it be for the poor, who have much less access to information? People make their choices based on what makes sense to them, but given that most of them have not had rudimentary high school biology and have no reason, as we saw, to trust the competence and professionalism of their doctors, their decision is pretty much a shot in the dark.

For example, the poor in many countries seem to have the theory that it is important that medicine be delivered directly to the blood—this is why they want injectables. To reject this (plausible) theory, you have to know something about the way the body absorbs nutrients through the digestive tract and something about why proper sterilization of needles requires high temperatures. In other words, you need at least high school biology.

To make matters worse, learning about health care is inherently difficult not only for the poor, but for everyone.[33] If patients are somehow convinced that they need shots to get better, there is little chance that they could ever learn they are wrong. Because most diseases that prompt visits to the doctor are self-limiting (i.e., they will disappear no matter what), there is a good chance that patients will feel better after a single shot of antibiotics. This naturally encourages spurious causal associations: Even if the antibiotics did nothing to cure the ailment, it is normal to attribute any improvement to them. By contrast, it is not natural to attribute causal force to inaction: If a person with the flu goes to the doctor, and the doctor does nothing, and the patient then feels better, the patient will correctly infer that it was not the doctor who was responsible for the cure. And rather than thanking the doctor for his forbearance, the patient will be tempted to think that it was lucky that everything worked out this time but that a different doctor should be seen for future problems. This creates a natural tendency to overmedicate in a private, unregulated market. This is compounded by the fact that, in many cases, the prescriber and the provider are the same person, either because people turn to their pharmacists for medical advice, or because private doctors also stock and sell medicine.

It is probably even harder to learn from experience about immunization, because it does not fix an existing problem, but rather protects against potential future problems. When a child is immunized against measles, that child does not get measles. But not all children who are not immunized actually contract measles (especially if others around them who are the potential source of infection are immunized), so it is very difficult to draw a clear link between immunization and the lack of disease. Moreover, immunization just prevents some diseases—there are many others—and uneducated parents do not necessarily understand what their child is supposed to be protected against. So when the child gets sick despite being immunized, the parents feel cheated and probably resolve not to go through with it again. They may also not understand why all the different shots in the basic immunization regime are needed—after two or three shots, parents might feel that they have done what they should. It is all too easy to get misleading beliefs about what might work in health.

Weak Beliefs and the Necessity of Hope

There is potentially another reason the poor may hold on to beliefs that might seem indefensible: When there is little else they can do, hope becomes essential. One of the Bengali doctors we spoke to explained the role he plays in the lives of the poor as follows: "The poor cannot really afford to get treated for anything major, because that involves expensive things like tests and hospitalization, which is why they come to me with their minor ailments, and I give them some little medicines which make them feel better." In other words, it is important to keep doing something about your health, even if you know that you are not doing anything about the big problem.

In fact, the poor are much less likely to go to the doctor for potentially life-threatening conditions like chest pains and blood in their urine than with fevers and diarrhea. The poor in Delhi spend as much on short-duration ailments as the rich, but the rich spend much more on chronic diseases.[34] So it may well be that the reason chest pains are a natural candidate for being a *bhopa* disease (an older woman once explained to us the dual concepts of *bhopa* diseases and doctor diseases—*bhopa* diseases are caused by ghosts, she insisted, and need to be treated by traditional healers), as are strokes, is precisely that most people cannot afford to get them treated by doctors.

It is probably for the same reason that in Kenya, traditional healers and preachers have been particularly in demand to cure HIV/AIDS (their services are proudly advertised on hand-painted billboards in every town). There was not much that allopathic doctors could really do (at least until anti-retrovirals became more affordable), so why not try the traditional healer's herbs and spells? They were cheap and at the very least gave the patient a sense of doing something. And since symptoms and opportunistic infections come and go, it is possible to believe, at least for a little while, that they have an effect.

This kind of grasping at straws is not specific to poor countries. This is also what the privileged few in poor countries and the citizens of the First World do when they face a problem that they do not know how to remedy. In the United States, depression and back pains are two conditions that are both poorly understood and debilitating. This is why Americans are constantly going between psychiatrists and spiritual healers, or yoga classes and chiropractors. Since both conditions come and go, sufferers go through cycles of hope and disappointment, each time wanting to believe for a moment at least that the new cure must be working.

Beliefs that are held for convenience and comfort may well be more flexible than beliefs that are held out of true conviction. We saw signs of this in Udaipur. Most people who go to the *bhopa* also go to the Bengali doctor and the government hospital and do not seem to stop to think about the fact that these represent two entirely different and mutually inconsistent belief systems. They do talk about *bhopa* diseases and doctor diseases, but when a disease persists they seem not to insist on this distinction, and are willing to use both.

The issue of what beliefs mean to people came up a lot when Seva Mandir was considering what it could do to improve immunization, after discovering that even its system of well-run monthly camps left four-fifths of children not fully immunized. Some local experts argued that the issue was rooted in people's belief systems. They claimed that immunization had no place in the traditional belief system—in rural Udaipur, among other places, traditional belief has it that children die because they catch the evil eye, and the way to catch the evil eye is by being displayed in public. This is why parents don't take their children outside for the first year of life. Given this, the skeptical experts argued, it would be exceedingly difficult to convince villagers to immunize their children without first changing their beliefs.

Notwithstanding these strong views, when Seva Mandir set up immunization camps in Udaipur, we managed to convince Neelima Khetan, Seva Mandir's CEO, to try something on a pilot basis: offer 2 pounds of dal (dried beans, a staple in the area) for each immunization and a set of stainless steel plates for completing the course. The doctor in charge of Seva Mandir's health program was initially quite reluctant to try this out. On the one hand, it seemed wrong to bribe people to do the right thing. They should learn on their own what is good for their health. On the other hand, the incentive we proposed seemed much too weak: If people do not immunize their children, given the huge benefits of doing so, they must have some strong reason behind it. If they believed, for example, that taking their children out would cause harm, 2 pounds of dal (worth only 40 rupees, or $1.83 USD PPP, less than half the daily wage earned by working in a public works site) was not going to persuade them. We had known people at Seva Mandir for long enough that we could persuade them that this was still an idea worth trying on a small scale, and thirty camps with incentives were established. They were a roaring success. The immunization rate in the village where the camps were set up increased sevenfold, to 38 percent. In all neighboring villages, within about 6 miles, it was also much higher. Seva Mandir discovered that offering the dal, paradoxically, actually lowered the cost per immunization by increasing efficiency, because the nurse, whose time was already paid for, was kept busy.[35]

Seva Mandir's immunization program is one of the most impressive we have ever evaluated, and probably the one that has saved the most lives. We are therefore working, with Seva Mandir and others, to encourage replications of this experiment in other contexts. Interestingly, we are running into some resistance. Doctors point out that 38 percent is far from the 80 percent or 90 percent required to achieve "herd immunity," the rate at which an entire community is fully protected: WHO targets 90 percent coverage nationally for the basic immunization, and 80 percent in every subunit. For some in the medical community, if full protection for the community is not going to be achieved, there is no reason to subsidize some households to do what they should do for their own good anyway. Although it would certainly be excellent to be able to get to full coverage, this "all or nothing" argument is only superficially sensible: Even if immunizing my own child does not contribute to eradicating the disease, it still protects not only my child but also others around him.[36] There is thus still a huge social benefit from increasing full immunization rates against basic diseases from 6 percent to 38 percent.

In the end, the mistrust of incentives for immunization comes down to an article of faith for both those on the right and the left of the mainstream political spectrum: Don't try to bribe people to do things that *you* think they ought to do. For the right, this is because it will be wasted; for the conventional left, which includes much of the public health community and the good doctor from Seva Mandir, this is because it degrades both what is given and the person who gets it. Instead, we should focus on trying to convince the poor of the benefits of immunization.

We think that both of these views are somewhat wrongheaded ways to think about this and other similar problems, for two reasons. First, what the 2-pounds-of-dal experiments demonstrate is that in Udaipur at least, the poor might appear to believe in all kinds of things, but there is not much conviction behind many of those beliefs. They do not fear the evil eye so much that they would pass up the dal. This must mean that they actually know they are in no position to have a strong basis to evaluate the costs and benefits of vaccines. When they actually know what they want—marrying their daughter to someone from the right caste or religion, to take an unfortunate but important example—they are not at all easy to bribe. So, although some beliefs the poor have are undoubtedly strongly held, it is a mistake to consider that it is always the case.

There is a second reason this is wrong. Both the right wing and the left wing seem to assume that action follows intention: that if people were convinced of the value of immunization, children would be immunized. This is not always true, and the implications are far-reaching.

New Year's Resolutions

One obvious sign that resistance to immunization is not very deep is that 77 percent of children received the first vaccine in the villages where the camps did not offer dal: People seem to be willing to start the immunization process, even without any incentives. The problem is to get them to complete it. This is also why the full immunization rate does not go beyond 38 percent—the incentives make people come a few more times, but not enough to get the full five shots, despite the free stainless steel plates that wait for them if they complete the course.

It seems that this might have a lot to do with the same reason that, year after year, we have trouble sticking to our New Year's resolution to go to the gym regularly, despite knowing that it may save us from a heart attack down the line. Research in psychology has now been applied to a range of economic phenomena to show that we think about the present very differently from the way we think about the future (a notion referred to as "time inconsistency").[37] In the present, we are impulsive, governed in large part by emotions and immediate desire: Small losses of time (standing in line to get the child immunized) or petty discomforts (glutes that need to be woken up) that have to be endured right now feel much more unpleasant in the moment than when we think about them without a sense of immediacy (say, after a Christmas meal that was heavy enough to rule out all thoughts of immediate exercise). The reverse, of course, goes for small "rewards" (candy, a cigarette) that we really crave in the present; when we plan for the future, the pleasure from these treats seems less important.

Our natural inclination is to postpone small costs, so that they are borne not by our today self but by our tomorrow self instead. This is an idea that we will see again in future chapters. Poor parents may even be fully convinced of the benefits of immunization—but these benefits will accrue sometime in the future, while the cost is incurred today. It makes sense, from today's perspective, to wait for tomorrow. Unfortunately, when tomorrow becomes today, the same logic applies. Likewise, we may want to postpone the purchase of a bed net or a bottle of Chlorin until later, because we have better use for the money right now (there is someone frying delicious conch fritters across the street, say). It is easy to see how this could explain why a small cost discourages the use of a life-saving device, or why small incentives encourage it. The 2 pounds of dal works because it is something that the mother receives today, which compensates her for the cost she bears for getting her child immunized (the couple of hours spent bringing her child to the camp or the low fever that the shot sometimes causes).

If this explanation is correct, it suggests a new rationale for mandating specific preventive health behaviors or for providing financial incentives that go beyond the traditional economic argument we have already suggested, which is that it makes sense for society to subsidize or enforce behaviors that have benefits for others. Fines or incentives can push individuals to take some action that they themselves consider desirable but perpetually postpone taking. More generally, time inconsistency is a strong argument for making it as easy as possible for people to do the "right" thing, while, perhaps, leaving them the freedom to opt out. In their best-selling book *Nudge: Improving Decisions About Health, Wealth, and Happiness,* Richard Thaler and Cass Sunstein, an economist and a law scholar from the University of Chicago, recommend a number of interventions to do just this.[38] An important idea is that of default option: The government (or a well-meaning NGO) should make the option that it thinks is the best for most people the default choice, so that people will need to actively move away from it if they want to. So people have the right to choose what they want, but there is a small cost of doing so, and as a result, most people end up choosing the default option. Small incentives, like giving dal for vaccines, are another way to nudge people, by giving them a reason to act today, rather than indefinitely postpone.

The key challenge is to design "nudges" tailored to the environment of developing countries. For example, the key challenge with chlorinating water at home is that you have to remember to do it: The bleach has to be purchased, and the right number of drops have to be put in before anyone drinks the water. This is what is so great about piped water—it comes chlorinated to our homes; we don't need to think about it. How does one nudge people to chlorinate their drinking water, where piped water is not available? Michael Kremer and his colleagues came up with one method: a (free) chlorine dispenser, called "one turn," installed next to the village well, where everybody goes to get water, which delivers the right quantity of chlorine at one turn of a knob. This makes the chlorination of water as easy as possible, and because that leads many people to add chlorine every time they collect water, this is the cheapest way to prevent diarrhea among all the interventions for which there is evidence from randomized trials.[39]

We were less fortunate (or, more likely, less competent) when we designed a program for the iron fortification of flour with Seva Mandir to deal with rampant anemia. We had tried to design the program with a built-in "default" option: A household had to decide once and only once whether it wanted to participate. The flour of a participating household would then always be fortified. But unfortunately, the incentive of the millers (who were paid a flat fee regardless of how much flour they fortified) was to start from the opposite default option: not to fortify unless the household required it. As we discovered, the small cost of having to insist on fortification was large enough to discourage most people.[40]

Nudging or Convincing?

In many cases, time inconsistency is what prevents our going from intention to action. In the specific case of immunization, however, it is hard to believe that time inconsistency by itself would be sufficient to make people permanently postpone the decision if they were fully cognizant of its benefits. For people to continuously postpone getting their children immunized, they would need to be constantly fooled by themselves. Not only do they have to think that they prefer to spend time going to the camp next month rather than today, they also have to believe that they will indeed go next month. We are certainly somewhat naïve and overconfident about our own ability to do the right thing in the future. But if parents actually believe in the benefits of immunization, it seems unlikely that they can keep fooling themselves month after month by pretending that they will do it next month until the entire two-year window runs out and it is too late. As we will see later in the book, the poor find ways to force themselves to save despite themselves, which requires a great deal of sophisticated financial thinking. If they really believed that immunization is as wonderful as WHO believes it to be, they would probably have figured out a way to overcome their natural tendency to procrastinate. The more plausible explanation is that they procrastinate *and* they underestimate the benefits.

Nudges may be especially helpful when, for whatever reason, households are somewhat dubious about the benefits of what is being proposed to them. This makes preventive care a doubly appropriate candidate for such policies: The benefits are in the future, and in any case, it is hard to understand exactly what they are. The good news is that nudges may also help with the convincing, which may jump-start a positive feedback loop. Remember the bed nets that were given to a poor Kenyan family? We argued earlier that, on its own, the income gain from the first bed net was not large enough to make the child who got one buy one for his own children: Even if the bed net led to an increase in income of 15 percent for a child, that income gain increases their probability to buy a net only by 5 percent. However, the income effect is not the whole story: The family may observe that when they use a net, their children are sick less often. Moreover, they may also learn that it is easier to use bed nets and less unpleasant to sleep under bed nets than they had initially believed. In one experiment, Pascaline Dupas tested this hypothesis by making a second attempt to sell bed nets to the families that were previously offered very cheap or free nets, as well as to the families that were offered nets at full price and mostly did not buy one.[41] She found that families that were offered a free or sharply reduced net were *more* likely to buy a second net (even though they had one already) than the families that were asked to pay full price for the first one. Moreover, she also found that knowledge travels: Friends and neighbors of those who were given a free net were also more likely to buy a net themselves.

THE VIEW FROM OUR COUCH

The poor seem to be trapped by the same kinds of problems that afflict the rest of us—lack of information, weak beliefs, and procrastination among them. It is true that we who are not poor are somewhat better educated and informed, but the difference is small because, in the end, we actually know very little, and almost surely less than we imagine.

Our real advantage comes from the many things that we take as given. We live in houses where clean water gets piped in—we do not need to remember to add Chlorin to the water supply every morning. The sewage goes away on its own—we do not actually know how. We can (mostly) trust our doctors to do the best they can and can trust the public health system to figure out what we should and should not do. We have no choice but to get our children immunized—public schools will not take them if they aren't—and even if we somehow manage to fail to do it, our children will probably be safe because everyone else is immunized. Our health insurers reward us for joining the gym, because they are concerned that we will not do it otherwise. And perhaps most important, most of us do not have to worry where our next meal will come from. In other words, we rarely need to draw upon our limited endowment of self-control and decisiveness, while the poor are constantly being required to do so.

We should recognize that no one is wise, patient, or knowledgeable enough to be fully responsible for making the right decisions for his or her own health. For the same reason that those who live in rich countries live a life surrounded by invisible nudges, the primary goal of health-care policy in poor countries should be to make it as easy as possible for the poor to obtain preventive care, while at the same time regulating the quality of treatment that people can get. An obvious place to start, given the high sensitivity to prices, is delivering preventive services for free or even rewarding households for getting them, and making getting them the natural default option when possible. Free Chlorin dispensers should be put next to water sources; parents should be rewarded for immunizing their children; children should be given free deworming medicines and nutritional supplements at school; and there should be public investment in water and sanitation infrastructure, at least in densely populated areas.

As public health investments, many of these subsidies will more than pay for themselves in the value of reduced illness and death, and higher wages—children who are sick less often go to school more and earn more as adults. This does not mean that we can assume that these will automatically happen without intervention, however. Imperfect information about benefits and the strong emphasis people put on the immediate present limit how much effort and money people are willing to invest even in very inexpensive preventive strategies. And when they are not inexpensive, there is of course always the question of money. As far as treatment is concerned, the challenge is twofold: making sure that people can afford the medicines they need (Ibu Emptat, for one, clearly could not afford the asthma medicine that her son needed), but also restricting access to medicines they don't need as a way to prevent growing drug resistance. Because regulating who sets up a practice and decides to call himself a doctor seems to be beyond the control of most governments in developing countries, the only way to reduce the spread of antibiotic resistance and the overuse of high-potency drugs may be to put maximal effort into controlling the sale of these drugs.

All this sounds paternalistic, and in a way, it certainly is. But then it is easy, too easy, to sermonize about the dangers of paternalism and the need to take responsibility for our own lives, from the comfort of our couch in our safe and sanitary home. Aren't we, those who live in the rich world, the constant beneficiaries of a paternalism now so thoroughly embedded into the system that we hardly notice it? It not only ensures that we take care of ourselves better than we would if we had to be on top of every decision, but also, by freeing us from having to think about these issues, it gives us the mental space we need to focus on the rest of our lives. This does not absolve us of the responsibility of educating people about public health. We do owe everyone, the poor included, as clear an explanation as possible of why immunization is important and why they have to complete their course of antibiotics. But we should recognize—indeed assume—that information alone will not do the trick. This is just how things are, for the poor, as for us.

4

Top of the Class

In summer 2009, in the village of Naganadgi in the state of Karnataka, India, we met Shantarama, a forty-year-old widow and mother of six. Her husband had died four years before, entirely unexpectedly, of appendicitis. His life was not insured, nor was there any pension that the family was entitled to. The three eldest children had each gone to school at least until eighth grade, but the next two—a ten-year-old boy and a fourteen-year-old girl—had dropped out. The girl was working in a neighbor's field. We assumed that the death of the father had forced the family to withdraw the children from school and send all the older ones to work.

Shantarama set us straight. After her husband died, she had rented out the fields they owned and started to work as a casual laborer. She earned enough to take care of their basic needs. The girl was indeed sent to work in the fields, but only after she dropped out, because the mother did not want her idling at home. The rest of the children had stayed on in school—out of the three oldest children, two were still students when we met them (the oldest, who was married and twenty-two, was expecting her first child). We learned that the oldest boy was in college in Yatgir, the nearest town, studying to be . . . a teacher. The two middle children were out of school only because they absolutely refused to go.

There were several schools near the village, including a government school and a few private schools. Those two children had been enrolled at the government school, but they had both run away countless times before their mother abandoned any hope of being able to make them attend. The ten-year-old boy, who was with his mother when we interviewed her, mumbled something about school being boring.

Schools are available. In most countries, they are free, at least at the primary level. Most children are enrolled. And yet in the various surveys that we have conducted around the world, child absentee rates vary between 14 percent and 50 percent.[1] Absence often does not seem to be driven by an obvious need at home. Although some of it might reflect ill health—for example, in Kenya when children were treated for intestinal worms, they missed fewer days of school[2]—much of it probably reflects children's unwillingness to be in school (which might well be universal, as most of us will remember from our childhood) and also the fact that their parents do not seem to be able, or willing, to make them go.

For some critics, this is a sign of the catastrophic failure of an establishment-led effort to increase education from the top down: Building schools and hiring teachers is useless if there is no strong underlying demand for education; conversely, if there is real demand for skill, a demand for education will naturally emerge, and supply will follow. However, this optimistic view seems to be inconsistent with the story of Shantarama's children. There is certainly no shortage of demand for educated people in Karnataka, whose capital is Bangalore, India's IT hub. The family, with a future teacher among its members, was both aware of the value of education and willing to invest in it.

So if the failure of schools in developing countries to attract children can't be explained by problems of access, or lack of demand for educated labor, or parental resistance to educating their children, then where is the snag?

SUPPLY-DEMAND WARS

Education policy, like aid, has been the subject of intense policy debates. As in the case of aid, the debate is not about whether education per se is good or bad (everyone probably agrees it is better to be educated than not educated). It centers instead on whether governments ought to, or know how to, intervene. And though the specific reasons invoked are different, the fault line divides the field essentially in the same place it divides it on the subject of aid, with the aid optimists being generally education interventionists, and the aid pessimists being in favor of laissez-faire.

A large majority of policy makers, at least in international policy circles, have traditionally taken the view that the problem is essentially simple: We have to find a way to get the children into a classroom, ideally taught by a well-trained teacher, and the rest will take care of itself. We will call these people, who emphasize the "supply of schooling," the "supply wallahs," appropriating the Indian term for "purveyor of" (as in the western Indian surnames Lakdawala [wood supplier], Daruwala [booze supplier], and Bandukwala [gun seller]), to avoid confusing them with supply-siders, the economists who think Keynes got everything wrong and are in fact largely opposed to any form of government intervention.

Perhaps the most visible articulation of the supply wallah position can be found in the UN's Millennium Development Goals (MDG), the eight goals that the world's nations agreed in 2000 to reach by 2015. The second and third MDGs are, respectively, to "ensure that, by 2015, children everywhere, boys and girls alike, will be able to complete a full course of primary schooling" and to "eliminate gender disparity in primary and secondary education, preferably by 2005, and in all levels of education no later than 2015." Most national governments seem to have bought into this idea. In India, 95 percent of children now have a school within a half mile or so.[3] Several African countries (including Kenya, Uganda, and Ghana) have made primary education free, and children have flooded the schools. According to UNICEF, between 1999 and 2006, enrollment rates in primary school in sub-Saharan Africa increased from 54 percent to 70 percent. In East and South Asia, they increased from 75 percent to 88 percent over the same period. Worldwide, the number of children of school age who were out of school fell from 103 million in 1999 to 73 million in 2006. In our eighteen-country data set, even among the extremely poor (those who live on less than 99 cents a day), enrollment rates are now above 80 percent in at least half the countries for which we have data.

Access to secondary school (ninth grade and above) is not part of the MDGs, but even there, progress has been made. Between 1995 and 2008, secondary gross enrollment ratios increased from 25 percent to 34 percent in sub–Saharan Africa, from 44 percent to 51 percent in South Asia, and from 64 percent to 74 percent in East Asia,[4] despite the fact that the costs of secondary schools are much higher: Teachers are expensive, because they need to be better qualified, and for parents and children the value of the forgone earnings, and the forgone labor-market experience, is much larger because teenage children can work and earn money.

Getting children into school is a very important first step: This is where learning starts. But it isn't very useful if they learn little or nothing once they're there. Somewhat bizarrely, the issue of learning is *not* very prominently positioned in international declarations: The Millennium Development Goals do not specify that children should learn anything in school, just that they should complete a basic cycle of education. In the final declaration of the Education for All Summit in Dakar in 2000, sponsored by the United Nations Educational, Scientific and Cultural Organization (UNESCO), the goal of improving the quality of education is mentioned only in the sixth position—out of six goals. The implicit assumption, presumably, was that learning would follow from enrollment. But unfortunately things aren't that simple.

In 2002 and 2003, the World Absenteeism Survey, led by the World Bank, sent unannounced surveyors to a nationally representative sample of schools in six countries. Their basic conclusion was that teachers in Bangladesh, Ecuador, India, Indonesia, Peru, and Uganda miss one day of work out of five on average, and the ratio is even higher in India and Uganda. Moreover, the evidence from India suggests that even when teachers are in school and are supposed to be in class, they are often found drinking tea, reading the newspaper, or talking to a colleague. Overall, 50 percent of teachers in Indian public schools are not in front of a class at a time they should be.[5] How are the children supposed to learn?

In 2005, Pratham, an Indian NGO focused on education, decided to go one step further and find out what children were really learning. Pratham was founded in 1994 by Madhav Chavan, a U.S.-educated chemical engineer with an unflappable belief that all children should, and can, learn to read and read to learn. He has taken Pratham from a small Mumbai-based UNICEF-sponsored charity to one of the largest NGOs in India, perhaps in the world: Pratham's programs reach close to 34.5 million children all over India and are now venturing into the rest of the world. Under the banner of the Annual State of Education Report (ASER), Pratham formed volunteer teams in all 600 Indian districts. These teams tested more than 1,000 children in randomly chosen villages in every district—700,000 children overall—and came up with a report card. One of the leading lights of the ruling Congress-led government, Montek Singh Ahluwalia, launched the report, but what he read could not have made him happy. Close to 35 percent of children in the seven-to-fourteen age group could not read a simple paragraph (first-grade level) and almost 60 percent of children could not read a simple story (second-grade level). Only 30 percent could do second-grade mathematics (basic division).[6] The math results are particularly stunning—all over the Third World, little boys and girls who help their parents in their family stall or store do much more complicated calculations all the time, without the help of pen and paper. Are schools actually making them unlearn?

Not everyone in the government was as gracious as Mr. Ahluwalia. The government of the state of Tamil Nadu refused to believe that it was really doing as badly as the ASER data seemed to imply and ordered its own teams to conduct a retest, which unfortunately only served to reinforce the bad news. These days in India, in an annual ritual in January, ASER results are released. Newspapers express dismay at the poor scores, academics talk about the statistics in panel discussions, and very little changes.

Unfortunately, India is not unique: Very similar results have been found in neighboring Pakistan, in distant Kenya, and in several other countries. In Kenya, the Uwezo Survey, modeled on ASER, found that 27 percent of children in fifth grade could not read a simple paragraph in English, and 23 percent could not read in Kiswahili (the two languages of instruction in primary school). Thirty percent could not do basic division.[7] In Pakistan, 80 percent of children in third grade could not read a first-grade-level paragraph.[8]

The Demand Wallahs' Case

For the "demand wallahs," a set of critics (including William Easterly) who believe that there is no point in supplying education unless there is a clear demand for it, these results encapsulate everything that has been wrong with education policy in the last few decades. In their view, the quality of education is low because parents do not care enough about it, and they don't because they know that the actual benefits (what economists call the "returns" to education) are low. When the benefits of education become high enough, enrollment will go up, without the state having to push it. People will send their children to private schools that will be set up for them, or if that is too expensive, they will demand that local governments set up schools.

The role of demand is indeed critical. School enrollment is sensitive to the rate of returns to education: During the Green Revolution in India, which raised the level of technical know-how needed to be a successful farmer and thereby increased the value of learning, education increased faster in regions that were better suited to the new seeds introduced by the Green Revolution.[9] More recently, there is the example of the offshore call centers. In Europe and the United States, they are usually vilified for taking away local jobs, but they have been part of a small social revolution in India by dramatically expanding young women's employment opportunities. In 2002, Robert Jensen of the University of California at Los Angeles teamed up with some of these centers to organize recruiting sessions for young women in randomly selected villages in rural areas where recruiters would typically not go, in three states in northern India. Not surprisingly, compared to other randomly chosen villages that did not see any such recruiting efforts, there was an increase in the employment of young women in business process outsourcing centers (BPOs) in these villages. Much more remarkably, given that this is the part of India probably most no-torious for discrimination against women, three years after the recruit-ing started, girls age five to eleven were about 5 percentage points more likely to be enrolled in school in the villages where there was re-cruiting. They also weighed more, suggesting that parents were taking better care of them: They had discovered that educating girls had eco-nomic value, and were happy to invest.[10]

Since parents are able to respond to changes in the need for an edu-cated labor force, the best education policy, for the demand wallahs, is no education policy. Make it attractive to invest in business requiring educated labor and there will be a need for an educated labor force, and therefore a pressure to supply it. And then, the argument contin-ues, since parents will start to really care about education, they will also put pressure on teachers to deliver what they need. If public schools cannot provide quality education, a private-school market will emerge. Competition in this market, they argue, will ensure that parents get the quality of schooling that they need for their children.

At the core of the demand wallahs' view is the idea that education is just another form of investment: People invest in education, as they invest in anything else, to make more money—in the form of in-creased earnings in the future. The obvious problem with thinking of education as an investment is that parents do the investing and children get the benefits, sometimes much later. And though many children do, in effect, "repay" parents for the investment by taking care of them in old age, many others do so only reluctantly, or they simply "default," abandoning their parents along the way. Even when the children turn out to be dutiful, it is not always clear that the extra bit of money that they earn because they spent that extra year in school translates into that much more for the parents—we have certainly come across parents who rue the day when their children became rich enough to move out to their own house, leaving them to their lonely elderly lives. T. Paul Schultz, a Yale economist, talks about his father, the famous economist and Nobel Laureate Theodore Schultz, whose parents were against ed-ucating him, because they wanted him to stay back on the farm.

It is true that many parents do take pride and pleasure in the fact that their children are doing well (and in sharing the good news with their neighbors). In this sense they may feel more than adequately repaid even when they don't get a penny from their children. So from the point of view of the parent, education is partly investment but also partly a "gift" that they offer their children. But there is also the flip side: Most parents are in a position of power relative to their children—they decide who goes to school, who stays home or goes out to work, and how their earnings are spent. Parents who are cynical about how much they would get out of a son's earnings once he is old enough to push back, and who do not value education for its own sake, may prefer to take him out of school and send him to work when he is ten. In other words, although the economic return to education (as measured by the extra earnings of an educated child) clearly matters, lots of other things probably matter as well, things like our hopes about the future, our expectations about our children, even how generous we are feeling toward them.

"Exactly," says the supply wallah. "This is why some parents need a push. A civilized society cannot allow a child's right to a normal childhood and a decent education to be held hostage to a parent's whims or greed." Building schools and hiring teachers is a necessary first step to lower the cost of sending a child to school, but it may not be enough. This rationale explains why most rich countries simply give parents no choice: Children have to be sent to school until a certain age, unless parents can prove they are educating them at home. But this clearly does not work where state capacity is more limited and compulsory education cannot be enforced. In such cases, the government must make it financially worthwhile for parents to send their children to school. This is the idea behind the new tool of choice in education policy: the conditional cash transfer.

The Curious History of Conditional Cash Transfers

Santiago Levy, a former professor of economics at Boston University, was deputy minister in the Mexican Ministry of Finance from 1994 to 2000, tasked with reforming the intricate welfare system, which was made of several distinct programs. He believed that by linking the receipt of welfare payments to investment in human capital (health and education), he could ensure that the money spent today could contribute to eradicating poverty, not only in the short term but in the long term as well, by fostering a healthy and well-educated generation. This inspired the design of PROGRESA, a transfer program "with strings attached." PROGRESA was the first conditional cash transfer (CCT) program: It offered money to poor families, but only if their children regularly attended school and the family sought preventive health care. They got more money if the children were in secondary school than in primary school and if it was a girl who went to school rather than a boy. To make it politically acceptable, the payments were presented as "compensation" to the family for the wages lost when their child went to school instead of working. But in reality, the goal was to nudge the family, by making it costly for the family to fail to send their children to school, regardless of what the family thought of education.

Santiago Levy had another goal—to make sure that the program survived the change of government every few years, since each new president usually canceled all his predecessors' programs before launching his own. Levy calculated that if the program was demonstrably a great success, the new government would not find it easy to get rid of it. So he set up a pilot project, which was offered only in a randomly chosen group of villages, making it possible to rigorously compare outcomes in chosen and non-chosen villages. The pilot demonstrated beyond reasonable doubt that such a program does substantially increase school enrollment, particularly at the secondary level. Secondary school enrollment increased from 67 percent to about 75 percent for girls, and from 73 percent to about 77 percent for boys.[11]

This was also one of the first demonstrations of the persuasive power of a successful randomized experiment. When the government duly changed, the program survived, albeit renamed OPORTUNIDADES. But Levy probably did not anticipate that he had given birth to two new traditions. First, CCTs spread like wildfire all over the rest of Latin America, and subsequently to the rest of the world. Mayor Michael Bloomberg even gave them a try in New York City. And second, when other countries launch their own CCTs, they now usually also carry out a set of randomized trials to evaluate them. In some of these experiments, features of the program are varied, to try to understand how to design it better.

Paradoxically, it was one of these replications, in Malawi, that led us to rethink the success of PROGRESA. The conditionality in PROGRESA is based on the principle that increased income is not enough and that parents need to be given an incentive. Researchers and practitioners started to ask whether an *unconditional* program could have the same effect as a conditional transfer. A World Bank study found, provocatively, that conditionality does not seem to matter at all: The researchers offered the families of school-age girls a transfer ranging between $5 and $20 USD PPP per month. In one group, the transfer was conditional on enrollment. In another, it wasn't. A third group (the control group) did not receive a transfer. The effects were large (after a year, dropout was 11 percent in the control group, and only 6 percent among those who benefited from the transfer), but they were the same for those who received the conditional transfer and for those who got the unconditional one, suggesting that parents did not need to be *forced* to send their children to school, they needed to be helped financially.[12] Subsequently, another study that compared conditional and unconditional transfers in Morocco found similar results.[13]

Several factors probably explain why the financial transfer made a difference in Malawi: Perhaps parents could not pay for school fees, or could not give up the money their children earned. Of course, borrowing to finance the schooling of their ten-year-old based on what she will make at twenty is entirely a pipe dream. The income transfer, by moving parents out of extreme poverty, may also have given the mental space to take a longer view of life: Schooling is something where the costs are paid now (you have to nag—or drag—your children into school now) and it only pays off when they are older.

For all these reasons, income per se matters for education decisions: Jamal will get less education than John because his parents are poorer, even if the income gains from education are the same for both. Indeed, in our eighteen-country data set we find that the share of spending on education increases as we move up from those who live on under 99 cents a day to those in the $6–$10 category. Given that the number of children born to each family goes down sharply with income, this means that education spending per child grows much faster than total consumption. This is the opposite of what we would expect in a world where education is an investment like any other, unless we are willing to believe that the poor are just incapable of getting educated.

This is important, because if parental income plays such a vital role in determining educational investment, rich children will get more education even if they are not particularly talented, and talented poor children may be deprived of an education. So leaving it purely to the market will not allow every child, wherever she comes from, to be educated according to her ability. Unless we can fully erase differences in income, public supply-side intervention that makes education cheaper would be necessary to get close to the socially efficient outcome: making sure that every child gets a chance.

Does Top-Down Education Policy Work?

The question, however, is whether this kind of public intervention, even if it is desirable in principle, is actually feasible. If parents do not care about education, isn't there a risk that such a top-down education drive would just lead to a waste of resources? In *The Elusive Quest for Growth*, Easterly argues, for example, that the investment in education in African countries has not helped these countries to grow.

Once again, the best way to answer this question is to study what happened when specific countries tried it. The good news is that despite the poor quality of education, schools are still useful. In Indonesia, after the first oil boom in 1973, the country's then dictator, General Suharto, decided to go on a school-building spree.[14] It was the classic top-down supply-driven program: Schools were built based on a pre-specified rule that gave strict precedence to areas where the number of unschooled children was the highest. If the lack of schools in this area reflected lack of interest in education, this program should have been a miserable failure.

In fact, the INPRES (Instruksi Presiden, or Presidential Instruction) program was a great success: To evaluate it, Esther compared the wages of adults who, as children, were young enough to have benefited from the newly constructed schools to what the immediately older generation (people who were just old enough to have missed their chance to go to these schools) was earning. She found that relative to the older generation, the wages of the younger one were significantly higher in areas where more schools were constructed. Putting together the effect on education and on wages, she concluded that every extra year of primary school due to the new school raised wages by about 8 percent. This estimate of the returns to education is very similar to what is commonly found in the United States.[15]

Another classic top-down program is compulsory schooling. In 1968, Taiwan instituted a law that made it mandatory for all children to complete nine years of schooling (the previous law only required six years of school attendance). This law had a significant positive effect on the schooling of both boys and girls, as well as on their employment prospects, especially for girls.[16] The benefits of education are not only monetary: The Taiwan program had a large effect on child mortality.[17] In Malawi, girls who did not drop out because of the cash transfer were also less likely to become pregnant. The same results were found in Kenya.[18] There is now a significant body of rigorous evidence testifying to the far-reaching effects of education.

Moreover, this research also concludes that every little bit of education helps. People who are comfortable with reading are more likely to read newspapers and bulletin boards and to find out when there is a government program available for them. People who go on to secondary education are more likely to get a formal-sector job, but even those who don't are able to run their businesses better.

It seems, then, that once again the polarized debate between philosophically opposed strategies largely misses the point. Supply and demand strategies have no reason to be mutually exclusive. Supply by itself does some good, but demand is important, too. There are indeed people who somehow find ways to get educated without any top-down help when the right jobs come to town, but for many others, the impetus from schools being built in their area can be critical.

None of this means that top-down strategies deliver as much as they could, or should. After all, as we saw, the quality of education delivered in public schools can be dismal. The fact that students are getting *some-thing* out of them does not mean they could not work significantly better. Could it be that demand-based approaches would work better? Private schooling is the canonical demand-driven strategy—the parents must spend their own hard-earned money to put their children into one, even though free public schools are available. Have private schools cracked the problem of the quality of education?

Private Schools

There is a surprising amount of agreement that private schools should play an important role in the process of filling the gaps in the education system. India's Right to Education Act, which was recently passed with strong support across the political spectrum (including the left, which, the world over, has traditionally opposed the role of the market), is a version of what is called voucher privatization—the government gives citizens "vouchers" to pay private-school fees.

Even before the education experts gave it the heads-up, many ambitious low-income parents around the world had decided that they had to get their children into private schools, even if they would have to scrimp for it. This has caused the surprising phenomenon of cut-price private schools all over South Asia and Latin America. The monthly fees in these schools can be as low as $1.50. The schools tend to be quite modest, often just a couple of rooms in someone's house, and the teachers are often local people who couldn't find another job and decided to start a school. One study[19] found that an excellent predictor of the supply of private schools in a Pakistani village is whether a secondary girl's school had been set up in the area a generation earlier. Educated girls, looking for an opportunity to make some money without having to leave the village, were increasingly entering the education business as teachers.

Despite their sometimes dubious credentials, private schools often work better than public schools. The World Absenteeism Survey found that in India, private schools were more likely to be found in villages where the public schools were particularly bad. Furthermore, on average, the private-school teachers were 8 percentage points more likely to be in school on a given day than public-school teachers in the same village. Children who go to private school also perform better. In India in 2008, according to ASER, 47 percent of government-school students in fifth grade could not read at the second-grade level, compared to 32 percent of private-school students. In the Learning and Educational Achievement in Pakistan Schools (LEAPS) survey, by third grade, children in private schools were 1.5 years ahead in English and 2.5 years in math relative to children in public schools. It is true that families who decide to send their children to private schools may be different. But this could not be entirely explained by the private schools' attracting kids from richer families: The gap in performance between private- and public-school students was close to ten times the average gap between the children from the highest and lowest socioeconomic categories. And though it is not quite so large, there is still a sizable gap between children enrolled in public and private school even within the same family[20] (this may still be an overestimate of the true benefit if parents send their most talented child to private school or also help that child in other ways).[21]

So children in private school learn more than children in public schools. This does not mean, however, that private schools are as efficient as they could be. We see that they are not when we compare the effect of being in private school to the effect of simple interventions.

Pratham Versus Private Schools

Pratham, the remarkable educational NGO that runs ASER, not only exposes the deficiencies of the educational system but also tries to fix them. We have been working with them for the last ten years, evaluating almost every new edition of their program for teaching children arithmetic and reading. Our association started in the year 2000 in western India, in the cities of Mumbai and Vadodara, where Pratham was running what they called the Balsakhi (meaning "children's friend") program. The program took the twenty children in each classroom who most needed help and sent them to work with the balsakhi, a young woman from the community, on their specific areas of weakness. Despite an earthquake and communal riots, the program generated very large gains in test scores for these children—in Vadodara, about twice the magnitude of the average gains from private schooling that have been found in India.[22] Yet these balsakhis were much less educated than the average private- (or public-) school teacher—many of them had barely ten years of schooling, plus a week's training by Pratham.[23]

Given these results, many organizations would have rested on their laurels. Not Pratham. The idea of resting anywhere, least of all on their laurels, is entirely foreign to Madhav's personality or that of Rukmini Banerji, the human dynamo who is the driving force behind Pratham's spectacular expansion. One way in which Pratham could reach more children was by having communities take over the program. In the Jaunpur District in the eastern part of Uttar Pradesh, India's largest state and one of the poorest, Pratham volunteers went from village to village testing children and encouraging the community to get involved in the testing to see for themselves what their children knew and didn't know. The parents were not thrilled by what they saw—their first instinct often was to try to smack their children—but eventually a set of volunteers from the community emerged, ready to take on the job of helping their little brothers and sisters. They were mostly young college students who held classes in the evening in their neighborhoods. Pratham gave them a week of training but no other compensation.

We evaluated this program as well, and the results were quite dramatic: By the end of the program, *all* the participating children who could not read before the program could at least recognize letters (in contrast, only 40 percent of those in the comparison villages could read letters by the end of the year). Those who could read only letters at the beginning were 26 percent more likely, by the end, to be able to read a short story if they had participated than if they had not.[24]

More recently, Pratham has shifted its focus to working with the government school system. In Bihar, India's poorest state and the state with the highest measured teacher absentee rate, Pratham organized a set of remedial summer camps for schoolchildren in which the teachers from the government school system were invited to come and teach. The results from this evaluation were surprising: The much-maligned government teachers actually taught, and the gains were comparable to the gains from the Jaunpur evening classes.

Pratham's results are striking enough that many school systems in India and around the world are reaching out to the organization. A version of the program is now being tested in Ghana, in a large-scale RCT run as collaboration between a research team and the government: Youth who are looking for a first job experience will be trained to provide remedial education in school. Delegations from the Ministry of Education in Senegal and Mali have visited Pratham's operations and are thinking of replicating the program.

This evidence poses a set of puzzles: If volunteer and semi-volunteer teachers can generate such large gains, private schools can clearly adopt the same kinds of practices and should do even better. Yet we know that in India a full one-third of fifth-graders in private schools cannot read at first-grade level. Why not? If government teachers can teach so well, why don't we see it in the school system? If such large learning gains are so easily available, why don't parents demand them? Indeed, why was it that in Pratham's Jaunpar program, only 13 percent of the children who could not read attended the evening classes?

No doubt, some of the usual reasons that markets do not work as well as they should are at work here. Perhaps there is not enough competitive pressure among private schools, or parents are not sufficiently informed about what they do. Broader issues of political economy that we will discuss later may explain the poor performance of government teachers. But one key issue is unique to education: The peculiar way in which *expectations about what education is supposed to deliver* distort what parents demand, what both public and private schools deliver, and what children achieve—and the colossal waste that ensues.

THE CURSE OF EXPECTATIONS

The Illusory S-Shape

Some years ago we had organized a parent-child collage session in an informal school run by Seva Mandir in rural Udaipur. We had brought a stack of colorful magazines and asked parents to cut some pictures out from them to represent what they thought education would bring to their children. The idea was for them to build a collage with the help of their children.

The collages all ended up looking rather similar: The pictures were studded with gold and diamond jewelry and various recent models of cars. There were other images available in the magazines—peaceful rural vistas, fishing boats, coconut trees—but if the evidence of the collages is to be believed, this is not what education is all about. Parents seem to see education primarily as a way for their children to acquire (considerable) wealth. The anticipated route to those riches is, for most parents, a government job (as a teacher, for example), or failing that, some kind of office job. In Madagascar, parents of children from 640 schools were asked what they thought a child who had completed primary education would do for a living, and what a child who had completed secondary education would do. Seventy percent thought that a secondary-school graduate would get a government job, when in fact 33 percent of them actually get those jobs.[25]

Yet very few of these children will make it to sixth grade, let alone pass the graduation exam that, these days, is typically the minimum qualification for any kind of job that has an education requirement. And it is not that parents are fully unaware of this: In Madagascar, where parents were asked their view of the returns to education, it was found that parents get it right *on average*. But they greatly overstate both the upside and the downside. They see education as a lottery ticket, not as a safe investment.

Pak Sudarno, a scrap collector in the slum of Cica Das in Bandung, Indonesia, who, very matter-of-factly told us that he was known to be the "poorest person in the neighborhood," explained this succinctly. When we met him in June 2008, his youngest son (the youngest of nine children) was about to enter secondary school. He thought that the most probable outcome was that after completing secondary school, the boy would get a job in the nearby mall, where his brother was already working. This is a job that he could have had already—but nevertheless, Pak Sudarno thought it was worthwhile for him to complete secondary school, even if it meant three years of forgone salary. His wife thought that the boy might be able to enter a university. Pak Sudarno felt that this was a pipe dream—but he thought that there was some chance that he could get an office job, the best job possible, for the security and respectability it offered. In his view, it was worth taking the chance.

Parents also tend to believe that the first few years of education pay much less than the next ones. For example, in Madagascar, parents believed that each year of primary education would increase a child's income by 6 percent, each year of junior high education by 12 percent, and each year of senior secondary education by 20 percent. We found a very similar pattern in Morocco. There, parents believed that each year of primary education would increase a boy's earning by 5 percent, and each year of secondary education by 15 percent. The pattern was even more extreme for girls. In the view of parents, each year of primary education was worth almost nothing for them: 0.4 percent. But each year of secondary education was perceived to increase earnings 17 percent.

In reality, available estimates show that each year of education increases earnings more or less proportionally.[26] And even for people who do not get a formal-sector job, education seems to help: For example, educated farmers earned more during the Green Revolution than uneducated ones.[27] Moreover, there are also all the other, nonfinancial benefits. In other words, parents see an S-shape where there really isn't one.

This belief in the S-shape means that unless parents are unwilling to treat their children differently from one another, it makes sense for them to put all their educational eggs in the basket of the child they perceive to be the most promising, making sure that she gets enough education, rather than spreading the investment evenly across all their children. A few doors down from Shantarama (the widow whose two children were not in school), in the village of Naganadgi, we met a farming household with seven children. None of them had studied past second grade, except the youngest, a twelve-year-old boy. They were not satisfied with the quality of the government high school, where had spent a year. So the boy was attending seventh grade in a private boarding school located in the village. A year at school cost the family more than 10 percent of its total income from farming, a considerable commitment for just one child and clearly an impossible expense for seven. The lucky boy's mother explained to us that he was the only intelligent child in the family. The willingness to use words like "stupid" and "intelligent" to refer to one's own children, often in their presence, is entirely consistent with a worldview that puts a large premium on picking a winner (and in getting everyone else in the family to back the winner). This belief creates a strange form of sibling rivalry. In Burkina Faso, a study found that adolescents were more likely to be enrolled in school when they scored high on a test of intelligence, but they were *less* likely to be enrolled in school when their siblings had scored high.[28]

A study of conditional cash transfer in the city of Bogotá, Colombia, found compelling evidence of the propensity to concentrate resources on one child. The program had limited funds, and parents were offered the option to enter any of their age-eligible children into a lottery. Parents of winners would get a monthly transfer as long as the child attended school regularly. Lottery winners were more likely to attend regularly, more likely to reenroll each academic year, and, in the version of the program where part of the transfer was conditional on college enrollment, much more likely to attend college. The disturbing finding was that in families that entered two or more children and one won, the child who lost the lottery was *less* likely to be enrolled in school than children in families where both lost. This is despite the increase in family income, which should have helped the other child. A winner was picked, and resources were concentrated on him (or her).[29]

Misperception can be critical. In reality, there should not be an education-based poverty trap: Education is valuable at every level. But the fact that parents *believe* that the benefits of education are S-shaped leads them to behave as if there were a poverty trap, and thereby inadvertently to create one.

Elitist School Systems

Parents are not alone in focusing their expectations on success at the graduation exam: The whole education system colludes with them. The curriculum and organization of schools often date back to a colonial past, when schools were meant to train a local elite to be the effective allies of the colonial state, and the goal was to maximize the distance between them and the rest of the populace. Despite the influx of new learners, teachers still start from the premise that their mandate remains to prepare the best students for the difficult exams that, in most developing countries, act as a gateway either to the last years of school or to college. Associated with this is a relentless pressure to "modernize" the curriculum, toward making it more scientific and science oriented, toward fatter (and no doubt weightier) textbooks—to the point where the Indian government now sets a limit of 6.6 pounds on the total weight of the book bag that first- and second-graders can be asked to carry.

We once followed some Pratham staff to a school in the city of Vadodara, in western India. Their visit was preannounced and the teacher clearly wanted to make a good impression: His idea was to draw an enormously complex figure on the board, representing one of the fiendishly clever proofs that Euclidian geometry is famous for, accompanied by a long lecture about the diagram. All the children (students in third grade) were neatly arranged in rows on the floor, and sat very quietly. Some might have been trying to draw a simulacrum of the figure on their tiny slates, but the quality of the chalk was so low that it was impossible to tell. It was clear that none of them had a clue what was going on.

This teacher was not an exception. We have seen countless examples of this kind of elite bias among teachers in developing countries. In collaboration with Pascaline Dupas and Michael Kremer, Esther helped design a reorganization of Kenyan classrooms, taking advantage of an extra teacher to divide the class in two. Each class was separated by prior achievement, to help children learn what they did not know yet. Teachers were then randomly assigned to the "top" or "bottom" track by a public lottery. Teachers who "lost" the lottery and were assigned to the bottom track were upset, explaining that they wouldn't get anything out of teaching and would be blamed for their students' low scores. And they adjusted their behavior accordingly: During random visits, teachers assigned to the bottom track were less likely to teach, and instead more likely to be having tea in the teachers' room, than those assigned to the top track.[30]

The problem is not the high ambition per se; what makes it really damaging is that it is combined with low expectations of what the students can accomplish. We once went to see some testing of children in Uttarakand, in the foothills of the Indian Himalayas. It was a brilliant fall day, and it was hard not to feel that the testing was something of an intrusion. The child we were trying to test certainly thought so. He vigorously nodded when we asked him whether he went to school and seemed agreeable enough when we told him we would ask him some questions, but when the interviewer handed him a sheet to read, he resolutely looked the other way, as only a seven-year-old can. The interviewer tried very hard to coax him to just glance at the sheet, promising nice pictures and a fun story, but his mind was made up; his mother kept muttering words of encouragement, but a certain half-heartedness in her efforts suggested that she did not expect him to change his mind. As we walked toward the car after the "interview," an elderly man in a short dusty dhoti (the loincloth farmers wear in the area) and a yellowing T-shirt fell into step with us. "Children from homes like ours . . . ," he said, leaving us to guess the rest. We had seen the same pessimism in the mother's face and in faces of many mothers like her: She was not going to say it, but we were wasting our time.

References to a certain old-fashioned sociological determinism, whether based on caste, class, or ethnicity, are rife in conversations involving the poor. In the late 1990s, a team led by Jean Dreze prepared a report on the state of education in India, the Public Report on Basic Education in India (PROBE). One of the findings was:

> Many teachers are anxious to avoid being posted in remote or "backward" villages. One practical reason is the inconvenience of commuting, or of living in a remote village with poor facilities. . . . Another common reason is alienation from the local residents, who are sometimes said to be squandering their money on liquor, to have no potential for education, or simply to "behave like monkeys." Remote or backward areas are also seen as infertile ground for a teacher's efforts.

A young teacher simply told the team that it was impossible to communicate with "children of uncouth parents."[31]

In a study designed to find out whether this prejudice influenced teachers' behavior with students, teachers were asked to grade a set of exams. The teachers did not know the students, but half of the teachers, randomly chosen, were told the child's full name (which includes the caste name). The rest were fully anonymous. They found that, on average, teachers gave significantly lower grades to lower-caste students when they could see their caste than when they could not. But interestingly, it was not the higher-caste teachers who were doing this. The lower-caste teachers were actually *more* likely to assign worse grades to lower-caste students. They must have been convinced these children could not do well.[32]

The combination of elevated expectations and little faith can be quite lethal. As we saw, the belief in the S-shape curve leads people to give up. If the teachers and the parents do not believe that the child can cross the hump and get into the steep part of the S-curve, they may as well not try: The teacher ignores the children who have fallen behind and the parent stops taking interest in their education. But this behavior *creates* a poverty trap even where none exists in the first place. If they give up, they will never find out that perhaps the child could have made it. And in contrast, families that assume that their children can make it, or families that don't want to accept that a child of theirs will remain uneducated, which tend to be, for obvious historical reasons, more elite families, end up confirmed in their "high" hopes. As one of his early teachers likes to recall, when Abhijit was falling behind in his schoolwork in first grade, everyone somehow managed to persuade themselves that this was because he was too far ahead of the class and bored. As a result he was sent up to the next grade, where, once again, he immediately fell behind, to the point where the teacher took to hiding his homework so that the higher-ups would not question the wisdom of having promoted him. If, instead of being the child of two academics, he had been a child of two factory workers, he would almost surely have been assigned to remedial education or asked to leave the school.

Children themselves use this logic when assessing their own abilities. The social psychologist Claude Steele demonstrated the power of what he calls "stereotype threat" in the U.S. context: Women do better on math tests when they are explicitly told that the stereotype that women are worse in math does not apply to this particular test; African Americans do worse on tests if they have to start by indicating their race on the cover sheet.[33] Following Steele's work, two researchers from the World Bank had lower-caste children in the Indian state of Uttar Pradesh compete against high-caste children in solving mazes.[34] They found that the low-caste children compete well against the high-caste children as long as caste is not salient, but once low-caste children are reminded that they are low castes competing with high-caste children (by the simple contrivance of asking them their full names before the game starts), they do much worse. The authors argue that this may be driven in part by a fear of not being evaluated fairly by the obviously elite organizers of the game, but it could just as well be the internalization of the stereotype. A child who expects to find school difficult will probably blame herself and not her teachers when she can't understand what is being taught, and may end up deciding she's not cut out for school—"stupid," like most of her ilk—and give up on education altogether, daydreaming in class or, like Shantarama's children, just refusing to go.

WHY SCHOOLS FAIL

Because in many developing countries, both the curriculum and the teaching are designed for the elite rather than for the regular children who attend school, attempts to improve the functioning of the schools by providing extra inputs have generally been disappointing. In the early 1990s, Michael Kremer was looking for a simple test case to perform one of the first randomized evaluations of a policy intervention in a developing country. For this first attempt, he wanted a noncontroversial example in which the intervention was likely to have a large effect. Textbooks seemed to be perfect: Schools in western Kenya (where the study was to be conducted) had very few of them, and the near-universal consensus was that the books were essential inputs. Twenty-five schools were randomly chosen out of 100, and textbooks (the officially approved books for those classes) were distributed. The results were disappointing. There was no difference in the average test scores of students who received textbooks and those who did not. However, Kremer and his colleagues did discover that the children who were initially doing very well (those who had scores near the top in the test given before study began) made marked improvement in the schools where textbooks were given out. The story started to make sense. Kenya's language of education is English, and the textbooks were, naturally, in English. But for most children, English is only the third language (after their local language and Swahili, Kenya's language), and they speak it very poorly. Textbooks in English were never going to be very useful for the majority of children.[35] This experience has been repeated in many places with other inputs (from flip charts to improved teacher ratios). As long as they're not accompanied by a change in pedagogy or in incentives, new inputs don't help very much.

It should now be clear why private schools do not do better at educating the average child—their entire point is to prepare the best-performing children for some difficult public exam that is the stepping- stone toward greater things, which requires powering ahead and covering a broad syllabus. The fact that most children are getting left behind is unfortunate, but inevitable. The school Abhijit went to in Calcutta had a more or less explicit policy of expelling the bottom of the class every year, so that by the time the graduation exam came around, it could claim a perfect pass record. Kenyan primary schools adopt the same strategy, at least starting in sixth grade. Because parents share these preferences, they have little reason to put pressure on the schools to behave otherwise. Parents, like everyone else, want schools to deliver what they understand to be an "elite" education to their child—despite the fact that they are in no position to monitor whether this is what is actually being delivered or give any thought to whether their children will benefit from it. For example, English-language instruction is particularly popular with parents in South Asia, but non-English-speaking parents cannot know whether the teachers can actually teach in English. The flipside of this is that parents have little interest in the summer camps and the evening classes—kids who need those classes are not going to win the lottery, so what is the point?

We can also see why Pratham's summer schools worked. The public-school teacher seems to know how to teach the weaker children and is even willing to put some effort into it during the summer, but during the regular school year this is not his job—or so he has been led to believe. Recently, also in Bihar, we evaluated a Pratham initiative to fully integrate remedial education programs into government schools, by training the teachers to work with their materials and also by training volunteers to work as teacher's assistants in these classrooms. The result was striking. In those (randomly chosen) schools that had both the teacher training and the volunteers, the gains are substantial, mirroring all the Pratham results we saw above. Where there was just teacher training, on the other hand, essentially nothing changed. The same teachers who did so well during the summer camps completely failed to make a dent: The constraints imposed by the official pedagogy and the particular focus on covering the syllabus seem to be too much of a barrier. We cannot just blame the teachers for this. Under India's new Right to Education Act, finishing the curriculum is required by law.

At the broader, societal level, this pattern of beliefs and behavior means that most school systems are both unfair and wasteful. The children of the rich go to schools that not only teach more and teach better, but where they are treated with compassion and helped to reach their true potential. The poor end up in schools that make it very clear quite early that they are not wanted unless they show some exceptional gifts, and they are in effect expected to suffer in silence until they drop out.

This creates a huge waste of talent. Among all those people who drop out somewhere between primary school and college and those who never start school, many, perhaps most, are the victims of some misjudgment somewhere: Parents who give up too soon, teachers who never tried to teach them, the students' own diffidence. Some of these people almost surely had the potential to be professors of economics or captains of industry. Instead they became daily laborers or shopkeepers, or if they were lucky, they made it to some minor clerical position. The slots that they left vacant were grabbed, in all likelihood, by mediocre children of parents who could afford to offer their children every possible opportunity to make good.

Stories about great scientists, from Albert Einstein to the Indian math genius Ramanujam, both of whom did not make it through the educational system, are of course well-known. The story of the company Raman Boards suggests that this experience may not just be limited to a few extraordinary people. A Tamil engineer named V. Raman started Raman Boards in Mysore in the late 1970s. The company made industrial-grade paper products such as the sheets of cardboard used in electrical transformers. One day, V. Raman found a young man, Rangaswami, outside the door of the factory, asking for a job. He was from a very poor family, he said, and he had some engineering education, but just a diploma, not a proper college degree. Compelled by his insistence that he could do good work, Raman gave him a quick intelligence test. Impressed by the results, he took the young man under his wing. When there was a problem, Rangaswami would be assigned the task, and working initially with Raman, but increasingly on his own, he would come up with a creative solution to it. Raman's firm was eventually bought up by the giant Swedish multinational, ABB—it is now the most efficient of the many plants that ABB runs the world over, including in Sweden. Rangaswami, the man who could not get an engineering degree, is the head of engineering. His colleague, Krishnachari, another of Raman's finds—an ex-carpenter with little formal education—is a key manager in the components division.

Aroon, Raman's son, who ran the company before it was sold, now runs a small R&D unit with a few people who were with him at Raman Boards. His core research team of four includes two people who never completed high school, and no qualified engineers. They are brilliant, he says, but at the beginning the problem was that they didn't have the confidence to speak up, so how could one know? It is only because it was a small firm, and yet one that did a lot of R&D, that they were discovered. And even then it took a lot of patient work to discover their capabilities and they needed constant encouragement.

This model is obviously not easy to replicate. The problem is that there are no straightforward ways to identify talent, unless one is willing to spend a lot of time doing what the education system should have been doing: giving people enough chances to show what they are good at. Yet Raman Boards is not the only firm that thinks there is a lot of undiscovered talent out there. Infosys, one of India's IT giants, has set up testing centers where people, including those without much formal qualification, can walk in and take a test that focuses on intelligence and analytical skills rather than textbook learning. Those who do well get to become trainees, and successful trainees get a job. This alternative route is a source of hope for those who fell through the gaping holes in the education system. When Infosys closed its testing centers during the global recession, it was front-page news in India.

A combination of unrealistic goals, unnecessarily pessimistic expectations, and the wrong incentives for teachers contributes to ensure that education systems in developing countries fail their two basic tasks: giving everyone a sound basic set of skills, and identifying talent. Moreover, in some ways the job of delivering quality education is getting harder. The world over, education systems are under stress. Enrollment has gone up faster than resources, and with the growth in the high-tech sectors, there is a worldwide increase in the demand for the kind of peoples who used to become teachers. Now they are becoming programmers, computer systems managers, and bankers instead. This is going to be a particularly serious issue for finding good teachers at the secondary level and beyond.

Is there a way out, or is the problem simply too difficult?

REENGINEERING EDUCATION

The good news, and it is very good news indeed, is that all the evidence we have strongly suggests that making sure that every child learns the basics well in school is not only possible, it is in fact fairly easy, as long as one focuses on doing exactly that, and nothing else.

A remarkable social experiment from Israel shows how much schools can do. In 1991, 15,000 more or less indigent Ethiopian Jews and their children were airlifted out of Addis Ababa in a single day and dispersed into communities all over Israel. There, these children, whose parents had had on average between one and two years of schooling, entered elementary schools with other Israeli children, both long-term settlers and recent immigrants from Russia, whose parents had had on average 11.5 years of schooling. The family backgrounds of the two groups could not have been more different. Years later, at the point when those who entered school in 1991 were about to graduate from high school, the differences had narrowed considerably. Sixty-five percent of the Ethiopian children had reached twelfth grade without grade repetition, compared to the only slightly higher 74 percent among the Russian emigrants. It turns out that even the most severe disadvantage in terms of family background and early life conditions can largely be compensated for, at least in Israeli schools, where the right conditions are met.[36]

Successful experiments have given us a number of ideas on how to create these conditions. A first factor is a focus on basic skills, and a commitment to the idea that *every child* can master them as long as she, and her teacher, expends enough effort on it. This is the fundamental principle behind the Pratham program, but it is also an attitude that is encapsulated by the "no excuse" charter schools in the United States.[37] These schools, such as the Knowledge Is Power Program (KIPP) schools, the Harlem Children's Zone, and others, mainly cater to students from poor families (particularly black children), with a curriculum that focuses on the solid acquisition of basic skills and continuous measurements of what children actually know: Without such diagnosis, it is impossible to evaluate their progress.

These schools have been shown, in several studies based on comparing those winners and losers of the admission lotteries, to be extremely effective and successful. A study of charter schools in Boston suggests that expanding fourfold the capacity of charter schools and keeping the current demographic profile of students the same would have the potential to erase up to 40 percent of the citywide gap in math test scores between white and black children.[38] The mechanism at play is exactly what we see in Pratham's programs: Children who are completely lost in the regular school system (their test scores are way behind those of other children when they enter charter schools) are given a chance to catch up, and many take it.

A second piece of good news from Pratham's work is that it takes relatively little training to be an effective remedial teacher, at least in the lower grades. The volunteers who had such dramatic effects were mostly college students and other people with a week or ten days of training in pedagogy. Moreover, this extends beyond teaching only reading and basic arithmetic. The same program in Bihar that put volunteers in classrooms also had them teach the children who could read well to use their reading skills to learn—Pratham calls this Reading to Learn, the sequel to its more basic Learning to Read—and the learning gains were substantial. Charter schools mainly use young, enthusiastic teachers, and they are able to significantly help both primary-school and middle-school children.

Third, there are large potential gains to be had by reorganizing the curriculum and the classrooms to allow children to learn at their own pace, and in particular to make sure the children who are lagging behind can focus on the basics. Tracking children is a way to do that. In Kenya, the study mentioned earlier compared two models to assign first-grade students to two separate classes. In one model, children were randomly assigned to a classroom. In the other, they were split up based on what the children already knew. When students were assigned according to their initial level, so that the teachers could address the children's needs better, students at all levels of initial achievement did better. And the gains were persistent: At the end of third grade, students who had been tracked in first and second grades were still doing better than those who had not been tracked.[39] Alternatively, one could find other ways to tailor the teaching to the needs of individual students. One possibility is to make the boundaries between the grades more fluid, so that a child whose age puts him in fifth grade but who needs to take second-grade classes in some subjects can do so without additional stigma.

More generally, a lot could be done to change the unrealistic expectations that everyone has. A program in Madagascar that simply told parents about the average income gains from spending one more year in school *for children from backgrounds similar to theirs* had a sizable positive effect on test scores, and, in the case of parents who found out that they had underestimated the benefits of education, the gains were twice as large.[40] An earlier study in the Dominican Republic produced similar results with high school students.[41] Since it is essentially free to have teachers simply pass on information to parents, this is so far the cheapest known way to improve test scores, among all the interventions that have been evaluated.

It may also be a good idea to try to set more proximate goals for both children and teachers. That way everyone can stop focusing so much on that one elusive outcome at the end of many years. A program in Kenya that offered a $20 USD PPP scholarship for the next year to girls who scored in the top 15 percent on an exam not only got the girls to do much better, but it also put pressure on the teachers to work harder (to help the girls), which meant that boys did better, too, even though there was no scholarship for them.[42] In the United States, rewarding children for achieving long-term goals (such as getting high grades) was not successful, but rewarding them for effort on reading proved extremely effective.[43]

Finally, given that good teachers are hard to find and information technology is getting better and cheaper by the day, it seems rational to use it more. The current view of the use of technology in teaching in the education community is, however, not particularly positive. But this is based mainly on experience from the rich countries, where the alternative to being taught by the computer is, to a large extent, being taught by a well-trained and motivated teacher. As we have seen, this is not always the case in poor countries. And in fact, the evidence from the developing world, though sparse, is quite positive. We did an evaluation of a computer-assisted learning program run in collaboration with Pratham in the government schools in Vadodara in the early 2000s. The program was simple. Pairs of third- and fourth-graders got to play a game on the computer. The game involved solving progressively difficult math problems; success in solving them gave the winner a chance to shoot some garbage into outer space (this was a very politically correct game). Despite the fact that they only got to play for two hours a week, the gains from this program in terms of math scores were as large as those of some of the most successful education interventions that have been tried in various contexts over the years, and this was true across the board—the strongest children did better, and so did the weakest children. This highlights what is particularly good about the computer as a learning tool: Each child is able to set his or her own pace through the program.[44]

This message of scaling down expectations, focusing on the core competencies, and using technology to complement, or if necessary substitute for, teachers, does not sit well with some education experts. Their reaction is perhaps understandable—we seem to be suggesting a two-tier education system—one for the children of the rich, who will no doubt get taught to the highest standards in expensive private schools, and one for the rest. This objection is not entirely unwarranted but unfortunately, the division exists already, with the difference that the current system delivers essentially nothing to a very large fraction of children. If the curriculum were radically simplified, if the teacher's mission were squarely defined as making everyone master every bit of it, and if children were allowed to learn it at their own pace, by repeating if necessary, the vast majority of children would get something from the years they spend in school. Moreover, the gifted would actually get a chance to discover their own gifts. It is true that it would take some work to put them on the same footing as those who went to elite schools, but if they had learned to believe in themselves, they might have a chance, especially if there is a willingness in the system to help them get there.[45] Recognizing that schools have to serve the students they do have, rather than the ones they perhaps would like to have, may be the first step to having a school system that gives a chance to every child.

5

Pak Sudarno's Big Family

S anjay Gandhi, the younger son of the Indian prime minister
Indira Gandhi and her heir apparent until his death in a plane
crash in 1981, was convinced that population control needed to
be an essential part of India's development plan. It was the central
theme of his many public appearances during the period called the
Emergency (mid-1975 until early 1977), when democratic rights were
temporarily suspended and Sanjay Gandhi, despite holding no official
position, was quite openly running things. The family-planning program must be given "the utmost attention and importance," he said in
a characteristically understated quote, "because all our industrial, economic, and agricultural progress would be of no use if the population
continued to rise at the present rate."[1]

India had had a long history with family planning, starting in the
mid-1960s. In 1971, the state of Kerala experimented with mobile
sterilization services, the "sterilization camps" approach that was to be
the cornerstone of Sanjay Gandhi's plan during the Emergency. Although most politicians before him had identified population control
as an important issue, Sanjay Gandhi brought to the problem both an
unprecedented level of enthusiasm and the ability (and willingness) to
twist as many arms as necessary to implement his chosen policies. In

April 1976, the Indian Cabinet approved a formal statement of national population policy that called for a number of measures to encourage family planning, notably, large financial incentives for those who agreed to be sterilized (such as a month's wages or priority on a housing list), and more frighteningly, authorization for each state to develop compulsory sterilization laws (for, say, everyone with more than two children). Although only one state proposed such a law (and that law was never approved), states were explicitly pressured to set sterilization quotas and fulfill them, and all but three states "voluntarily" chose targets greater than what was proposed by the central government: The targets totaled 8.6 million sterilizations for 1976–1977.

Once laid out, the quotas were not taken lightly. The chief of the Uttar Pradesh bureaucracy wrote by telegraph to his principal field subordinates: "Inform everybody that failure to achieve monthly targets will not only result in the stoppage of salaries but also suspension and severest penalties. Galvanise entire administrative machinery forthwith repeat forthwith and continue to report daily progress by crash wireless to me and secretary to Chief Minister." Every government employee, down to the village level, and not excluding railway inspectors and school teachers, was supposed to know the local target. Parents of schoolchildren were visited by teachers, who told them that in the future, their children may be denied enrollment in school if they did not agree to get sterilized. People traveling by train without a ticket— a widely accepted practice among the poor until then—were handed heavy fines unless they chose sterilization. Not surprisingly, the pressure occasionally went much further. In Uttawar, a Muslim village near the capital city of Delhi, all male villagers were rounded up one night by the police, sent to the police stations on bogus charges, and sent from there to be sterilized.

The policy appears to have achieved its immediate target, although the incentives probably also led to some overreporting in the number of actual sterilizations. In 1976–1977, 8.25 million people were reportedly sterilized, 6.5 million of them during just the period July–December 1976. By the end of 1976, 21 percent of Indian couples were sterilized. But the violations of civil liberties that were an integral part of the implementation of the program were widely resented, and

when in 1977, India finally held elections, discussions of the sterilization policy were a key part of the debate, as captured most memorably
by the slogan "*Indira hatao, indiri bachao* (Get rid of Indira and save your
penis)." It is widely believed that Indira Gandhi's defeat in the 1977
elections was in part driven by popular hatred for this program. The
new government immediately reversed the policy.

In one of those ironic twists in which historians delight, it is not in-
conceivable that in the longer term, Sanjay Gandhi actually contributed to the faster growth of India's population. Tainted by the
emergency, family-planning policies in India retreated into the shadows and in the shadows they have remained—some states, such as Rajasthan, do continue to promote sterilization on a voluntary basis, but
no one except the health bureaucracy seems to have any interest in it.
In the meantime, however, generalized suspicion of the motivations of
the state seems to be one of the most durable residues of the Emergency; for example, one still routinely hears of people in slums and villages refusing pulse polio drops because they believe it is a way to
secretly sterilize children.

This particular episode and China's draconian one-child policy are
the most well-known examples of severely enforced population control measures, but most developing countries have some form of population policy. In an article published in *Science* in 1994, John Bongaarts,
from the Population Council, estimated that in 1990, 85 percent of the
population of the developing world lived in countries where the government had the explicit view that their population was too large and
needed to be controlled through family planning.[2]

There are certainly many reasons for the world at large to be worried about population growth today. Jeffrey Sachs talks about them in
his book *Common Wealth*.[3] The most obvious is its potential impact on
the environment. Population growth contributes to the growing car-
bon dioxide emissions and hence to global warming. Drinking water is
getting scarcer by the day in some parts of the world, in part directly
because there are more people drinking and in part because having
more people means growing more food and therefore using more water for irrigation (70 percent of fresh water is accessed for irrigation).
The World Health Organization estimates that one-fifth of the world's

population lives in areas where fresh water is scarce.[4] These are of course vitally important issues, and individual families deciding how many children to have probably do not fully take them into account, which is precisely why a population policy might be needed. The problem is that it is impossible to develop a reasonable population policy without understanding why some people have so many children: Are they unable to control their own fertility (due to lack of access to contraception, for example), or is it a choice? And what are the reasons for those choices?

WHAT IS WRONG WITH LARGE FAMILIES?

Richer countries have lower population growth. For example, a country like Ethiopia, where the total fertility rate is 6.12 children per woman, is fifty-one times poorer than the United States, where the total fertility rate is 2.05.

This strong relationship has convinced many, including academics and policy makers, of the validity of an old argument first popularized by the Reverend Thomas Malthus, a professor of history and political economy at the East India Company College, near London, at the turn of the eighteenth century. Malthus believed that the resources countries have are more or less fixed (his favorite example was land), and he therefore thought that population growth was bound to make them poorer.[5] By this logic, the Black Death, believed to have killed half of Britain's population between 1348 and 1377, should get credit for the high-wage years that followed. Alwyn Young, an economist at the London School of Economics, recently reinstated this argument in the context of the current HIV/AIDS epidemic in Africa. In an article entitled "The Gift of the Dying," he argued that the epidemic would make future generations of Africans better off by reducing fertility.[6] This reduction of fertility occurs both directly, through the reluctance to engage in unprotected sex, and indirectly, because the resulting labor scarcity makes it more attractive for women to work rather than have babies. Young calculated that in South Africa in the coming decades, the "boon" of a reduced population would be large enough to outweigh the fact that many of the AIDS orphans would not get a proper education; South Africa could be 5.6 percent richer in perpetuity as a direct consequence of HIV. He concluded by observing, no doubt for the benefit of his more squeamish readers, "One cannot endlessly lament the scourge of high population growth in the developing world and then conclude that a reversal of such processes is an equal economic disaster."

Young's article generated a heated controversy that centered on whether the HIV/AIDS epidemic indeed causes a decline in fertility. Careful follow-up[7] has since refuted this claim. However, people were mostly willing to concede his other premise—that a cut in fertility would make everyone richer.

Yet this is less obvious than it sounds. After all, there are many times more people on the planet today than when Malthus first formulated his hypothesis and most of us are richer than Malthus's contemporaries. Technological progress, which did not figure in Malthus's theories, has a way of making resources appear from nowhere; when there are more people around, there are more people looking for new ideas, and so perhaps technological breakthroughs are more likely. Indeed, for most of human history (starting in 1 million BC), regions or countries that had more people were growing *faster* than the rest.[8]

The case is therefore unlikely to be settled on purely theoretical grounds. And the fact that today, countries with higher fertility rates are poorer, doesn't tell us that they are poorer because of high fertility: It could instead be that they have high fertility because they are poor, or some third factor could cause both high fertility and poverty. Even the "fact" that periods of rapid economic growth often coincide with sharp declines in fertility, as in Korea and Brazil in the 1960s, is ambiguous at best. Did families start having fewer children when growth accelerated, perhaps because they had less time to take care of them? Or did the reduction in fertility free up resources for other investments?

As we have had to do many times already, we need to shift perspective, leave the large question aside, and focus on the lives and choices of poor people—if we want to have any hope of making progress on this issue. One way to start is by looking at what happens within the family: Are large families poorer because they are large? Are they less able to invest in the education and health of their children?

One of Sanjay Gandhi's favorite slogans was "A small family is a happy family." Accompanied by a cartoon image of a beaming couple with their two plump children, it was one of the most universal sights in late 1970s India. This could have been the illustration of an influential argument offered by Gary Becker, a Nobel Prize–winner in economics. Families, Becker argued, face what he called a "quality-quantity trade-off." That is, when there are more children, each of them will be of lower "quality" because the parents will devote fewer resources to feeding and schooling each of them properly.[9] This would be particularly true if the parents believed, rightly or wrongly, that it is worth investing more in the most "gifted" of their children, which, as we have already discussed, is what happens in the S-shaped world. Some children could then end up being entirely denied their life chances. If children born into large families are less likely to receive proper education, nutrition, and health care (what economists call investment in human capital), and if poor families are more likely to be large (say, because they cannot afford contraception), this creates a mechanism for the intergenerational transmission of poverty, in which poor parents beget (many) poor children. Such a poverty trap could potentially provide a rationale for a population policy, an argument that Jeffrey Sachs makes in *Common Wealth*.[10] But is it actually true? Do children who grow up in larger families have obvious disadvantages? In our eighteen-country data set, children born into large families do tend to have less education, though this is not true everywhere—rural Indonesia,[11] Côte d'Ivoire, and Ghana[12] are among the exceptions. However, even where it is true, there is no presumption that it is *because* the children have many siblings that they are poor and less educated. It could just be that poor families who choose to have many children also do not value education as much.

To test Becker's model and find out whether an increase in family size leads to reduced investment in children's human capital, researchers have tried to focus on instances where the increase was in part beyond the control of the family. Their results are surprising: In such cases, they found no evidence that children born in smaller families are really more educated.

One example of a situation where a family ends up with more children than it expected, given that most of the world's poor do not use fertility-enhancing therapies, is the birth of twins: If the family was planning to have two children, for example, but twins are born at the second birth, the first child then has one more sibling than he or she would otherwise have had. The sex composition of children is another factor. Families often want to have both a boy and a girl. This means that a couple whose second child was of the same gender as their first is more likely to plan for a third than a family that already has a boy and a girl.[13] In many developing countries, parents are also more likely to have an additional child if they have not yet had a boy. Compare a girl who is a first child, and has one female sibling, with one who has a male younger sibling: The former is more likely to grow up with two or more siblings than the latter, for the purely accidental reason (at least till the advent of child sex-selection technologies) that she had a younger sister rather than a younger brother. A study in Israel that focused on these sources of variation in family size found, surprisingly, that large family size appears to have had no adverse effects on the education of the children, even among Israeli Arabs, who are mostly very poor.[14]

Nancy Qian found an even more provocative result when she looked at the effect of the one-child policy in China. In some areas, the policy was relaxed to allow a family whose first child was a girl to have a second child. She found that girls who, because of this policy, got a sibling they would not otherwise have had received *more* education, not less,[15] in apparent defiance of Becker's theorem.

Another piece of evidence comes from Matlab, Bangladesh. This area was the setting for one of the most impressive experiments in voluntary family planning in the world. In 1977, a sample of half of 141 villages was selected to receive an intensive family-planning outreach program called the Family Planning and Maternal and Child Health Program (FPMCH). Every two weeks, a trained nurse brought family-planning services to the homes of all married women of childbearing age who were willing to receive her. She also offered help with prenatal care and immunizations. Perhaps not surprisingly, the program led to a sharp reduction in the number of children. By 1996, women in the program areas between the ages of thirty and fifty-five had about 1.2 fewer children than those in the areas that didn't get the program.

This change was accompanied by a drop in child mortality by one-fourth, but since the program also directly intervened to improve child health, there is no reason to attribute the increase in child survival to the change in fertility. Yet despite the facts that fertility decreased and lots more money was spent on making children healthier, by 1996, there was no significant difference in the height, weight, school enrollment, or years of education achieved for either boys or girls. Again, the quality-quantity relationship seems to be absent.[16]

Of course, these three studies alone may not be the last word, and there is certainly a need for more research, but for now, our reading of the evidence, contrary to what Sachs argues in *Common Wealth*, is that there is no smoking gun to prove that larger families are bad for children. As such, it is hard to justify top-down family planning as a means of protecting children from having to grow up in large families.

That family size does not adversely affect children seems counterintuitive, however: If the same resources have to be shared among more people, some of them at least should end up with less. If children do not suffer, who does? One possible answer is the mother.

The Profamilia program in Colombia suggests that this is definitely something to worry about. Launched by a young obstetrician named Fernando Tamayo in 1965, Profamilia was the major provider of contraception in Colombia over the next few decades and is one of the longest-standing family-planning programs in the world. By 1986, 53 percent of Colombian women of reproductive age were using contraceptives, mainly obtained through Profamilia. And women who had access to family planning as teenagers through this program had more schooling and were 7 percent more likely to work in the formal sector than those who did not.[17]

Along similar lines, the Bangladeshi women who benefited from the program in Matlab were heavier and taller than those in the comparison group and also earned more. The availability of contraception gives women more control over their reproductive lives—they can decide not just how many babies to have but also when to have them. And there is clear evidence that getting pregnant too early in life is very bad for the health of the mother.[18] Moreover, early pregnancy, or even getting married, often results in dropping out of school.[19] But to locate the case for family planning in society's desire to protect the mother raises an obvious question: If getting pregnant at the wrong time is not in her interest, why does it happen? More generally, how do families make fertility decisions, and how much control do women have over these decisions?

DO THE POOR CONTROL THEIR FERTILITY DECISIONS?

One reason the poor may not be able to control their fertility is that they may not have access to modern contraception methods. According to the official UN report on progress toward the Millennium Development Goals, filling "unmet demand" for modern contraceptives could "result in a 27 percent drop in maternal deaths each year by reducing the annual number of unintended pregnancies from 75 million to 22 million."[20] Poor and uneducated women are much less likely to use contraception than richer and more educated women. Moreover, in the last decade, there has been no increase in the use of modern contraception among poor women.

Yet, low *usage* is not necessarily a sign of *lack of access*. The same kinds of demand-supply wars that have animated the field of education have their equivalents in the family-planning arena and, perhaps not surprisingly, the supply and demand wallahs are often the same people. The supply wallahs (such as Jeffrey Sachs) emphasize the importance of access to contraception, noting that people who use modern contraceptive methods have much lower fertility rates; the demand wallahs retort that this relationship just reflects the fact that those who want to reduce fertility mostly find their way to the right kind of contraception without any outside help, so just making contraception available will not do very much.

To find out whether it was the case, Donna Gibbons, Mark Pitt, and Mark Rosenzweig painstakingly matched the data on the number of family-planning clinics available at three points in time (1976, 1980, and 1986) in each of several thousand Indonesian subdistricts to village-level survey data on fertility.[21] Unsurprisingly, they found that regions that had more clinics had lower fertility. However, they also found that the decline in fertility over time was unrelated to the increase in the number of clinics. They concluded that family-planning facilities were provided where people wanted them, but that they had no direct effect on fertility. Demand wallahs, 1; supply wallahs, 0.

The Matlab program has long been the poster child for the supply wallahs. Here at least, they argue, there is incontrovertible evidence that the availability of contraceptives makes a difference. As we saw, women age thirty to fifty-five in 1996 had on average 1.2 fewer children in treatment areas than those in control areas. But the program in Matlab was doing much more than just making contraceptives available. One of its key components was the biweekly visit by a female health worker to households where women were in purdah and therefore limited in their mobility, bringing the discussion of contraception to places where it used to be taboo. (This also made the program expensive— Lant Pritchett, then a World Bank economist, estimated that the Matlab program cost thirty-five times more per fertile woman and per year than the typical family-planning program in Asia.)[22] Thus, it is plausible that the program directly altered the households' desired number of children, rather than just giving them some tools they could use to control their fertility. Moreover, since about 1991, fertility has stopped falling in the program areas, and the difference between program areas and other control areas has started to narrow. In 1998, the last year for which we have data, the total fertility rate was 3.0 in the program areas, 3.6 in the control areas, and 3.3 in the rest of Bangladesh.[23] The Matlab program may have simply accelerated a trend toward fertility reduction that was happening in the rest of the country. So at best, this one seems to be a draw.

The study of the Colombian Profamilia program also concludes that the program had very little effect on overall fertility. Access to Profamilia led women to have only about 5 percent fewer children in their lifetimes, which is less than one-tenth of the total fertility decline since the 1960s. Demand wallahs, 2; supply wallahs, 0.

Thus, the data seem to squarely hand victory to the demand wallahs: Contraceptive access may make people happy by giving them a much more convenient way to control their fertility than the available alternative. But it appears to do, in itself, little to reduce fertility.

Sex, School Uniforms, and Sugar Daddies

What better access to contraceptives can do, however, is help teenagers postpone pregnancies. The Profamilia program did that in Colombia and helped women get better jobs down the line. Unfortunately, in many countries, teenagers are barred from accessing the family-planning services unless their parents give official consent. Teenagers may be the most likely to have an unmet need for contraception, mainly because many countries do not recognize the legitimacy of their sexual desires or assume that they have so little control that they would not be able to use contraception properly. The result is that teenage pregnancy rates are extremely high in many developing countries, particularly in sub-Saharan Africa and in Latin America. According to WHO, the rate of teen pregnancy is above 10 percent in Côte d'Ivoire, Congo, and Zambia; and Mexico, Panama, Bolivia, and Guatemala have rates between 8.2 and 9.2 births per 100 adolescent women (in the United States, which has one of the highest teen pregnancy rates in the developed world, there are 4.5 births per 100 adolescent women).[24] Further, the little that seems to be done about this issue or the related issue of the spread of sexually transmitted diseases (including HIV/AIDs) tends to completely miss the mark.

Esther found a clear example of the consequences of this kind of misguided effort in Kenya. With Pascaline Dupas and Michael Kremer, she followed schoolgirls—initially ages twelve to fourteen, who had never been pregnant.[25] One, three, and five years down the road, average pregnancy rates among them were 5 percent, 14 percent, and 30 percent, respectively. Early pregnancies are not only undesirable in and of themselves, but they are also a marker for risky sex, which in Kenya means a higher risk of contracting HIV/AIDS. The official strategy to address this problem in Kenya, the result of a delicate balancing act negotiated among civic groups, various churches, international organizations, and the government, mostly emphasizes that sexual abstinence is the only foolproof solution. The standard message spells out a clear hierarchy of strategies: Abstain, Be faithful, use a Condom . . . or you Die (or in other words, ABCD). In schools, children are taught to avoid sex until marriage, and condoms are not discussed. For many years, this trend was encouraged by the U.S. government, which focused its AIDS prevention money on abstinence-only programs.[26]

This strategy presumes that adolescents are not responsible or smart enough to weigh the costs and benefits of sexual activity and condom use. If this were indeed the case, scaring them away from sex altogether (or at least from sex outside marriage) would be the only way to protect them. But several simultaneous experiments that Esther, Pascaline Dupas, and Michael Kremer conducted in Kenya suggest that, quite to the contrary, adolescents make carefully calculated, if not fully informed, choices about whom to have sex with and under what conditions.

In the first study, the ABCD strategy was evaluated by arranging for teachers in 170 randomly chosen schools to be trained in teaching the ABCD curriculum. Not surprisingly, this training increased the time spent on AIDS education in schools, but there were no changes in reported sexual behavior or even in knowledge about AIDS. In addition, when measured one, three, and five years after the intervention, pregnancy rates among adolescents were the same in schools where teachers were trained and where they were not, suggesting no change in the extent of risky sex.

The effects of the two other strategies that were tried in the same schools could not be more different. The second strategy just involved telling the girls something they did not know: the fact that older men are more likely to be infected with HIV than younger ones. A striking feature of HIV is that women from the ages of fifteen to nineteen are five times more likely to be infected than young men in the same cohort. This seems to be because young women have sex with older men, who have comparably high infection rates. The "sugar daddies" program simply informed students about what kind of people are more likely to be infected. Its effect was to sharply cut down sex with older men (the "sugar daddies") but, also interestingly, to promote protected sex with boys their own age. After a year, the pregnancy rates were 5.5 percent in schools that had not received the program and 3.7 percent in schools that had received it. This reduction was mainly attributable to a reduction by two-thirds in pregnancies where an older male partner was involved.[27]

The third program just made it easier for girls to remain in school by paying for a school uniform. Teenage pregnancy rates in the schools where uniforms were offered fell from 14 percent to 11 percent after a year. To put it slightly differently, for every three girls who stayed in school because of the free uniform, two delayed their first pregnancy. Intriguingly, this effect was entirely concentrated in the schools where the teachers had not been trained in the new sex-education curriculum. In schools that had both the HIV/AIDS and the uniforms programs, girls were no less likely to become pregnant than those in the schools that had nothing. The HIV/AIDS education curriculum, instead of reducing sexual activity among adolescents, actually *undid* the positive effect of the uniform distribution.

Putting these different results together, a coherent story starts to emerge. Girls in Kenya know perfectly well that unprotected sex leads to pregnancy. But if they think that the prospective father will feel obliged to take care of them once they give birth to his child, getting pregnant may not be such a bad thing after all. In fact, for the girls who cannot afford a school uniform and therefore cannot stay in school, having a child and starting a family of her own may be a relatively attractive option, compared to just staying at home and becoming the general "Hey, you" for the whole family, the usual outcome for unmarried out-of-school teenage girls. This makes older men more attractive partners than young boys who cannot yet afford to get married (at least when the girls don't know that they are more likely to have HIV). Uniforms reduce fertility by giving girls the ability to stay in school, and thus a reason not to be pregnant. But the sex-education program, because it discourages extramarital sex and promotes marriage, focuses the girls on finding a husband (who more or less has to be a sugar daddy), undoing the effect of the uniforms.

One thing is relatively clear: For the most part, poor people, even adolescent girls, make conscious choices about their own fertility and sexuality and find ways—though perhaps not pleasant ways—to control it. If young women get pregnant even though it is extremely costly for them, it must reflect someone's active decision.

Whose Choice?

One issue that immediately arises when we think about fertility choice, however, is whose choice? Fertility decisions are made by a couple, but women end up paying most of the physical costs of bearing children. Not surprisingly, their preferences for fertility end up being quite different from those of men. In surveys on desired family size in which men and women are separately interviewed, men usually report a larger ideal family size and consistently a lower demand for contraception than their wives. Given the potential for disagreement, how much say a woman has within the household will clearly matter. It is plausible, for example, that a woman who is much younger than her husband or much less educated (both consequences of early marriage) will find it harder to stand up to her husband. But it also depends on whether she can find a job, her freedom to divorce, and her survival options in the case of divorce. These contingencies, in turn, depend on the legal, social, political, and economic environment she and her husband inhabit, which can be affected by public policy. In Peru, for example, when former squatters were handed out property rights, fertility declined in households that got a title (compared to those that got nothing), but only if the woman's name was included on the title along with that of the man.[28] One likely explanation is that with her name on a property title, the woman acquired more bargaining power in the family and was therefore able to weigh more heavily in the decision on family size.

The conflict between husbands and wives also implies that whereas the availability of contraceptives per se may not do very much to reduce fertility, small changes in the *way* in which they are made available can potentially have larger effects. Nava Ashraf and Erica Field provided 836 married women in Lusaka, Zambia, with a voucher guaranteeing free and immediate access to a range of modern contraceptives through a private appointment with a family-planning nurse. Some women received the voucher in private. Some received the voucher in the presence of their husbands. Ashraf and Field found that this made a huge difference: Compared to cases where husbands were involved, women who were seen alone were 23 percent more likely to visit a family-planning nurse, 38 percent more likely to ask for a relatively concealable form of contraception (injectable contraceptives or contraceptive implants), and 57 percent less likely to report an unwanted birth nine to fourteen months later.[29] One of the reasons the Matlab program changed fertility choices more than other family-planning programs is probably also that by visiting the women in their houses, presumably when the husbands were away, the female health worker may have enabled some of them to adopt family planning without his knowledge. In contrast, women whose mobility was restricted by the custom of purdah (which forbids a woman to leave the house without her husband) would have had to be accompanied by their husbands to go receive the services at a central location, and this might have changed their decision.

A possible explanation for the relatively large effects of the Matlab program, especially early on, is that it accelerated social change. One reason the fertility transition takes time is that people other than the wife and husband have a say about it. Fertility is in part a social and a religious norm, and deviations from it do get punished (by ostracism, ridicule, or religious sanctions). Therefore, it matters what the community deems to be appropriate behavior. In the treatment areas in Matlab, this change was faster than elsewhere—the community health workers, who tended to be relatively well-educated and assertive women, were both the embodiment of the new norm and the carrier of news about the shifting norms in the rest of the world.

Kaivan Munshi studied the role of social norms in the contraception decisions in Matlab. He cites a young woman who described how her peer group discussed "how many children we would have, what method would be suitable for us . . . whether we should adopt family planning or not, all these topics. . . . We used to know from people that they used (contraceptives). If a couple takes any such method, the news somehow spreads."[30]

Munshi found that in Matlab villages where there was a community health worker, women were more likely to adopt contraceptives if village members of their own religious group had had higher contraceptive use over the previous six months. Even though both Hindus and Muslims within the village had access to the same health worker and had exactly the same access to contraceptives, Hindus adopted contraceptive use when other Hindus were doing so and Muslims adopted contraceptives when other Muslims did. The contraceptive adoption by Hindus had no effect on the adoption by their Muslim neighbors, and vice versa. This pattern, Munshi concludes, must mean that the women were progressively learning about what was acceptable behavior within their communities.

Negotiating shifts in the social norm within traditional societies can be a very complex business. It is not easy, for example, to ask certain questions (Is contraception against religion? Will it make me permanently barren? Where can I find it?) because the act of asking itself reveals your inclinations. As a result, people often pick up things from the most unlikely sources. In Brazil, a Catholic country, the state has carefully stayed away from encouraging family planning. However, television is very popular, in particular the telenovelas (soap operas) that air on prime time on one of the main channels, Rede Globo. From the 1970s through the 1990s, access to the Rede Globo channel expanded dramatically, and with it the viewership of the telenovelas. At the telenovelas' peak popularity in the 1980s, the characters in the soaps tended to be very different from the average Brazilian in terms of both class and social attitudes: Whereas the average Brazilian woman had almost six children in 1970, in the soap operas most female characters under the age of fifty had none, and the rest had one. Right after soaps became available in an area, the number of births would drop sharply; moreover, women who had children in those areas named their children after the main characters in the soap.[31] The novelas ended up projecting a very different vision of the good life than the one that Brazilians were used to, with historic consequences. This was not entirely accidental—in Brazil's straitlaced society, the soap opera ended up being the outlet of choice for many creative and progressive artists.

At the risk of sounding, perhaps one time too many, like the "two-handed economists" that irritated Harry Truman, the answer to the question "Do the poor control their family decisions?" thus seems to proceed in two steps. At the most obvious level, they do: Their fertility decisions are the product of a choice, and even the lack of availability of contraception does not seem to be a big constraint. At the same time, what leads them to make these choices may be in part factors that are outside their immediate control: Women, in particular, may be pressured by their husbands, their mothers-in-law, or social norms to bear more children than they would like. This suggests a very different set of policies than those adopted by Sanjay Gandhi, or by the well-intentioned international organizations today: Making contraception available will not be sufficient. Affecting social norms may be more difficult, although the example of TV in Brazil shows it can be done. But the social norms may also reflect economic interests in a society. To what extent do the poor want many children simply because it is a sound economic investment?

CHILDREN AS FINANCIAL INSTRUMENTS

For many parents, children are their economic futures: an insurance policy, a savings product, and some lottery tickets, all rolled into a convenient pint-size package.

Pak Sudarno, the scrap collector from the Cica Das slum in Indonesia, who was sending his youngest child to secondary school because that seemed to him to be a worthwhile gamble, had nine children and a large number of grandchildren. When we asked him whether he was happy that he had had so many children, he said "absolutely." He explained that with nine children, he could be sure that at least a couple of them would turn out fine and take care of him when he was old. Clearly, having more children also increases the risk that something will go wrong with at least one of them. In fact, one of Pak Sudarno's nine children suffered from severe depression and had disappeared three years before. He was sad about that, but at least he had the other eight to console him.

Many parents in rich countries don't need to think in quite these terms because they have other ways to deal with their waning years—there is Social Security, there are mutual funds and retirement plans, and there is health insurance, public or private. We will discuss at some length why many of these options are not really available to someone like Pak Sudarno in the coming chapters. For the time being, we will just observe that for most of the world's poor, the idea that children (and family beyond children—siblings, cousins, and so forth) will take care of parents in old age and during times of need is the most natural thing. In China, for example, more than half the elderly lived with their children in 2008, and that fraction increases to 70 percent for those who had seven or eight children (this was before family planning, when having many children was actually politically favored).[32] Elderly parents also received regular financial help from their children, particularly boys.

If children are in part a way to save for the distant future, we would expect that when fertility drops, financial savings go up. China, with its government-enforced restriction on family size, provides us with the starkest example of this phenomenon. After encouraging high fertility rates immediately after the revolution, China started encouraging family planning in 1972, then introduced the one-child policy in 1978. Abhijit, with two Chinese-born coauthors, Nancy Qian (an only child born in the one-child policy era) and Xin Meng (one of four children born before it began) examined what happened to savings rates after the introduction of family planning.[33] Households that had their first child after 1972 have one less child on average than those who had that child before 1972, and their savings rates are approximately 10 percentage points higher. These results imply that up to one-third of the phenomenal increase in savings rates in China in the past three decades (the household savings ratio increased from 5 percent in 1978 to 34 percent in 1994) can potentially be explained by the reduction in fertility induced by family-planning policies; the effect was particularly strong for households that had a daughter rather than a son at first birth, consistent with the view that sons are supposed to be the ones who take care of parents.

This is a huge effect, but of course the Chinese "experiment" is somewhat extreme: It was a large, sudden, and involuntary reduction in family size. Something similar happened in the Matlab area in Bangladesh, however. By 1996, families in villages where contraception had been made available had significantly more assets of all kinds (jewelry, land, animals, house improvements) than families in the comparable villages where it was not available. On average, a household in the treatment area had 55,000 takas' more worth in assets ($3,600 USD

PPP, more than twice the GDP per capita of Bangladesh) than those in control areas. There is also a link between fertility and the amount of money given to parents by their children: Those in the treatment areas received on average 2,146 takas less in transfers from their children every year.[34]

The very strong substitution between family size and savings may help us explain the surprising finding that having fewer children does not translate into healthier or better-educated children: If parents who have fewer children expect lower money transfers in the future, they also need to save more in anticipation, and this cuts into the funds they have available for investing in the children they have. Indeed, if investing in children tends to have a much higher return than investing in financial assets (after all, feeding a child is not that expensive), families may actually be poorer in a lifetime sense when they have fewer children.

The same logic also tells us that if parents don't expect their daughters to be nearly as useful in taking care of them as their sons—say, because they have to pay a dowry to get their daughters married or because women are expected to get married and once married, their husbands have economic control over them—parents will be less invested in the lives of their daughters. Families not only choose an optimal number of children, they also choose the gender composition. We typically think of our children's gender as something we don't get to decide, but that turns out to be untrue: Sex-selective abortions, which are now widely available and extremely cheap, allow parents to choose whether they would rather abort a female fetus. As the stickers pasted on the dividers in Delhi's main road advertising (illegal) sex-determination services put it: "Spend 500 rupees now and save 50,000 rupees later" (on dowries). And even before sex-selective abortion was an option, in environments where a whole range of childhood diseases can easily turn fatal if not properly dealt with, there was always neglect, deliberate or otherwise, which can be an effective way to get rid of any unwanted children.

Even if their children don't die before or after birth, when parents prefer boys, they may have children until they have the number of boys they want. This means that girls will tend to grow up in larger families, and many of the girls will be born in a family that really wanted boys. In India, girl babies stop getting breast-fed earlier than boys, which means that they start drinking water earlier and have accelerated exposure to waterborne life-threatening diseases like diarrhea.[35] This is mostly the unintended consequence of the fact that breast-feeding acts as a contraceptive. After the birth of a girl (particularly if she has no brothers), parents are more likely to want to stop breast-feeding earlier in order to increase the wife's chances of getting pregnant again.

Whatever the exact mechanics of discrimination against baby girls (or potential baby girls), the fact remains that the world has many fewer girls than human biology would predict. In the 1980s, in a now classic article in the *New York Review of Books*, Amartya Sen calculated that there were 100 million "missing women" in the world.[36] This was before sex-selective abortion was available—and things have only gotten worse since. In some regions in China, there are today 124 boys for every 100 girls. Between 1991 and 2001 (the date of the latest census in India), the number of boys under seven per 100 girls the same age increased from 105.8 to 107.8 for India as a whole. In Punjab, Haryana, and Gujarat, three of India's richest states but also three of the states where discrimination against girls is believed to be the greatest, there were respectively 126.1, 122.0, and 113.8 boys per 100 girls in 2001.[37] Even according to self-reports, which almost certainly underestimate the phenomenon, the number of abortions is particularly high in those states: In families with two daughters, 6.6 percent of pregnancies ended in an induced abortion and 7.2 percent in a "spontaneous" abortion.

But this is less of a problem where girls are more valuable either in the market for marriage or in the labor market. In India, girls are not supposed to get married within their own villages. Typically, there are designated areas, not too close to the village but not too far away, into which a majority of the girls will marry and move. As a result, it is possible to look at what happens when there is economic growth in this marriage "catchment" area, which presumably makes it easier to find a prosperous family to marry a daughter into. Andrew Foster and Mark Rosenzweig studied this and found that the mortality differential between boys and girls decreases when a girl's marriage prospects are brighter; in contrast, economic growth *in the village,* which increases the value of investing in boys (because they stay home), leads to a widening of the mortality gap between boys and girls.[38]

Perhaps the most striking illustration of how a household's treatment of girls responds to the relative values of boys and girls comes from China, which has one of the largest imbalances between boys and girls. During the Maoist era, centrally planned agricultural production targets focused on staple crops. In the early reform era (1978–1980), households were allowed to produce cash crops, including tea and orchard fruits. Women tend to be more useful than men in the production of tea, which needs to be plucked with delicate fingers. In contrast, men are more useful than women in the production of orchard fruits, which involves lifting heavy loads. Nancy Qian showed that when we compare children born in the post- and pre-reform periods, the number of girls in the tea plantation regions (hilly and rainy) increased, but it went down in the regions that were more suitable for orchards.[39] In regions that were not particularly suitable to either tea or orchards, where agricultural income increased across the board without favoring either gender, the gender composition of children did not change.

What all of this underscores is the violence, active and passive, subsumed within the functioning of the traditional family. This was, until fairly recently, ignored by most (though not all) economists, who preferred to leave that black box closed. Yet most societies rely on the goodwill of the parents to make sure that children get fed, schooled, socialized, and taken care of more generally. Given that these are the same parents who contrive to let their little girls die, how much faith should we place in their ability to get this done effectively?

THE FAMILY

For the sake of their models, economists often ignore the inconvenient fact that the family is not the same as just one person. We treat the family as one "unit," assuming that the family makes decisions as if it were just one individual. The paterfamilias, the head of the dynasty, decides on behalf of his spouse and his children what the family consumes, who gets educated and for how long, who gets what kind of bequest, and so on. He may be altruistic, but he is clearly omnipotent. But as anybody who has been part of a family knows, this isn't quite how families work. This simplification is misleading, and there are important policy consequences from ignoring the complicated dynamics within the family. We already saw, for example, that giving women access to a formal property title is important for fertility choices, not because it changes her view on how many children she wants but because it makes her views count more.

The realization that the simplest model was missing important aspects of how the family works led to a reassessment in the 1980s and 1990s:[40] Family decisionmaking came to be seen as the result of a bargaining process among family members (or at least between the two parents). Both partners negotiate over what to buy, where to go on vacation, who should work how many hours, and how many children to have, but do so in a way that serves both of their interests as well as possible. In other words, even if they disagree on how the money should be spent, if one of them can be made happier without hurting the other one's well-being, they would make sure it is done. This view of the family is usually referred to as the "efficient household" model. It recognizes that there is something special about the family—its members, after all, did not meet just yesterday and are presumably tied together for the long term. It should therefore be possible (and in their interest) to negotiate over all their decisions to make sure that they do as well as they can, as a family. For example, if the family runs a small enterprise (be it a farm or a small business), it should always try to make as much money from it as possible, and only afterward find a way to split up the gains among its members.

Christopher Udry tested this prediction in rural Burkina Faso, where each household member (the husband and the wife, or wives) works on a separate plot.[41] In an efficient household, all inputs (family labor, fertilizer, and so forth) should be allocated to the various plots in a way that maximizes total family earnings. The data squarely rejected this view: Instead, plots farmed by women were allocated systematically less fertilizer, less male labor, and less child labor than plots farmed by men. As a result, these households systematically produced less than they could have. Using a little bit of fertilizer on a plot increases its productivity a great deal, but increasing the amount beyond that initial level does not do very much—it is more effective to use a little bit of fertilizer on all the plots than a lot of fertilizer on just one plot. But most of the fertilizer in the Burkina Faso households was used on the husband's plot: By reallocating some of the fertilizer plus a bit of labor to the wives' plots, the family could increase its production by 6 percent without spending an extra penny. Families were literally throwing money away because they could not agree on the best way to use the resources they had.

The reason they were doing so also seems clear: Even though they are part of the same family, what the husband grows on his own plot seems to determine what he gets to consume, and likewise for his wife.[42] In Côte d'Ivoire, women and men traditionally grow different crops. Men grow coffee and cocoa, whereas women grow bananas, vegetables, and other staples. Different crops are affected differently by the weather: A particular rainfall pattern may result in a good year for the male crops and a bad year for the female crops. In a study with Udry, Esther found that in good "male" years, more is spent on alcohol, tobacco, and personal luxury items for men (such as traditional items of clothing). In good "female" years, more resources are spent on little indulgences for women but also on food purchases for the household. What is particularly odd about these results is that spouses do not seem to be "insuring" each other. Knowing that they will be together for a long time, the husband could gift his wives some extra goodies in a good male year in return for some extras when the weather goes the other way. Informal insurance arrangements of this kind *between households* of the same ethnic group are not uncommon in Côte D'Ivoire,[43] so why do they not operate within the family?

One finding in Côte d'Ivoire gives us a useful hint about why families are different. There is a third "player" in the family drama—the modest yam, nutritious and easy to store, a staple food in the area. Yams are typically a "male" crop. But as the French anthropologist Claude Meillassoux explains, it is not a crop that the husband can freely sell and spend.[44] Yams are meant for the basic sustenance of the household. They can be sold, but only to pay for school fees or medical care for the children, not to buy a new blouse or some tobacco. And indeed, when there is a good year for yams, the family does consume more yams, which is perhaps not surprising, but spending on food purchased in the market and on education also increases. The yam makes sure that everyone in the family is properly fed and educated.

Thus, what makes the family special is not that its members are effective in negotiating with each other: Quite the contrary—they operate by observing simple, socially enforceable rules such as "Thou shalt not sell thy child's yam to buy new Nikes" that safeguard their basic interests, without having to negotiate all the time. Other results also make more sense viewed in this light. We saw that when women make more money on their plots, the family eats more. This may be a product of another rule that Meillassoux describes: It is the woman who is in charge of feeding the family; her husband gives her a fixed amount of money for that, but then it is her job to figure out how to do it best.

The family is bound together then, not in perfect harmony or by the ability to always divide up resources and responsibilities efficiently, but by a very incomplete, very coarse, and often very loose "contract" that defines the responsibilities of each member toward the other members. It is likely that the contract has to be socially enforced, because children cannot negotiate with parents, or wives with husbands, on an equal basis, but society gains from all members of the family having something like a fair share of resources. The incomplete nature of the contract probably reflects the difficulty of enforcing anything more sophisticated. There is no way for anyone to make sure that parents feed their children the right number of yams, but society may be able to sanction or show disapproval of parents who are seen selling yams to buy sneakers.

One problem with rules that rely on social norms for enforcement is that these norms change slowly, and therefore there is always the risk that the rules are entirely out of sync with reality, sometimes with tragic consequences. In Indonesia in 2008, we met a middle-aged couple at their house, a small white-and-green bamboo structure built on pillars. Right next to it stood another white-and-green house, much larger, airy, made of concrete. It belonged to their daughter, who worked as a maid in the Middle East. The couple was obviously very poor: The husband had a persistent cough and a headache that never seemed to go away, which made it hard for him to work. But he could not afford to see a doctor. Their younger child had dropped out of school after middle school because they could not afford his bus fare to the city. Suddenly, a four-year-old came into the room: She was visibly healthy, well fed, and dressed nicely in a pretty dress, with shoes that had little lights in them that went on and off as she ran around the room. It turned out that her grandparents were taking care of her while their daughter was away. Her mother sent money for the child, but nothing extra for the husband and wife. It seemed that they were the victims of some norm that had not yet shifted—married daughters were still not expected to take care of their parents, despite the obvious inequity it implied, but grandparents continued to feel obligated to take care of their granddaughters.

Despite the many obvious limitations of the family, society does not have another viable model for bringing up children, and though one day social pension programs and health insurance might free the elderly in today's poor countries from relying on their children for old-age care, it is not entirely obvious that it would make them (or their children) happier. The right space for policy is not so much to replace the family as it is to complete its action and, sometimes, protect us from its abuses. Starting from the right understanding of how families function is crucial in being able to do so effectively.

It is, for example, now widely recognized that public support programs that put money in the hands of women, like the Mexican program PROGRESA, for example, may be much more effective in directing resources toward children. In South Africa, at the end of apartheid, all men over sixty-five and women over sixty who did not have a private pension became eligible for a generous public pension. Many of these old people lived with their children and grandchildren, and the money was shared with the families. But it is only when a grandmother lived with a granddaughter that the granddaughter benefited: Those girls were significantly less likely to be stunted. Pensions received by a grandfather had no such effect. And there is more: Only if the pension was received by the girl's *maternal* grandmother was this effect seen.[45]

At least one of the two of us is inclined to interpret this evidence as saying that men are just a lot more selfish than women. But it may also be that this is where the norms and social expectations, which we argued play an important role in family decisionmaking, kick in. Perhaps women are expected to do things for the family when they get some windfall cash and men are not. If this is the case, not only who gets the money, but how it is earned, will also matter: Women may not feel that the money they have earned from their own work or their small business "belongs" to their family or their children. Paradoxically, it may be precisely because of women's traditional role in the family that public policy can get some mileage by empowering them.

We now return to the question of whether the poor really want such large families. Pak Sudarno wanted nine children. His large family was not the product of lack of self-control, lack of access to contraception, or even a norm imposed by society (although the fact that he got to make this decision may have been; his wife did not tell us what she would have wanted herself). At the same time, he believed that having nine children made him poor. So he did not really "want" so many children. He only needed nine children because there was no other way for him to be sure that at least one of them would support him later in his life. In an ideal world, he would have had fewer and tried to raise them as well as he could, but he would not have had to depend on them later.

Although many elderly people in the United States would prefer to spend more time with their children and grandchildren (at least if sitcoms are to be believed), the fact that they have the option of surviving on their own—thanks in part to Social Security and Medicare—may be very important for their dignity and their sense of self. It also means that they do not need to have lots of children in order to ensure that there will be someone to take care of them. They can have the number of children they really want, and if it turns out that none of them are willing or able to take care of them, there is always the public fallback.

The most effective population policy might therefore be to make it unnecessary to have so many children (in particular, so many male children). Effective social safety nets (such as health insurance or old age pensions) or even the kind of financial development that enables people to profitably save for retirement could lead to a substantial reduction in fertility and perhaps also less discrimination against girls. In the second part of the book, we turn to how this can be done.

PART II

Institutions

6

Barefoot Hedge-Fund Managers

R isk is a central fact of life for the poor, who often run small businesses or farms or work as casual laborers, with no assurance of regular employment. In such lives a bad break can have disastrous consequences.

In summer 2008, Ibu Tina lived with her disabled mother, her two brothers, and her four children ages three to nineteen in a tiny house in Cica Das, the vast urban slum in Bandung, Indonesia. The three younger children were at least nominally in school, but the oldest had dropped out. Her two unmarried brothers, a daily wage-earning construction worker and a taxi driver, kept the family from entirely going under, but there never seemed to be enough money for school fees, food, clothes for her children, and care for her aging mother.

Yet this had not always been Ibu Tina's life. When she was young, she worked in a garment factory. After she got married, she joined her husband's garment business. They had four employees, and the business was doing well. Their problems started when a business acquaintance they trusted gave them a bad check worth 20 million rupiah ($3,750 USD PPP). They went to the police. Policemen demanded 2.5 million rupiah in bribes even to agree to start investigating; after they were paid, they did manage to arrest the defaulter. He ended up spending a week in prison before he was released, after promising to repay what he owed. After reimbursing 4 million rupiah to Ibu Tina (of which the police claimed another 2 million) and promising to repay the rest over time, he disappeared and has not been heard from since. Ibu Tina and her husband had paid 4.5 million rupiah in bribes to recoup 4 million.

For the next three or four years, they tried very hard to bounce back and eventually managed to get a loan of 15 million rupiah ($2,800 USD PPP) from PUKK, a government lending program. They used the loan to start a garment-trading business. One of their first large orders was for shorts. They purchased the shorts from the garment makers and had them ironed and packaged for sale, but then the retailers backed off, leaving them with thousands of shorts that no one wanted.

The sequence of disasters put enormous stress on their marriage, and shortly after the second mishap, they got divorced. Ibu Tina moved in with her mother, bringing with her the four children and the stacks of shorts. When we met her she was still trying to recover from that trauma and said that she did not really have the energy to start again. She thought that when she felt better, she would open a small grocery shop in part of her mother's house, and maybe sell some of the shorts for Idur Fitri, the Muslim holiday.

To make matters worse, her eldest daughter needed a lot of attention. Four years earlier, when she was about fifteen, she had been abducted by a homeless person who lived next to their house. He released her after a few days, but the girl was traumatized by that episode and had stayed home since, unable either to work or go to school.

Was Ibu Tina particularly unlucky? To some extent, certainly. She thought that the abduction of her daughter was a freak accident (though even that situation had something to do with the fact that their house was near the railway line, where many homeless people lived), but she also firmly believed that her business misfortunes were symptomatic of the lives of small business owners.

THE HAZARDS OF BEING POOR

A friend of ours from the world of high finance always says that the poor are like hedge-fund managers—they live with huge amounts of risk. The only difference is in their levels of income. In fact, he grossly understates the case: No hedge-fund manager is liable for 100 percent of his losses, unlike almost every small business owner and small farmer. Moreover, the poor often have to raise all of the capital for their businesses, either out of the accumulated "wealth" of their families or by borrowing from somewhere, a circumstance most hedge-fund managers never have to face.

A high fraction of the poor run small businesses or farms. In our eighteen-country data set, an average of 50 percent of the urban poor have a non-agricultural business, whereas the fraction of the rural poor who report running a farm business ranges between 25 percent and 98 percent (the one exception is South Africa, where the black population was historically excluded from farming). In addition, a substantial fraction of these households also operate a non-agricultural business. Moreover, most of the land farmed by the poor is not irrigated. This makes farm earnings highly dependent on the weather: A drought, or even a delay in the rains, can cause a crop failure on non-irrigated land, and half the year's income might vanish.

Business or farm owners are not the only ones exposed to income risk. The other main form of employment for the poor is casual labor, paid by the day: Over half of those who are employed among the extremely poor in rural areas are casual workers. In urban areas, it is about 40 percent. When day laborers are lucky, they find jobs that last for several weeks or even a few months on a construction site or a farm, but often a job might just be for a few days or a couple of weeks. A casual worker never knows whether there will be a job when the current spell ends. If there is a problem with the business, these jobs are the first to be eliminated: It didn't take much time for Pak Solhin, whom we met in Chapter 2, to lose his job when fertilizer and oil prices went up and farmers cut back on labor. As a result, casual laborers tend to work fewer days in a year than regular workers, and a good portion of them work very few days in a year. A survey in Gujarat, India, found that casual workers worked on average 254 days per year (as against 354 for salaried workers, and 338 for the self-employed), and that the bottom one-third worked only 137 days.[1]

Big agricultural disasters, such as the Bangladesh drought of 1974 (when wages fell by 50 percent in terms of purchasing power and, according to some estimates, up to 1 million people died)[2] or food crises in Africa (such as the Niger 2005–2006 drought), naturally attract particular attention from the media, but even in "normal" years, agricultural incomes vary tremendously from year to year. In Bangladesh, in any normal year, agricultural wages could be up to 18 percent above or below their average levels.[3] And the poorer the country, the greater this variability. For instance, agricultural wages in India are twenty-one times more variable than in the United States.[4] This is no surprise: American farmers are insured, receive subsidies, and benefit from the standard social insurance programs; they don't need to fire their workers or cut wages when they have a bad harvest.

As if the vagaries of the elements were not bad enough, agricultural prices fluctuate enormously. There was an unprecedented rise in food prices from 2005 to 2008. They have collapsed during the global financial crisis, only to rise to the pre-crisis level over the last two years. High food prices should in principle favor producers (the rural poor) and hurt consumers (the urban poor). In summer 2008, however, a record year for the prices of both food and fertilizer, everyone we talked to in countries such as Indonesia and India felt that they were holding the short end of the stick: Farmers thought that their costs had increased more than their prices; workers complained that they could not find work because farmers were saving money; at the same time, city dwellers were struggling to pay for food. The problem was not just the level of prices, but also the uncertainty. Farmers, for example, who were paying high prices for fertilizer were not sure whether the price of their produce would still be high when they were ready to harvest.

For the poor, risk is not limited to income or food: Health, which we discussed in a previous chapter, is one major source of risk. There is also political violence, crime (as in the case of Ibu Tina's daughter), and corruption.

There is so much risk in the everyday lives of the poor that somewhat paradoxically, events that are perceived to be cataclysmic in rich countries often seem to barely register with them. In February 2009, the World Bank's president, Robert Zoellick, warned the world's leaders: "The global economic crisis [sparked by the collapse of Lehman Brothers in September 2008] threatens to become a human crisis in many developing countries unless they can take targeted measures to protect vulnerable people in their communities. While much of the world is focused on bank rescues and stimulus packages, we should not forget that poor people in developing countries are far more exposed if their economies falter."[5] The World Bank note on the subject added that with the drop in global demand, the poor would lose the market for their agricultural products, their casual jobs on construction sites, and their jobs in factories. Government budgets for schools, health facilities, and relief programs would be cut under the simultaneous pressure of reduced tax receipts and a collapse in international assistance.

In January 2009, we went with Somini Sengupta, then the *New York Times* correspondent in India, on a trip to Maldah, a rural district in West Bengal. She wanted to write a story on how the poor were affected by the global crisis. Sengupta, who grew up in California but speaks perfect Bengali, was told that a lot of the laborers at many construction sites in Delhi were from Maldah, and she knew that construction was slowing in Delhi. So we went from village to village, asking young men about their migration experiences.

Everyone knew someone who had migrated. Many of the migrants themselves were home for the month of Muharram, observed by many Indian Muslims. Everyone was happy to talk to us about migration experiences. Mothers told us about distant cities in southern or northern India, places like Ludhiana, Coimbatore, and Baroda, where their sons and nephews now lived and worked. There were of course some tragedies—one woman talked about her son who had died in Delhi of some mysterious disease—but the tone was overwhelmingly upbeat. "Are there jobs in the city?" Sengupta would ask. Yes, lots of jobs. "Have you heard of cutbacks?" No, no cutbacks in Mumbai, things are great. And so on. We went to the train station to see if anyone had come back after having lost his job. There we met three young men on their way to Mumbai. One of them had never been there; the others, veterans, were assuring him that finding a job was no problem. In the end, Sengupta never wrote the story about how the poor had suffered from the global downturn.

The point is not that construction jobs were not lost during the crisis in Mumbai—some surely were—but for most of these young men, the salient fact for the time being was the opportunity. There were still jobs to be had, jobs that paid more than twice what they could make in a day in the village. Compared to what they had endured—the routine anxiety about not getting any work at all, the seemingly interminable wait for the rains to come—life as a migrant construction worker sill seemed pretty attractive.

Of course the global crisis increased risk for the poor, but it added little to the overall risk they have to deal with daily, even when there is no crisis for the World Bank to worry about. During the Indonesian crisis of 1998, the rupiah lost 75 percent of its value, food prices went up 250 percent, and GDP fell by 12 percent, but rice farmers, who tend to be among the poorest people, actually gained in terms of purchasing power.[6] It was government employees and other people with relatively fixed cash incomes who ended up worse off. Even in 1997–1998, the year of the great Thai financial crisis, when the economy shrank by 10 percent, two-thirds of the nearly 1,000 people surveyed said that the main reason for the fall in their income was a drought.[7] Only 26 percent named loss of employment, and the job losses were almost surely not all a result of the crisis. For the most part, it seems that, once again, things were not a lot worse for the poor than in any other year, precisely because their situation is always rather bad. They were dealing with problems that were all too familiar. For the poor, every year feels like being in the middle of a colossal financial crisis.

Not only do the poor lead riskier lives than the less poor, but a bad break of the same magnitude is likely to hurt them more. First, a cut in consumption is more painful for someone who consumes very little to start with. When a not-so-poor household needs to cut back on consumption, members may sacrifice some cell phone minutes, buy meat less often, or send the children to a less expensive boarding school. This is clearly painful. But for the poor, a large cut in income might mean cutting into essential expenditures: Over the previous year, adults in 45 percent of the extremely poor households we surveyed in rural Udaipur District had to cut the size of their meals at some point. And cutting meals is something the poor hate: Respondents who had to cut

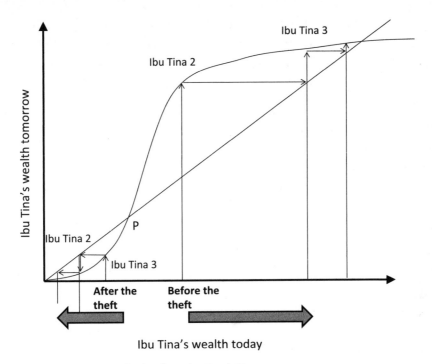

Figure 1: The Effect of a Shock on Ibu Tina's Fortunes

the size of their meals reported themselves to be much unhappier than those who did not need to do it.

Second, when the relationship between income today and future income is S-shaped, the effect on the poor of a bad break may actually be much worse than temporary unhappiness. In Figure 1, we have plotted the relationship between income today and income in the future for Ibu Tina, the Indonesian businesswoman.

In Chapter 1, we saw that there is the possibility of a poverty trap when investments pay off relatively little for those who can invest little, and more if they can invest enough. Ibu Tina was clearly in this situation. In her case, the relationship between income tomorrow and income today had an S-shape because her business needed a minimum scale to be profitable (in Chapter 9, we will see that this is a central feature of the businesses the poor run, so her case was not unique). Before the theft, she and her husband had four employees, and they had enough money to buy raw material and use their sewing machines and employees to make garments. This was very profitable. Afterward, all they could manage was to buy ready-made shorts and package them, an activity that was much less profitable (or not profitable at all). Before the debacle of the bounced check, Ibu Tina and her husband were outside the poverty-trap zone. If we follow their path over time, we see that they were on the trajectory to eventually arrive at a decent income. But the theft wiped out all their assets. This had the effect of moving them to the poverty-trap zone. Thereafter, they made so little money that they kept getting poorer over time: When we met her, Ibu Tina was reduced to living off her brothers' charity. One bad break in this S-shaped world can have permanent consequences. When the relationship between income today and income tomorrow is S-shaped, a family can plunge from being on a path to middle class to being permanently poor.

This process is often reinforced by a psychological process. Loss of hope and the sense that there is no easy way out can make it that much harder to have the self-control needed to try to climb back up the hill. We saw it with Pak Solhin, the onetime farm worker and now occasional fisherman in Chapter 2, and with Ibu Tina. They did not seem to be in the mental shape needed to pick themselves up and start over. In Udaipur we met a man who said in response to a standard survey question that he had been so "worried, tense, or anxious" that it interfered with normal activities like sleeping, working, and eating for more than a month. We asked him why. He said that his camel had died, and he had been crying and tense ever since. Somewhat naïvely perhaps, we then went on to ask whether he had done something about his depression (like talk to a friend, a health-care practitioner, or a traditional healer). He seemed irked: "I have lost the camel. Of course I should be sad. There is nothing to be done."

There may be other psychological forces at work as well: Facing risk (not only income risk but also the risk of death or disease) makes us worry, and worrying makes us stressed and depressed. Symptoms of depression are much more prevalent among the poor. Being stressed makes it harder to focus, which in turn may make us less productive. In particular, there is a strong association between poverty and the level of cortisol produced by the body, an indicator of stress. And conversely, the cortisol levels go down when households receive some help. The children of the beneficiaries of PROGRESA, the Mexican cash transfer program, have, for example, been found to have significantly lower levels of cortisol than comparable children whose mothers did not benefit from the program. This is important, because it turns out that cortisol directly impairs cognitive and decisionmaking ability: The stress-induced release of cortisol affects brain areas such as the prefrontal cortex, the amygdala, and the hippocampus, which are important in cognitive functioning; in particular, the prefrontal cortex is important in suppression of impulsive responses. It is therefore no surprise that when experimental subjects are artificially put under stressful conditions in the laboratory, they are less likely to make the economically rational decision when faced with choosing among different alternatives.[8]

THE HEDGE

What can the poor do to cope with these risks? A natural reaction when faced with a drop in wages or earnings is to try to work more. But this may sometimes be self-defeating. If all the poor laborers want to work more when times are bad (for example, because there is a drought or input prices have gone up), they compete with each other, which drives wages down. The situation is intensified if they cannot find a job outside the village. The result is that the same kind of drought has a more negative effect on wages in those villages in India that are more isolated, where it is harder for workers to go outside to look for work. In those places, working more is not necessarily an effective way of coping with getting paid less.[9]

If coping by working more after the shock hits is not really a good option, the best bet is often to try to limit exposure to risk by building, like a hedge-fund manager, a diversified portfolio, and it is clear that the poor invest a lot of ingenuity in doing so. The only difference is that they diversify activities, not just financial instruments. One striking fact about the poor is the sheer number of occupations that a single family seems to be involved in: In a survey of twenty-seven villages in West Bengal, even households that claimed to farm a piece of land spent only 40 percent of their time farming.[10] The median family in this survey had three working members and seven occupations. Generally, though most rural families have something to do with agriculture, it is rarely their sole occupation. This can be a way to reduce risk—if one activity falters, others can keep them going—though as we will see, there may be other reasons as well.

Holding multiple plots in different parts of the village, rather than one single large plot, also provides some risk diversification. When a blight or infestation hits one section of the village, other areas may escape; when the rains fail, the crops on plots with better access to groundwater have a better chance of surviving; and most surprisingly, different parts of the same village may actually have different microclimates, determined by exposition, slope, elevation, and moisture.

Temporary migration can also be interpreted in this light. It is relatively uncommon for an entire family to move together to the city. Usually, some members—mostly men and teenage boys in India or Mexico, but older daughters in China, the Philippines, and Thailand—migrate, while the rest stay behind. This ensures that the family's fortune does not rest entirely on one person's job in the city, while also allowing the family to maintain its village connections, which, as we will see, often turn out to be useful.

Another way the poor limit risk is by being very conservative in the way they manage their farms or their businesses. For example, they may know that a new and more productive variety of their main crop is available but choose not to adopt it. One advantage of sticking to the traditional technology is that farmers don't need to buy new seeds—they just save enough seed from last season's crop to replant—whereas the new seeds often cost a significant amount of money. Even if the new seeds repay the investment many times over when things go well, there is always a small chance that the crop will fail (say, because the rains don't arrive) and the farmer will lose the extra investment he has made in new seed.

The family is also used in creative ways to spread risk. Farming households in India use marriage as a way to diversify the "risk portfolio" of their extended families. When a woman moves to her in-laws' village after marriage, this creates a link between the household she came from and the household she married into, and the two families are able to call on each other when in trouble.[11] Farming households tend to marry off their daughters in villages that are close enough to maintain a relationship, but far enough away to have a slightly different weather pattern. In this way, if the rain fails in one village but not the other, they can help each other out. Another way to buy safety may be to have many children. Remember, Pak Sudarno had nine children to ensure at least one of them would take care of him.

All of these ways in which the poor cope with risk tend to be very costly. This has been well documented for agriculture: In India, poor farmers use farm inputs in a more conservative but less efficient way when they live in areas where rainfall is more erratic.[12] Poor farmers' profit rates go up by as much as 35 percent when they live in areas where the yearly rainfall pattern is very predictable. Furthermore, risk affects only the poor in this way: In the case of the richer farmers, there is no relationship between farm profit rates and variability in rainfall, presumably because they can afford a loss of harvest and therefore are willing to take risks.

Another strategy that poor farmers often adopt is to become someone's share tenant, meaning that the landlord pays a part of the cost of farming and claims a part of the output. This limits the farmer's risk exposure at the cost of incentives: Knowing that the landlord will take half (for example) of whatever comes out of the ground, the farmer has less reason to work very hard. A study in India showed that farmers put in 20 percent less of their own effort on land that they sharecrop compared to land where they are entitled to the entire crop.[13] As a result, these plots are farmed less intensively and less efficiently.

Having multiple occupations, as many poor people do, is also inefficient. It is hard to become a specialist in anything without specializing in it. Women who run three different businesses and men who cannot commit to a fixed job in the city because they want to keep the option of returning to the village every few weeks give up the opportunity to acquire skills and experience in their main occupations. By passing up these opportunities, they also pass up the gains from specializing in what they are really good at.

The risk borne by the poor is thus not only costly once a shock hits: The fear that something bad might happen has a debilitating effect on poor people's ability to fully realize their potential.

Helping Each Other Out

Another, and potentially much better, way to deal with risk is for villagers to help each other out. Most poor people live in villages or neighborhoods and have access to an extensive network of people who know them well: extended families, communities based on religion or ethnicity. Whereas some shocks may strike everyone in the network (a bad monsoon, for example), others are more specific. If those who are doing well now help out those who are having a bad time, in return for similar help when the roles are reversed, everyone can be made better off: Helping each other out does not have to be charity.

A study by Christopher Udry shows both the power and the limits of such informal insurance. Over an entire year that he spent in rural Nigeria, Udry got his fellow villagers to record every gift or informal loan that they gave to each other, as well as the terms under which they repaid those loans.[14] He also asked them every month if something bad had happened to them. He found that at any point in time, the average family owed or was owed money by 2.5 other families. Furthermore, the terms of the loans were adjusted to reflect the situations of both the lender and the borrower. When the borrower suffered a shock, he would reimburse less (often less than the original loan amount), but when it was the lender who had hit a rough patch, the borrower would actually repay *more than he owed*. The dense network of mutual borrowing and lending did a lot to reduce the risk that any individual was facing. Nevertheless, there was some limit to what this informal solidarity could achieve. Families still suffered a drop in consumption when they experienced a shock, even when the total income of everyone in their network put together had not changed.

A large body of research on informal insurance, which has investigated this phenomenon in places ranging from Côte d'Ivoire to Thailand, finds the same thing: While traditional solidarity networks do help in absorbing shocks, the insurance they provide is far from perfect.

If risk were well insured, it should be possible for a family to always consume more or less the same amount, dictated by its average earning capacity: In good times, they would help others, and in bad times, others would help them in turn. This is not what we usually see.

Health shocks, in particular, are very badly insured. In Indonesia, consumption drops 20 percent when a household member falls severely ill.[15] A study in the Philippines documents that intra-village solidarity functions particularly poorly in the case of nonfatal severe illnesses.[16] When a family has a bad harvest, or when someone loses his or her job, other families in the village come to the rescue. The affected family receives gifts, interest-free loans, and various other forms of assistance. But when individuals suffer a health shock, this is apparently not the case. The family is left to deal with it.

The lack of insurance for health shocks is very surprising, given that families do help each other in other ways. In a previous chapter, we talked about Ibu Emptat, a woman we met in a small village in Java, whose husband had had a problem with his eyes. Her child had had to drop out of school because she could not afford the medicine for his asthma. Ibu Emptat had borrowed 100,000 rupiah ($18.75 USD PPP) from the local moneylender to pay for a cure for her husband's eyes and when we met her, with accumulated interest she owed 1 million rupiah. She was very worried because the moneylender was threatening to take away everything they had. However, in the course of the interview, we discovered that one of her daughters had just given her a television. The daughter had just bought herself a new one for about 800,000 rupiah ($150 USD PPP) and decided to give her old one (which was still very nice) to her parents. We were a little surprised by this exchange: Wouldn't it have made sense for the daughter to have kept her old TV and given the parents the money to pay the moneylender? We asked her, "Can't one of your children help you with the debt?" Ibu Emptat shook her head and replied that they had their own problems, their own families to take care of—she implied that it was not for her to question the form of the gift. She seemed to think it was normal that no one would offer to help out with her health expenses.

What stops people from doing more to help one another? Why are some forms of risk not covered, or not covered well?

There are good reasons we may be unwilling to offer unconditional help to our friends and neighbors. For one thing, we may worry that the guarantee of help might create a temptation to slack off—this is what insurers call *moral hazard*. Or that people may claim that they are in need even when they are not. Or simply that the promise of mutual help may not be carried through: I help you, but when your turn comes around, you are too busy.

These are all explanations for why we may want to hold back our help a little, but it is not clear whether this could explain not offering help to those who just became very sick, because falling ill is presumably not a choice. The other possibility is that the way most economists think about informal insurance, as situations where we help others because we might need their help in the future, may not be the whole story. It could be that we would help our neighbors in extremis even when we had no expectation of being in a similar position, for example, just because it is immoral to let your neighbors starve. Betsey Hartman and Jim Boyce's book about life in rural Bangladesh in the mid-1970s[17] describes two neighboring families, one Hindu and one Muslim, that were not particularly close to each other. The Hindu family lost its main earner and was starving; in desperation, the woman of that family would creep across the fence into the other family's yard and steal some edible leaves from time to time. Hartman discovered that the Muslim family knew what was going on but decided to turn a blind eye. "I know her character isn't bad," the man said. "If I were in her position, I would probably steal, too. When little things disappear, I try not to get angry. I think 'The person who took this is hungrier than me.'"

The fact that people may help each other out in hard times out of a sense of moral obligation, rather than because they necessarily expect to be helped in the future, can help explain why informal networks are not equipped to deal with health shocks. When even a very poor household that has enough to feed itself sees a neighbor who does not, it just shares what it has. But helping people to pay for hospitalization, for example, requires going beyond this basic act of sharing: Many households would need to chip in, given how expensive hospitalization can be. As a result, it makes sense to exclude expensive health events from the basic moral imperative to help neighbors in need, because it would require a much more elaborate social contract to carry it through.

This view of insurance as mainly a moral duty to help someone in need explains why, in the Nigerian villages, villagers helped each other out on an individual basis, instead of all contributing to a common pot, despite the fact that sharing risk in this other way would be more efficient. It might also explain why Ibu Emptat's daughter gave her mother a TV but did not cover her health costs. She did not want to be the one child who was responsible for her parents' health care (and didn't want to presume the generosity of her siblings). So she chose to do something nice for them without biting off more than she could chew.

WHERE ARE THE INSURANCE COMPANIES FOR THE POOR?

Given the high cost of risk and the limitation of the insurance anyone can get from informal solidarity networks, one must wonder why the poor do not have more access to formal insurance, that is, insurance supplied by an insurance company. Formal insurance of any kind is a rarity among the poor. Health insurance, insurance against bad weather, and insurance against the death of livestock, which are standard products in the lives of farmers in rich countries, are more or less absent in the developing world.

Now that microcredit is something that everyone knows about, insurance for the poor seems like an obvious target of opportunity for the high-minded creative capitalist (a *Forbes* op-ed called it an "unpenetrated natural market").[18] The poor face an enormous amount of risk and should be willing to pay a reasonable insurance premium to insure their lives, their health, their cattle, or their harvest. With billions of poor people waiting to be insured, even a tiny profit per policy could make it a tremendous business proposition, and at the same time, it would also be a big help to the world's poor. All that seems to be lacking is someone to organize this market: This has prompted international organizations (such as the World Bank) and large foundations (likes the Gates Foundation) to invest hundreds of millions of dollars to encourage the development of insurance options for the poor.

There are of course a number of obvious difficulties with providing insurance. These problems are not specific to the poor. They are fundamental problems, but they are amplified in poor countries, where it is more difficult to regulate insurers and monitor the insured. We have already mentioned "moral hazard": People may change their behavior (farm less carefully, spend more money on health care, and so forth) once they know that they will not bear the full consequences. Consider some of the problems of providing health insurance, for example. We have seen that even without health insurance, the poor visit some forms of health providers all the time. What will they do if visits become free? And won't the doctors also have reason to prescribe unnecessary tests and drugs, especially if they also own a lab (which a lot of doctors do, both in the United States and in India) or get kickbacks from the drugstore? It seems that everything pushes in the same direction: Patients want to see action, so they tend to prefer doctors who are prescription happy, and the doctors often make more money if they prescribe more. Offering reimbursement-based health insurance for outpatient care in a country where health care is at best weakly regulated, and where anybody can set up shop as a "doctor," seems like the first step toward bankruptcy.

Another issue is "adverse selection." If insurance is not mandatory, those who know that they are likely to have a problem in the future may be more likely to get insurance. This would be fine as long as the insurer also knows that, because it could be factored into the premium. But if the insurance company is unable to identify those who are joining because they want care now, all they can do is raise the premium on everyone. The higher price, however, makes things worse, as it drives away those who know they will probably not need the insurance, thus exacerbating the original problem. This is why, in the United States, getting health insurance at reasonable prices is very difficult for those who cannot get it through their employers. And this is why affordable health insurance programs tend to be mandatory—if everyone is required to join, the insurer does not get stuck with just the high-risk types.

A third problem is outright fraud: What is to prevent a hospital from presenting to the insurer a large number of bogus claims or charging the patient substantially more than the cost of care received? And if a farmer purchases insurance for his water buffalo, what is to stop him from claiming that the buffalo had died? Nachiket Mor and Bindu Ananth from ICICI Foundation are the two people in the Indian financial sector most committed to designing better financial services for the poor. They recounted to us, with self-deprecating humor, their first disastrous attempt, many years ago, to provide cattle insurance: After the first lot of policyholders universally claimed to have lost their cattle, they decided that in order to claim that an animal had died, the owner would need to show the ear of the dead cow. The result was a robust market in cows' ears: Any cow that died, insured or not, would have its ear cut off and the ear would then be sold to those who had insured a cow. That way they could claim the insurance and keep their cow. In summer 2009, we went to a meeting where Nandan Nilekani, founder and ex-CEO of the Indian software giant Infosys, who had been charged by the government to provide every Indian with a "unique ID," was explaining his plan for unique identification. He assured listeners that ten fingerprints and a picture of the irises are essentially enough to uniquely identify anyone. Mor was listening intently. When Nilekani paused, he spoke up: "It's too bad that cattle don't have fingers."

Some types of risk ought to be easier to insure than others. Consider weather, for example. A farmer should value a policy that pays him a fixed amount (based on the premium he paid) when the rainfall measured at the nearby weather station falls below a certain critical level. Because no one controls the weather and there is no judgment to be made about what should be done (unlike in medical care, where someone must decide which tests or treatment is needed), there is no scope for moral hazard or fraud.

Within health care, insuring catastrophic health events—major illnesses, accidents—seems much easier than covering outpatient care. Nobody wants to have surgery or chemotherapy just for the heck of it, and the treatment is easily verified. The danger of overtreatment remains, but the insurer can cap what it will pay for each treatment. The big issue that remains is selection: The insurance company does not want only sick people signing up.

To avoid adverse selection, the trick is to start from a large pool of people who came together for some other reason than health—employees of a large firm, microcredit clients, card-carrying Communists . . . and try to insure all of them.

This is why many microfinance institutions (MFIs) thought of offering health insurance. They have a large pool of borrowers who could be offered insurance products. And because catastrophic health problems sometimes drive the otherwise highly compliant microcredit clients into default, health insurance for them would be a little bit of insurance for the MFI as well. Moreover, it would be easy to collect premiums from the clients, since loan officers already meet with them every week—in effect, they could just fold the premium into the loan.

In 2007, SKS Microfinance, then the largest microfinance institution in India, introduced "Swayam Shakti," a pilot health-insurance program offering maternity, hospitalization, and accident benefits. It was made mandatory for the groups to which it was offered to avoid adverse selection. To deal with the potential for fraud, benefits were capped and clients were strongly encouraged to use those hospitals with which SKS had a long-term networking arrangement. To sweeten the deal, clients who went to these hospitals were offered a "cashless facility": They would not need to pay anything as long as their treatment was for a covered illness—SKS would pay the hospitals directly.

When SKS first introduced the product, the company tried to make it mandatory for its clients. But the clients rebelled, so SKS decided to make the product mandatory only at the first renewal. The result was that some clients decided not to renew the loans, and SKS started losing clients in the areas where they were offering the insurance. After a few months, renewal rates for SKS loans had fallen from about 60 percent to about 50 percent. A CEO of a competing microfinance institution was asking us about our work with SKS, and when we said we were working on evaluating the impact of offering mandatory health insurance to microcredit clients, she laughed and said, "Oh, I know the effect! Everywhere SKS made this product mandatory, we got many more clients. People are leaving SKS to join our organization!" About one-fourth of the clients, eager to continue borrowing from SKS while avoiding being insured, found a loophole. They prepaid their loan just before the end of the one-year premium. This way, when they renewed their loan, they still technically had coverage, and therefore they did not have to pay the new premium. Faced with this resistance, SKS decided to make the product voluntary. But a voluntary product taken by only a few clients is again susceptible to adverse selection and moral hazard. The charges per covered client exploded, and ICICI Lombard, the company on behalf of which SKS was offering the insurance, decided it was losing money and asked SKS to stop insuring new clients. Other organizations attempting similar schemes have encountered very similar problems with client resistance to mandatory enrollment.

Micro health insurance is not the only form of insurance that has run into trouble. A group of researchers, including Robert Townsend, our colleague at MIT, tried to measure the impact of access to a very simple weather insurance scheme. Much like the one we described above, it pays a given amount of money when it rains less than a specific amount.[19] The product was marketed in two regions in India— Gujarat and Andhra Pradesh—both dry and drought-prone. In both cases, it was sold through a well-respected and well-known microfinance organization. The company tried various ways to offer and present the insurance to farmers. Overall, the sign-up rates were extremely low: At most, 20 percent of farmers bought some insurance, and that level of sign-up only occurred when someone from those very well-known MFIs went door to door to sell the product. Moreover, even those who bought some insurance bought very little: Most farmers purchased policies that would cover only 2 percent to 3 percent of their losses if the rains did fail.

Why Don't Poor People Want Insurance?

A first possibility for the low demand for insurance is that the government has spoiled the market. This is the familiar demand-wallah argument: When markets do not work, overprovision by the government or international institutions is probably to blame. The specific argument is that when disaster strikes, these kindly souls step in to help, and as a result, people actually don't need insurance.

It is true that during bad monsoon years, Indian districts compete to be designated "drought affected" because this opens the door for government help. Jobs are provided on government construction sites, food gets distributed, and so on. But it should be clear that this is a very small part of what the poor need. For one thing, the government intervenes only in cases of large-scale disasters, not when a buffalo dies or someone is hit by a car. And even disaster relief is, in most cases, vastly insufficient by the time it gets to the poor.

Another possibility is that the poor do not understand the concept of insurance very well. It is true that insurance is unlike most transactions that the poor are used to. It is something that you pay for, hoping that you will never need to make use of it. When talking to SKS clients, we met many people who were upset when their health insurance premiums were not reimbursed even though they hadn't made any claims over the past year. It is certainly possible to explain the concept of insurance better, but it is hard to imagine that a population that ingeniously found a loophole in the SKS system couldn't figure out the basic principle of insurance. Townsend, as a part of his effort to sell weather insurance, carried out an exercise to figure out whether people understand how the insurance works. While visiting each farmer, the salesman read aloud a brief description of a hypothetical insurance product (temperature insurance) and then asked the potential client several simple hypothetical questions about when the policy would pay out. The respondents had the correct answers three-fourths of the time. It is not clear that the average American or French person would do much better. It is therefore no surprise that the attempts to explain the rainfall insurance product better had no impact on farmers' willingness to purchase.[20]

The farmers were able to understand the main concept of insurance and how it functions, but they were simply not interested in buying it. They were, however, swayed in their decision by relatively small things. A simple home visit, without any particular effort at marketing, raises the fraction of people who buy weather insurance by a factor of four. In the Philippines, households that were randomly selected to complete a baseline survey containing many questions on health were more likely to eventually subscribe to health insurance than comparable households that had not completed the baseline survey. Presumably, answering all these questions about the possibility of health problems had reminded them of what could happen.[21]

Given the very high stakes, why aren't poor people more enthusiastic about the advantages of being insured, even without these little nudges?

The key problem, we think, is that because of the problems we mentioned earlier, the type of insurance the market can offer only covers people against catastrophic scenarios. This creates a number of issues.

Credibility is always a problem with insurance products: Because the insurance contract requires the household to pay in advance, to be repaid in the future at the discretion of the insurer, the household must trust the insurer completely. In the weather insurance case, the team marketing the product sometimes went with someone from Basix, an organization that the farmers know well, and sometimes they went on their own. They found that the presence of a member of Basix had a fairly large effect on sign-up rates, suggesting that trust is an issue.

Unfortunately this lack of credibility may be endemic, given the nature of the products and the way insurance companies react to any possibility of fraud. In winter 2009, we visited some of the SKS clients who had decided not to renew their health insurance. One woman said that she decided not to renew after SKS refused to reimburse her when she went to the hospital with a stomach infection. Since the policy covered only catastrophic events, a stomach infection, horrible as it can be, did not qualify. But it was not clear that she understood the distinction—after all, she went to the hospital and was treated there. She also talked about a woman from another borrowing group (like most MFIs, SKS has its clients organized into groups) whose husband died of a severe infection, but not before his wife spent quite a bit of money on medicines and doctors. After his death, she submitted her bills to the insurance company, but the company refused to pay up on the grounds that he had never spent a night in the hospital. Appalled by the incident, an entire group of women decided to stop paying the premium. From a purely legal point of view, the insurer was clearly within its right to refuse payment. On the other hand, what could be more catastrophic?

Weather insurance has many of the same problems. The crop may have dried up and the farmers may be starving, but if the rainfall is above the cutoff at the rainfall station, no one in that area will get any payment. Yet there are many microclimates: In any year when the average rainfall in the area is just above the drought cutoff, many individual farmers must face droughtlike conditions, just by the laws of chance. It is not going to be easy for suffering farmers to accept the verdict of the weather station, especially in an environment where corruption is not unknown.

The second issue is the problem of time inconsistency, which we already encountered in our chapter on health. When deciding whether or not to buy the insurance, we need to do the thinking now (and pay the premium), but the payout, if any, would take place in the future. We have already seen that this is a type of reasoning human beings are particularly bad at doing. The problem is made even harder when the insurance is against a catastrophic event: The payout would take place not only in the future, but in a particularly unpleasant future that no one really wants to think about. Not spending too much time anticipating these events may be a natural protective reaction, and this may explain why people were more likely to buy insurance after they were forced to think about it by answering a survey.

For these reasons, micro insurance may not become the next billion-client market opportunity: There seem to be deep reasons that most people don't yet feel very comfortable with the kinds of insurance products that the market is willing to offer. On the other hand, the poor clearly bear unacceptable levels of risk.

There is thus a clear role for government action. This does not mean the government needs to substitute for a private insurance market, but for a real market to have a chance to emerge, the government will probably need to step in. Private companies could continue to sell exactly the kinds of insurance they are currently willing to sell (catastrophic care with a strict cap, indexed weather insurance, and so forth). But for the time being, the government should pay a part of insurance premiums for the poor. There is already evidence that this could work: In Ghana, when weather insurance was offered to farmers with a large subsidy on the premium, almost all farmers to whom it was offered took it up. Because the fear of bad shocks leads the poor to costly mitigation strategies, subsidizing insurance could pay for itself in terms of higher incomes for the poor. In Ghana, farmers who had received cheap insurance were more likely to use fertilizer on their crops than those who had not received it, and they were better off as a result. They reported, for example, being much less likely to have missed a meal.[22] It is possible that over time, as people start to see how insurance works and the market starts to grow, the subsidy could be phased out. But even if that is not possible, given the enormous potential gains that could be achieved if the poor did not need to be the hedge-fund managers of their own lives, this seems like a great place to use public funds to promote the common good.

7

The Men from Kabul and the Eunuchs of India: The (Not So) Simple Economics of Lending to the Poor

The sight of countless fruit and vegetable sellers standing side by side on street corners is common to cities in most developing countries. Each of the sellers (usually a woman) has a small cart or just a sheet of tarp on the pavement on which she has piled tomatoes, onions, or whatever she happens to be selling. The vendors buy their stock in the morning from a wholesaler, usually on credit, and sell it during the day, reimbursing the wholesaler at night. Sometimes, the cart that they use to carry and display the vegetables is also rented for the day.

This is the way many businesses in rich countries operate, too: They get a working capital loan to produce and purchase goods and then repay the loans out of their revenues. What is striking is how much the poor repay, compared to the rich. In Chennai, India, when the typical fruit seller reimburses the wholesaler at night for the 1,000 rupees' ($51 USD PPP) worth of vegetables she got in the morning, she gives him 1,046.9 rupees on average. This interest payment is 4.69 percent *per day*.[1] To see what this means, try the following calculation: If you borrowed 100 rupees ($5.10 USD PPP) today and kept it until tomorrow, you would need to repay 104.69 rupees. If you kept this amount a further twenty-four hours and repaid it the following day, you would need to repay 109.6 rupees. After thirty days, you would owe almost 400 rupees, and after a year, 1,842,459,409 rupees ($93.5 million USD PPP). So the equivalent of a $5 loan, if it goes unrepaid for a year, leaves a debt of nearly $100 million.

These very high interest rates were the call to action for the founders of microfinance. For instance, Padmaja Reddy, the CEO of Spandana, one of the largest microfinance institutions (MFI) in India, told us that she got the inspiration for starting Spandana after striking up a conversation with a ragpicker in the city of Guntur, in Andhra Pradesh. She realized that if only the ragpicker could come up with the funds to buy one cart, she could be in a position to buy "scores of carts" in just a few weeks with the money saved from not having to pay the daily rental fee. But the ragpicker did not have enough money to buy a cart. *Why*, Padmaja asked herself, *is no one lending her the money to buy one cart?* According to Padmaja, the ragpicker explained that the bank would not lend to someone like her. She could have gotten a loan from a moneylender, but the rates would have been so high that it would not have been worth it. In the end, Padmaja decided to give her a loan. The ragpicker reimbursed it faithfully and flourished. Soon after, people were lining up at Padmaja's doorstep for loans, and she decided to quit her job to start Spandana. Thirteen years later, in July 2010, Spandana had 4.2 million loan clients, with an outstanding portfolio of 42 billion rupees.

The story Padmaja tells is not very different from that told by Muhammad Yunus, hailed as the father of modern microfinance: Banks are unwilling to touch the poor. Into this banking void step exploitative moneylenders and traders who charge outrageously high interest rates. Microfinance, in this narrative, is a wonderfully simple idea. Someone who is not out to make money off the poor can enter the market, charging the poor enough in interest to be financially sustainable, and perhaps make a modest profit, but no more. By the power of compounding, a small decrease in the interest rate can transform the clients' lives. Consider the fruit sellers: Imagine they can get a 1,000-rupee ($51 USD PPP) loan, even at a relatively hefty rate of, say, 10 percent monthly. They can now buy the vegetables in cash, rather than on credit. In one month, they would each already have saved 4,000 rupees ($203 USD PPP) in interest paid to the wholesaler, more than enough to repay the microfinance agency. They could grow their businesses and escape poverty in a matter of months, at least in theory.

Yet even this simple story raises questions. There are many fruit wholesalers in Chennai. Why didn't one of them, or an enterprising moneylender, decide to slightly drop the interest rate charged to the women? That individual should have been able to capture the entire market, still keeping a reasonable margin. Why did the fruit sellers have to wait for people like Muhammad Yunus or Padmaja Reddy?

In this sense, the advocates of microfinance are being too modest: They must be doing something more than introducing competition where there was a monopoly. On the other hand, they may also be too sanguine about the potential of small loans to lift people out of poverty. For all the individual anecdotes of fruit sellers turning into fruit magnates that can be found on the various Web sites of microfinance institutions, there are still many poor fruit sellers in Chennai. Many of them do not borrow from microfinance institutions, even though there are several in their town. Are they forgoing their tickets out of poverty, or is microfinance less of a miracle than we have been told?

LENDING TO THE POOR

Very few poor households get loans from a proper lending institution like a commercial bank or a cooperative. In the survey we conducted in Udaipur, in rural India, about two-thirds of the poor had a loan. Of these, 23 percent were from a relative, 18 percent from a moneylender, 37 percent from a shopkeeper, and only 6.4 percent from a formal source. The low share of bank credit is not due to the lack of physical access to banks, because a similar pattern occurs in urban Hyderabad, where households living below $2 a day primarily borrow from moneylenders (52 percent), friends or neighbors (24 percent), and family members (13 percent). Only 5 percent of their loans are with commercial banks. In all the countries we have in our eighteen-country data set, less than 5 percent of the rural poor have a loan from a bank, and less than 10 percent of the urban poor do.

Credit from informal sources tends to be expensive. In the Udaipur survey, those living on less than 99 cents a day pay on average 3.84 percent per month (which is equivalent to an annual rate of 57 percent) for the credit they receive from informal sources. Even credit card debt in the United States, which is notoriously expensive, pales in comparison. Bank of America's standard credit card has an interest rate of about 20 percent per year. Those who spend between 99 cents and $2 a day per capita pay a little less: 3.13 percent per month. There are two reasons for this difference in interest rates. First, the slightly less poor rely less on informal sources of credit and more on formal sources than the extremely poor, and the formal sources are cheaper. But second, the interest rates charged by informal sources tend to be higher for the poor than for the less poor. The average interest rate from an informal source drops by 0.4 percent per month for each additional hectare of land owned by the person taking out the loan.

Interest rates vary across sectors and countries, but the bottom line is always the same: Yearly interest rates in the 40 to 200 percent range (or even higher) are the norm, and the poor pay more than the rich. The implications of the fact that many people do borrow at these rates are quite staggering. There are millions of people willing to borrow at a rate that the average U.S. saver would dearly love to be paid. Why aren't investors rushing to them with bags of money?

This is not for lack of trying. From the 1960s until the late 1980s, many developing countries had government-sponsored credit programs, usually with subsidized interest rates, targeted at the rural poor. For example, in India starting in 1977, for every branch that a bank opened in a city, the bank had to open four additional branches in rural locations that did not have a bank. Moreover, banks were directed to lend 40 percent of their portfolios to the "priority sector": small firms, agriculture, cooperatives, and the like. Robin Burgess and Rohini Pande showed that where more bank branches were opened as a result of this policy, poverty decreased faster.[2]

The problem was that these forced lending programs didn't work very well as lending programs. Default rates were staggeringly high (40 percent during the 1980s). Lending was often driven more by political priorities than by economic need (a lot of loans were made to farmers just before elections in districts where the contest was expected to be tight).[3] And the money had a tendency to end up in the hands of the local elites. Even Burgess and Pande's generally favorable study concluded that it costs much more than 1 rupee to increase the incomes of the poor by 1 rupee through opening bank branches. Moreover, further work suggested that in the longer term, regions that got more branches may in fact have become poorer.[4] In 1992, in the wave of reforms that liberalized India, the requirement to start branches in rural areas was dropped and a similar trend of eroding government support for public lending programs can be seen in most other developing countries.

Perhaps the social banking experiment was a failure because the government should not be in the business of subsidized lending. Politicians find it too attractive to use the loans as giveaways, and there is no better giveaway than a loan one does not need to repay. But why don't private bankers want to lend to small entrepreneurs? Given that they are willing to pay up to 4 percent a month, which is many times what a bank makes on its average loan, wouldn't it make sense to try to lend to them? Some Web sites in the United States now enable potential lenders in rich countries to lend to entrepreneurs in poor countries. Could it be that they have finally understood something that everyone else missed?

Or alternatively, perhaps there is something that informal moneylenders can do that banks cannot. What could that be? And why is it cheaper to lend to richer people?

The (Not So) Simple Economics of Lending to the Poor

One standard explanation for why some people might have to pay high interest rates is that they are more likely to default. This is simple arithmetic: If a moneylender must get back on average 110 rupees for every 100 rupees he lends just to stay in business (for instance, because this is his cost of funds), without default, he could charge a 10 percent interest rate. But if half of his borrowers default, then he must get back at least 220 rupees from the half that actually do repay and hence charge a 120 percent interest rate overall. However, rates of default on informal loans, unlike those on government-sponsored bank lending, are not very high. Such loans are often repaid with some delay, but not repaying at all is actually rare. A study of rural moneylenders in Pakistan found that the median rate of default across moneylenders is just 2 percent, even though the average interest they charge is 78 percent.[5]

The problem is that these low default rates are anything but automatic; they require hard work on the lender's part. Enforcing credit contracts is never easy. If the borrower is allowed to misspend the loan proceeds, or somehow has bad luck and has no available cash, there will be nothing to collect. At that point, there is precious little the lender can do to collect on the loan. Given this, it is tempting for the borrower to contrive to appear to have no money even when she does, which makes matters worse for the lender. If this is allowed to go unchecked, the lender will never be repaid, even if the borrower's project actually succeeds.

The way lenders all over the world protect themselves against the different forms of willful default is by asking for a down payment, some collateral, or what is sometimes called the promoter's contribution, which is the part of the firm's capital that comes from the entrepreneur's pocket. If the borrower defaults on the loan, the lender can punish her by seizing the collateral. The more the borrower has at stake, the less tempting it is to take off with the borrowed money. But this means that the more the borrower can pledge, the larger the lender can make the loan. And thus we have the familiar (at least before the go-go days of no-down-payment mortgages) rule that ties the size of the loan to the amount of money the borrower already has. As the French put it, *"On ne prête qu'aux riches"* ("One lends only to the rich").

This means that poorer borrowers will be able to borrow less but it does not, by itself, explain why the poor should pay such high interest rates or why banks would refuse to lend to them. But there is something else that kicks in. In order to be able to collect on the loan, the lender needs to know many things about the borrower. Some are things the lender would like to find out before deciding to lend, such as whether the borrower is trustworthy. Others, such as the borrower's whereabouts and nature of the borrower's business, help in collecting on the loan should there be a problem. The lender may also want to keep an eye on the borrower, visiting her from time to time to make sure the money is being used as promised and nudging the business in the desired direction if need be. All of these efforts take time, and time is money. The interest rate has to go up to cover them.

Moreover, many of these expenses do not scale with loan size. There is no way to avoid collecting some basic information about the borrower, even if the loan is very small. As a result, the smaller the loan, the larger the monitoring and screening costs will be as a fraction of loan size, and because these costs have to be covered by the interest collected, the higher the interest rate will be.

To make matters worse, this creates what economists call a *multiplier effect*. When the interest rate goes up, the borrower has more reason to try to find a way not to repay the loan. That means the borrower needs to be monitored and screened more carefully, which adds to the cost of lending. This pushes the interest rate up even further, which necessitates more scrutiny, and so on. The upward pressure feeds on itself, and interest rates can skyrocket. Or, as often happens in practice, the lender may decide that it is not viable to lend to the poor: Their loans would be too small to make it worthwhile.

Once we understand this, many things fall into place. Because the main constraint on lending to the poor is the cost of gathering information about them, it makes sense that they would mostly borrow from people who already know them, such as their neighbors, their employers, the people they trade with, or one of the local moneylenders, and that is exactly what happens. Strange as it might seem, this emphasis on contract enforcement could also drive the poor to borrow from those who have the power to really hurt them if they were to default, since such lenders would not need to spend as much time monitoring (their borrowers wouldn't dare to stray) and the loans would be cheaper. In Calcutta in the 1960s and 1970s, a lot of the moneylenders were Kabuliwalas (men from Kabul)—tall men in Afghan clothes with a cloth bag slung across their shoulders who would go from door to door, ostensibly selling dried fruits and nuts, but actually mostly using that as a cover to carry out their lending operations. But why couldn't someone more local do the lending? The most likely answer is that these men had a reputation for being fierce and implacable, a stereotype sealed by a story that all Bengali schoolchildren have in their textbooks, in which a good-hearted but violent Kabuliwala kills someone who was trying to cheat him. The same logic also explains why the Mob in the United States was for many people the "lender of last resort."

A more baroque illustration of the power of threat can be seen in a story from London's *Sunday Telegraph*, dated August 22, 1999, titled "Pay Up—or We Will Send the Eunuchs to See You."[6] The report describes debt collectors in India making use of the old social prejudice against eunuchs to collect from long-standing defaulters. Because people believe that seeing a eunuch's genitals brings bad luck, the eunuchs were instructed to show up at the defaulter's house and threaten a "showing" if they continued to be uncooperative.

The high costs of collecting information on a borrower also help explain why even when there are several moneylenders in each village, competition does not drive the price of credit down. Once a lender has paid the cost of vetting a borrower, and the borrower has established a good reputation with him, leaving is difficult. If the borrower did go elsewhere for credit, the new lender would have to do the due diligence all over again, which would be expensive and would drive interest rates even higher. Moreover, the lenders would be suspicious of such a new client: Why did someone feel the need to abandon an existing relationship, when it is obviously costly to do so? The moneylender would then be doubly careful, which could further raise interest rates. Thus, despite the apparent choice of lenders, borrowers are somewhat bound to the one they know already. And moneylenders can exploit this advantage to raise interest rates.

This also explains why banks do not lend to the poor. Bank officers are not very well placed to do all the necessary due diligence: They don't stay in the village, they don't know the people, and they rotate frequently. Respectable banks are not in a position to compete with Kabuliwalas. They cannot easily threaten to break people's kneecaps or even send them eunuchs. The Indian branch of Citibank got into serious trouble when it was discovered that it was using *"goondas"* (local hooligans) to threaten borrowers who did not repay vehicle loans. And the courts are not really an option, either. In 1988, the Law Commission of India reported that 40 percent of the cases for asset liquidation (of bankrupt borrowers) were more than eight years pending.[7] Think of what this means from the lenders' point of view: They know that even if they are sure to win their case against a defaulting firm, they will only be able to claim the pledged assets in several years' time (with plenty of opportunities for the borrower to divert the assets). Of course, this means that from the point of view of the lenders, the value of the borrower's assets at the time the loan begins will be all that much lower. Nachiket Mor, who was then one of the vice presidents of ICICI Bank, once described to us what he had thought was an absolutely brilliant way to get farmers to repay their agricultural loan. Before disbursing each loan, he would ask them for a postdated check for the same amount. The great insight was that if the farmer did not repay, the bank would then be able to send the police to collect on the check, because not honoring a check is a criminal offense. This worked for a while, but then it began to unravel. When the police realized that they had hundreds of bounced checks to track, they politely told the bank that, really, this was not their job.

Even when the bank manages to get its money back, things can backfire: Banks do not like headlines associating them with "farmer suicides." And to cap it all off, when elections are around the corner, governments love to write off outstanding loans. Given all this, it is no surprise that banks find it easier to stay away from lending to the poor altogether, leaving the field to moneylenders. However, although the moneylenders have an advantage in getting their money back, they have to pay a lot more for the money they lend out than the banks. This is because we are happy to give our savings to the bank for safekeeping even if it pays us little or nothing in interest, but few people would think of depositing their savings with a moneylender. This, combined with the multiplier effect and the monopoly power that moneylenders often enjoy, explains why the poor face such high interest rates.

The innovation of people like Muhammad Yunus and Padmaja Reddy, then, was not just the idea of lending to the poor at more reasonable rates. It was figuring out *how* to do it.

MICRO INSIGHTS FOR A MACRO PROGRAM

From its modest beginnings with the Bangladesh Rehabilitation Assistance Committee (universally known as BRAC) and the Grameen Bank in the mid-1970s in Bangladesh, microcredit is now a global phenomenon. It has reached anywhere between 150 and 200 million borrowers, mainly women, and is available to many more. It is sometimes described, almost like a character in a Greek myth, as a beast with two teats—a profit mission and a social mission—and by all accounts it has known impressive successes on both fronts. On the one hand, the Nobel Prize for Peace, which was awarded to Muhammad Yunus and the Grameen Bank, crowned a series of public accolades; on the other hand, the Initial Public Offering (IPO) of Compartamos, a large Mexican MFI, in spring 2007 was a (controversial) triumph of the commercial side. The offering raised $467 million for Compartamos, although it also drew attention to the 100-percent-plus interest rates it charges. (Yunus publicly expressed his discontent, calling the CEOs of Compartamos the new usurers, but other MFIs are already following in their footsteps: In July 2010, the IPO of SKS Microfinance, India's largest microfinance institution, raised $354 million.)

One can see why Yunus may not like the association with usury, but in a (good) sense microcredit *is* moneylending reinvented for a social purpose. Like traditional moneylenders, MFIs rely on their ability to keep a close check on the customer, but they do so in part by involving other borrowers who happen to know the customer. The typical MFI contract involves loans to a group of borrowers, who are liable for each other's loans and hence have a reason to try to make sure that the others repay. Some organizations expect the borrowers to know each other when they come to borrow, whereas others bring them together by making them come to weekly meetings. The very act of meeting together every week helps clients know each other better and become more willing to help out a group member who faces a temporary difficulty.[8]

Like the moneylender, MFIs threaten to cut off all future lending to anyone who defaults outright and do not hesitate to use their connections within village social networks to put pressure on recalcitrant borrowers. Unlike moneylenders, their official policy is never to use actual physical threats.[9] However, the power of shame seems to be sufficient. A borrower we met in Hyderabad was struggling to repay loans from several MFIs. But she said she never missed a payment, even if it meant borrowing money from her children or going without a meal for a day: She loathed the idea of having the credit officer come to her doorstep and "make a nuisance" in front of the whole neighborhood.

Where MFIs clearly diverge from traditional moneylending is in removing almost all flexibility. Moneylenders will allow their borrowers to choose how they borrow and the way they repay—some repay once a week, but others repay whenever they have money in hand. Some repay only the interest until they are ready to repay the entire principal. An MFI client, by contrast, typically has to repay a fixed amount every week, starting one week after the loan is given out, and, at least for first loans, everyone usually receives the same amount. Moreover, the borrower has to make the payment at the weekly meeting, which is always at a fixed time for each group. The advantage of this is that keeping track of repayments is very easy: The loan officer just counts to see if he has the total amount he was supposed to get from that group and if he does, which is almost always the case, he is finished and can start on the next group. This allows a loan officer to collect repayment from 100 to 200 people every day, whereas a moneylender has to wait around not knowing when the money is coming in. Moreover, since the transaction is so simple, the loan officer does not need to be particularly well educated or trained, which also keeps costs down. In addition, loan officers are paid on steep incentive contracts, based on recruiting new clients and making sure that everyone repays.

All of these innovations contribute to reducing the administrative costs of lending, which, as we argued above, get blown up by the multiplier effect and make lending to the poor so very expensive. This is how most MFIs in South Asia manage to make money by lending to the poor at interest rates of around 25 percent per year, whereas the local moneylenders typically charge two to four times as much. Interest rates are higher in other parts of the world (one likely explanation is that loan officer salaries are higher), sometimes even higher than 100 percent per year, but remain much lower than the other alternatives for poor people. In urban Brazil, for example, MFIs offer microcredit at the rate of about 4 percent a month (60 percent a year), and the easiest alternative, which is credit-card-debt refinancing, costs between 12 percent and 20 percent per month (289 percent to almost 800 percent per year). Defaults, famously, are extremely rare, at least outside politically motivated crisis. The "portfolio at risk" (loans that *may* default, but not all will) was less than 4 percent in South Asia and no more than 7 percent in most Latin American and African countries in 2009.[10] And so microfinance, with its 150 to 200 million clients, has earned its place as one of the most visible anti-poverty policies. But does it work?

DOES MICROCREDIT WORK?

The answer obviously depends on what you mean by "work." According to the more enthusiastic backers of microfinance, it means transformation of people's lives. The Consultative Group to Assist the Poor (CGAP), an organization housed at the World Bank and dedicated to promoting microcredit, reported at some point in the FAQ section of its Web site that "there is mounting evidence to show that the availability of financial services for poor households—microfinance—can help achieve the MDGs"[11] (including universal primary education, child mortality, and maternal health, for example). The basic idea is that it puts economic power in the hands of women, and women care about these things more than men do.

Unfortunately, contrary to CGAP's claims, until very recently, there was in fact very little evidence either way on these questions. What CGAP called evidence turned out to be case studies, often produced by the MFIs themselves. For many supporters of microcredit, this appears to be enough. We met a prominent Silicon Valley venture capitalist and investor, and supporter of microcredit (he was an early backer of SKS), who told us that he needed no more evidence. He had seen enough "anecdotal data" to know the truth. But anecdotal data do not help with the skeptics out there, including large sections of governments everywhere that worry that microcredit might be the "new usury." In October 2010, just two months after SKS's successful IPO, the Andhra Pradesh government blamed SKS for the suicide of fifty-seven farmers, who allegedly were put under unbearable pressure by the loan officers' coercive recovery practices. A few loan officers from SKS and Spandana were arrested, and the government passed a law making the weekly collection of loans difficult—among other things, by requiring repayment to take place in the presence of an elected official—thereby sending the clear signal that borrowers did not need to repay. By early December, all credit officers of the major MFI (SKS, Spanda, Share) were still sitting idle and losses were mounting. The anecdotes, and the assurance by Vikram Akula, the CEO of SKS, that the fifty-seven farmers who committed suicide were not in default so they could not possibly have been driven to death by SKS loan officers, did little to help them out.

One reason the MFIs were lacking a powerful argument in their defense is that they had been reluctant to gather rigorous evidence to prove their impact. When we approached MFIs (starting around 2002) to propose to work together on an evaluation, their usual reaction was, "Why do we need to be evaluated any more than an apple seller does?" By which they meant that as long as the clients came back for more, microcredit had to be beneficial to them. And because MFIs are financially sustainable, and do not depend on the generosity of donors, evaluating exactly *how* beneficial they are is unnecessary. This is a bit disingenuous. Most MFIs are subsidized by the generosity of donors and the enthusiastic efforts of their staff, largely based on the belief that microcredit is *better than other ways to help the poor*. Sometimes they are also subsidized by policy. In India, microfinance qualifies as a "priority sector," which gives banks powerful financial incentives to lend to them at concessional rates, which is a massive implicit subsidy.

Furthermore, it is not obvious that people are entirely rational when they make long-term decisions like taking out a loan—the U.S. press is full of stories about people who got themselves into trouble by overusing their credit cards. Perhaps people do need protection from lenders, as many regulators seem to believe. The government's position in Andhra Pradesh was precisely that the borrowers did not know what they were getting into when they took loans that they could not repay.

Partly as a result of such criticism, and partly because many leaders of MFIs genuinely want to know whether they are helping the poor, several MFIs have started evaluating their own programs. We were involved in one such evaluation, Spandana's program in Hyderabad. Spandana is believed to be one of the most profitable organizations in the industry and has been one of the main targets of government activism in Andhra Pradesh. Padmaja Reddy, Spandana's founder and CEO, is a small, vibrant, and ferociously intelligent woman. She was born into a prosperous farming family from the Guntur area. Her brother was the first person in the village to complete high school, and he went on to become a very successful doctor. He persuaded his parents to let Padmaja go to college and then to do an MBA. She wanted to help the poor, so she started working with an NGO. This was when she met the ragpicker we described earlier, who prompted her to start a microcredit operation. When the NGO she worked for refused, she opened Spandana. Despite her success and her commitment to microfinance, Padmaja Reddy describes the potential benefits modestly. For her, access to microfinance is important because it gives the poor a way to map out the future in a way that was not possible for them before, and this is the first step toward a better life. Whether they are buying machines, utensils, or a television for their home, the important difference is that they are working toward a vision of a life that they want, by saving and scrounging and working extra hard when needed, rather than simply drifting along.

It was perhaps because she had always been careful not to overpromise that she agreed to work with us on an evaluation of the Spandana program. The evaluation took advantage of Spandana's expansion into some areas of the city of Hyderabad.[12] Out of 104 neighborhoods, fifty-two were chosen at random for Spandana to enter. The rest were left as a comparison group.

When we compared the households in these two sets of neighborhoods, some fifteen to eighteen months after Spandana started lending, there was clear evidence that microfinance was working. People in the Spandana neighborhoods were more likely to have started a business and more likely to have purchased large durable goods, such as bicycles, refrigerators, or televisions. Households that did not start a new business were consuming more in these neighborhoods, but those who had started a new business were actually consuming less, tightening their belts to make the most of the new opportunity. There was no clear evidence of the reckless spending that some observers feared would happen. In fact, we saw exactly the opposite; households started spending less money on what they themselves saw as small "wasteful" expenditures such as tea and snacks, perhaps a sign that, as Padmaja has predicted, they now had a better sense of where they were heading.

On the other hand, there was no sign of a radical transformation. We found no evidence that women were feeling more empowered, at least along measurable dimensions. They were not, for example, exercising greater control over how the household spent its money. Nor did we see any differences in spending on education or health, or in the probability that kids would be enrolled in private schools. And even when there was detectable impact, such as in the case of new businesses, the effect was not dramatic. The fraction of families that started a new business over the fifteen-month period went up from about 5 percent to just over 7 percent—not nothing, but hardly a revolution.

As economists, we were quite pleased with these results: The main objective of microfinance seemed to have been achieved. It was not miraculous, but it was working. There needed to be more studies to make sure that this was not some fluke, and it would be important to see how things panned out in the long run, but so far, so good. In our minds, microcredit has earned its rightful place as *one* of the key instruments in the fight against poverty.

Interestingly, this is not how the main results played out in the media and the blogosphere. The results were mainly quoted for the negative findings and as proof that microfinance was not what it was made out to be. And though some MFIs accepted the results for what they were (chief among them, Padmaja Reddy, who said this was exactly what she had expected, and financed a second wave of the work to study the longer-term impacts), the big international players in microfinance decided to go on the offensive.

The representatives of the "big six" (Unitus, ACCION International, Foundation for International Community Assistance [FINCA], Grameen Foundation, Opportunity International, and Women's World Banking), the largest MFIs worldwide, held a meeting in Washington, DC, shortly after our study was made public. They invited us to participate, and our colleague Iqbal Dhaliwal went, thinking that there would be some conversation on what the results meant. Instead, it turned out that all the big six wanted was to know when the results from other randomized impact studies were expected, so they could put together a SWAT team that would be in a position to respond (they were apparently convinced all the studies would be negative). A few weeks later, the SWAT team produced its first attempt at damage control. The MFIs responded to the evidence from the two studies (ours, and another by Dean Karlan and Jonathan Zinman, with even more lukewarm results)[13] with six anecdotes on successful borrowers. This was followed by an op-ed in the *Seattle Times* by Brigit Helms, CEO of Unitus, that simply declared, "These studies are giving the inaccurate impression that increasing access to basic financial services has no real benefit."[14] It was somewhat surprising to read, since our evidence shows, quite to the contrary, that microfinance is a useful financial product. But that apparently is not enough. Trapped by decades of overpromising, many of the leading players in the microfinance world have apparently decided they would rather rely on the power of denial than take stock, regroup, and admit that microfinance is only one of the possible arrows in the fight against poverty.

Fortunately, this is not the way the rest of the industry seems to be going. At a conference in New York City in fall 2010, where similar results were presented, all the attendees agreed that microcredit as we know it has its strengths and its limits, and that the next order of business was to see what microfinance organizations could do to deliver more to their clients.

THE LIMITS OF MICROCREDIT

Why didn't microcredit deliver more than it did? Why didn't more families start new businesses, given that they now had access to capital at affordable rates? In part, the answer is that many poor people are not willing, or able, to start a business, even when they can borrow (why this is the case is one of the central themes of Chapter 9, on entrepreneurship). What is much more puzzling is that even though three or more MFIs were offering credit in the slums of Hyderabad, only about one-fourth of the families borrowed from them, whereas more than one-half borrowed from moneylenders at much higher rates and that fraction was more or less unaffected by the introduction of microcredit. We don't claim to be able to explain in full why microcredit is not more popular, but it probably has something to do with precisely what makes it able to lend relatively cheaply and effectively—namely, its rigid rules and the time costs it imposes on its clients.

The rigidity and specificity of the standard microcredit model mean, for one thing, that since group members are responsible for each other, women who don't enjoy poking into other people's business don't want to join. Group members may be reluctant to include those they don't know well in their groups, which must discriminate against newcomers. Joint liability works against those who want to take risks: As a group member you always want all other group members to play it as safe as possible.

Weekly repayments starting a week after the loan is disbursed are also not ideal for people who need money urgently but aren't exactly sure when they will be able to start repaying. MFIs do recognize this and sometimes make exceptions for emergency health-care expenses, but that is just one of the many possible reasons one might need an emergency loan. What happens, for example, when your son is suddenly offered a chance to take a course that would really help with his career, but the course fee is 1 million rupiah ($179 USD PPP), to be paid by next Sunday? Presumably, you borrow from the local moneylender, pay up, and then start looking for an extra job that will allow you to pay for the loan. Microcredit would not offer you this flexibility.

The same requirement must also discourage taking on projects that only pay off after some time, since there needs to be enough cash flow every week to make the scheduled payments. Rohini Pande and Erica Field persuaded an Indian MFI, the Kolkata-based Village Welfare Society, to allow a randomly chosen set of clients to start their prescribed repayments two months after they got the loan, instead of one week. When they compared the clients who got to repay later to those who stayed on the standard repayment schedule, they found that the former were more likely to start riskier and larger businesses, for example, buying a sewing machine instead of just buying some saris to resell.[15] This presumably means that, down the line, they would be able to make more money. However, despite a clear increase in client satisfaction, the MFI decided to go back to its traditional model because the default rates in the new groups, though still very low, were 8 percentage points higher than under the original plan.

One way to summarize all these results is to observe that, in many ways, the focus on "zero default" that characterizes most MFIs is too stringent for many potential borrowers. In particular, there is a clear tension between the spirit of microcredit and true entrepreneurship, which is usually associated with taking risks and, no doubt, occasionally failing. It has been argued, for example, that the American model, where bankruptcy is (or at least was) relatively easy and does not carry much of a stigma (in contrast with the European model, in particular), has a lot to do with the vitality of its entrepreneurial culture. By contrast, the MFI rules are set up not to tolerate any failure.

Are MFIs right to insist on zero default? Could they do better, both socially and commercially, by setting up rules that leave scope for some default? Most leaders of the MFI community firmly believe that this is not the case, and that relaxing their guard on defaults could have disastrous consequences. And they may well be exactly right. After all, they are still operating in environments where they have very little recourse if a client decides not to reimburse them, which means that exactly like the banks, they would have to rely on the slow and creaky court system. In many ways, their success comes from making repayment an implicit social compact, in which the community ensures that loans will be repaid and the MFI continues to provide further loans. This gradual building of trust may be one reason many MFIs have gradually moved away from the formal requirement of joint liability. And indeed, a study found no difference in repayment whether clients are formally under joint liability contracts or not, as long as they continue to meet regularly (when they don't meet weekly, but instead monthly, another study found that social connections within the group do not build up as fast, and eventually default rates do creep up).[16]

But a social equilibrium based on the combination of collective responsibility and an ongoing relationship is necessarily somewhat fragile. If the two reasons I repay are that everyone is repaying and that I will get a new loan in the future, then whether I repay or not gets tied to what I believe about what everyone else is doing and the future of the organization. Indeed, if I were convinced that everyone else was about to default, I would assume that the organization was about to go under and would therefore give up on getting any further funds from it. As a result, the situation can quickly unravel when there is a shift in beliefs.

This is what happened to Spandana in the Krishna District of Andhra Pradesh, the epicenter of India's microfinance movement. Some bureaucrats and politicians in the district were keen to promote their own brand of microfinance and decided that they needed to get rid of the competition. Suddenly, sometime in 2005, the local-language newspapers (or by some accounts, fake newspapers made to look like the real thing) filled with stories about Padmaja Reddy. In some, she was reported to have fled to America; in others, to have killed her husband. The implication was that Spandana had no future and hence there was no point in repaying a loan the company might have given. We saw one "newspaper" page claiming that Padmaja herself had suggested that they default, since she had made enough money and was quitting.

It was a masterful effort to shift beliefs in exactly the way that could totally undermine the organization: Convincing people that an MFI has no future is the easiest way to make sure that it in fact does not have one—since it becomes in everyone's best interest to default. Padmaja was distraught (though she laughed at the idea that she would flee to America to avoid facing her obligations—after all, it was the borrowers who had her money, not the other way around), but she was determined to fight. She drove across the state, appearing at meetings in every little town and large village, saying, "I am still here, I am not going anywhere."

This particular crisis was thus averted. But a few months later, in March 2006, a new "scandal" broke out which exposed a different dimension of fragility. This time, Spandana and Share, one of its competitors, were accused of being the reason a number of farmers had committed suicide. According to a new series of articles in the press, loan officers had pushed the clients to overborrow, then put unfair pressure on them to repay. The MFIs obviously denied the charges, but before anything could be resolved, the district commissioner of Krishna (the administrative head of the district) decreed that repaying one's loan to Spandana or Share was . . . *illegal*. Within days, almost *all* the clients in Krishna had stopped repaying. At the time of the crisis, Spandana had approximately 590 million rupees ($34.5 million USD PPP) of principal outstanding in the Krishna District, which represented 15 percent of Spandana's gross loan portfolio across India in 2006.

The heads of the various MFIs went to the commissioner's superiors and got the order rescinded quickly, but the damage was done. People repay because other people repay, so once people stop, it is hard to get them to restart. One year later, 70 percent of the outstanding loans had yet to be repaid. Since then, Spandana loan officers have gone back to each of the affected villages and offered their customers new loans if they would only pay back the old ones (with no extra interest). These offers do work in some villages, and they have now managed to recover half of the outstanding loans, but the pressure to act as others do is evident.[17] In some villages, everyone repays. In others, everyone refuses, even those who were only a couple of payments away from getting a new loan. Even among those who had just one more repayment to make to get a fresh loan (so that a payment of about 150 rupees would get them an extra 8,000 rupees, which they could either repay or even pocket, by defaulting again), one-fourth of loans with only one payment remaining have not been repaid. These defaulters tend to be members of groups in which no one else was repaying.

The Krishna repayment crisis was repeated, though without obvious political interference, in Karnataka and in Orissa respectively in 2008 and 2009, provoking the bankruptcy of KAS, another large microfinance institution. Everyone stopped repaying after KAS lost access to liquidity and could not disburse new loans. The crisis of fall 2010 in Andhra Pradesh was almost a repeat, on a grander scale, of the 2006 crisis. Once again, farmer suicides were used as an argument for politicians to attack the MFIs, and once again, repayments entirely stopped once the government stepped in. It brought some of the biggest microfinance institutions (SKS, Spandana, and Share) to the brink of bankruptcy. Such episodes suggest that MFIs might be right to focus on managing beliefs, and therefore it might make sense for them to insist on prioritizing repayment discipline over everything else. Opening the door to defaults, even as a way to encourage necessary risk taking, may lead to an unraveling of the social contract that allows them to keep repayment rates high and interest rates relatively low.

The necessary focus on repayment discipline implies that microfinance is not the natural or best way to finance entrepreneurs who want to go beyond micro-enterprises. For each successful entrepreneur in the Silicon Valley or elsewhere, many have had to fail. The microfinance model, as we saw, is simply not well designed to put large sums of money in the hands of people who might fail. This is not an accident, nor is this due to some shortcoming in the microcredit vision. It is the necessary by-product of the rules that have allowed microcredit to lend to a large number of poor people at low interest rates.

Moreover, microcredit may not even be an effective way to discover entrepreneurs who will then go on to set up large businesses. Microfinance gives its clients every incentive to play it safe, so it is not well suited to discover who has an appetite for risk taking. Of course, there are always counterexamples—every microfinance agency boasts on its Web site about corner shops turning into retail chains, but the instances are few and far between. The average loan that Spandana gives out increases only from 7,000 rupees ($320 USD PPP) in the first cycle to 10,000 rupees ($460 USD PPP) after three years, and there are almost no loans greater than 15,000 rupees ($686 USD PPP). After more than thirty years of operation, Grameen Bank's loans remain, for the most part, very small.

HOW CAN LARGER FIRMS BE FINANCED?

But maybe it does not matter that microcredit is not designed to lend to larger borrowers. As we saw, credit constraints are likely to be much tighter for very poor borrowers than for somewhat richer ones. Perhaps there is a natural graduation process—start by borrowing from an MFI, grow your business, and then move on to a bank.

Unfortunately, it does not seem that more established businesses find it that much easier to get credit. In particular, they run the risk of being too large for the traditional moneylenders and microfinance agencies, but too small for the banks. In summer 2010, Miao Lei was a prosperous businessman in the city of Hangzhou, China. An engineer by training, he had gone into the business of setting up computer systems at various local firms. The problem was that he had to buy the hardware and software first and only after he set up the system would he get paid. No one would give him a loan. Once, he got a chance to bid on a particularly lucrative contract but it was clear that it would take more cash than he had on hand. However, the temptation was strong and he went ahead and bid. He remembers the days after his firm won the contract, running everywhere to try to raise the money, but nothing seemed to work. Defaulting on the contract would be the end of his career. In desperation, he decided to try to pull off an even bigger gamble. There was another contract up for bid, from a state-owned company, and he knew that if he won the contract he would get an advance, which he could use to finance the first contract. Then, perhaps, he could use the money from the first to pay for the second. He decided to put in a very aggressive bid—he was happy to lose some money to win it. He still remembers the evening when he was waiting to hear if his bid had been accepted. He sent the staff home early and spent hours pacing the empty office. In the end, his bid won, and somehow it all worked out. Money flowed in, and bankers with loans followed (once his revenues crossed 20 million yuan, bankers started coming to his door). By the time we met him, he was running four separate businesses.

Miao Lei, with a good degree and a reasonable business model, had to gamble to survive. Narayan Murthy and Nandan Nilekani, despite their degrees from the ultra-prestigious Indian Institute of Technology, could not get a loan to start the firm Infosys because the banker objected that the bank could see no inventory to lend against. Infosys today is one of the largest software firms in the world. It is hard not to assume that there are a lot more people like these three, but who just couldn't make it because they didn't get the right financing at the right time.

Even those businesses that do manage to get started, survive, and grow to a certain size don't seem able to escape from being constrained in their access to capital. The town of Tirupur, South India, is India's T-shirt capital (70 percent of India's knitted garments are produced there). The firms operating in the region have a worldwide reputation: Buyers the world over go there to place large orders for their collections. Naturally, the town has attracted talented textile entrepreneurs from all over India. It also has many local entrepreneurs, the scions of wealthy farming families (from the Gounder caste). The outsiders are, not surprisingly, the experts in this line of business. The firms they run are much more efficient than those started by Gounders. For any level of capital, they produce and export more. What is more surprising, though, is that the average firm owned by a Gounder starts out with about three times more capital than those started by outsiders.[18] Instead of lending money to the outsiders who were the experts in this line of business, wealthy Gounders started their own firms, despite the fact that they had no experience at all. Why did they do that? Or for that matter, why didn't banks jump in and help the outsiders set up larger businesses? The answer is that even largish firms like these (the average firm owned by an outsider had a capital stock of 2.9 million rupees, or $347,000 USD PPP) are subject to the problems we described earlier. The Gounders started their own firms because they trusted their own community, and they were not sure the outsiders would repay them.

Recognizing this problem, developing countries have tried to use regulations to get banks to lend to these somewhat larger enterprises. India has a "priority sector" regulation, which constrains banks to lending 40 percent of their portfolios to the priority sector, consisting of agriculture, microfinance, and small and medium enterprises, which can include quite large firms (the largest eligible firms are larger than 95 percent of Indians' firms). And firms were clearly able to invest some of these funds productively. When the priority sector was expanded in 1998 to include somewhat larger firms, the firms that were newly eligible invested the extra loans they got by virtue of being in the priority sector and made a lot of money. A 10 percent increase in loans led to an increase in profits of 9 percent, *after repaying the loan.*[19] This is a fantastic rate of return. However, the fashion nowadays is very much to eliminate this kind of mandatory lending, in part because banks complain that lending to these firms is expensive and too risky.

There exist some people who are trying to identify promising new businesses and fund them. Miao Lei, the businessman from China, does precisely that, perhaps because of his own experience. He buys equity in promising young businesses. But we are far from seeing the equivalent of the microfinance revolution for small and medium firms; nobody has yet figured out how to do it profitably on a large scale. Changes in the business environment, such as improvements in the functioning of courts, may well make a difference. In India, the introduction of faster court action led to much faster loan recovery, larger loans, and lower interest rates. However, this is not a magic bullet, either. When the debt recovery tribunals were introduced, lending to the largest firms increased, but lending to the smaller firms actually went down.[20] This appears to be because the bank officer found it relatively more profitable to lend to the largest firms now that the bank could be sure it could collect on the asset the firm had pledged.

Ultimately, this problem stems from the structure of banks. Because they are, by nature, large organizations, it is hard for them to provide incentives to their employees to screen the firms, monitor projects, and make worthwhile investments. For example, if they decide to punish loan officers for default (which, to a point, they must), loan officers start looking for the absolutely safest projects, which are unlikely to be small, unknown firms. A *future* Miao Lei or Narayan Murthy may well go unfinanced.

The microfinance movement has demonstrated that, despite the difficulties, it is possible to lend to the poor. Although one may debate the extent to which MFI loans transform the lives of the poor, the simple fact that MFI lending has reached its current scale is a remarkable achievement. There are very few other programs targeted at the poor that have managed to reach so many people. However, the structure of the program, which is the source of its success in lending to the poor, is such that we cannot count on it to be a stepping-stone for larger businesses to be created and financed. Finding ways to finance medium-scale enterprises is the next big challenge for finance in developing countries.

8

Saving Brick by Brick

Driving from the city center toward the less affluent suburbs in almost any developing country, one is struck by the number of unfinished houses. There are houses with four walls but no roof, houses with a roof but no windows, would-be houses that might have an unfinished wall or two, houses with beams sticking out of their roofs, walls that someone started painting but never finished. Yet there are no cement mixers or masons in sight. Most of these houses have not been worked on for months. In some of the newer neighborhoods of Tangiers, Morocco, this is so endemic that the finished and freshly painted houses are the ones that stand out.

If you ask owners why they keep an unfinished house, they generally have a simple answer: This is how they save. The story is familiar. When Abhijit's grandfather earned some extra cash, he would add a room to the house. This is how, one room at a time, more or less, the house where his family still lives was built. Poorer people cannot afford a whole room. Abhijit's family used to have a driver who would occasionally ask for a day's leave. He would buy a sack of cement, a sack of sand, and a stack of bricks and would take a day off to lay some brick. His house was built over many years, 100 bricks at a time.

At first sight, unfinished houses don't seem to be the most attractive savings instrument. One cannot live in a roofless house; a half-built house can collapse in the rains; and if money is needed for an emergency before the house is finished and it has to be sold incomplete, the partial construction may be worth less than what it originally cost to buy the bricks. For all these reasons, it would seem more practical to save cash (say, in a bank) until enough money has accumulated, and then build at least an entire room, complete with a roof, in one go.

If the poor still save brick by brick, it must be because they have no better way to save. Is it because banks have not found a way to collect the savings of the poor, and there is a "microsaving revolution" waiting to happen? Or is there something we haven't yet thought of that makes an unfinished house an attractive investment? And should we be impressed by the extraordinary patience of people, often living on less than 99 cents a day, who will deprive themselves of some of the little pleasures of life for years in order to complete their houses? Or surprised by the fact that, if building the house brick by brick is the only way to get to own a house, they don't try to save more to build it faster?

WHY THE POOR DON'T SAVE MORE

Given that the poor have little access to credit to finance their ventures, and limited insurance to cope with risks, shouldn't they try to save as much as they can? Saving would give them a buffer against a bad year in the field or an illness. It could also hold the key to starting a business.

At this point, one common reaction is, "How could the poor save— they have no money?" But this is only superficially sensible: The poor should save because, like everybody else, they have a present and a future. They have little money today, but unless they expect to stumble on a pile of cash during the night, they presumably also expect to have little money tomorrow. Indeed, they should have more reason to save than the rich, if there is at least some possibility that, in the future, a little bit of buffer could shield them from a disaster. Such a financial cushion would, for example, allow the poor families in India's Udaipur

District to avoid cutting meals when money runs out, which they claim makes them extremely unhappy. Likewise in Kenya, when a market vendor falls ill with malaria, the family ends up spending a part of the business working capital to pay for medicine, but that makes it hard for the recovering patient to go back to work because now he has little or nothing to sell. Couldn't they avoid all that if they had some money set aside to pay for the drugs?

The Victorians thought that was just how the poor were—much too impatient and unable to think far enough ahead. Consequently, they believed that the only way to keep the poor from sinking into a life of sloth was to threaten them with extreme misery if they ever strayed from the straight and narrow. So they had the nightmarish poorhouse (where the indigent were housed) and the debtors' prisons that Charles Dickens wrote about. That view of the poor as essentially different people, whose innate inclination toward shortsighted behavior is what keeps them poor, has persisted over the years in slightly different forms. We see a version of the same view today among the critics of microfinance institutions who accuse the MFIs of preying on the profligacy of the poor. In a very different vein, Gary Becker, the Nobel Prize winner and father of the modern economics of the family, argued in a 1997 paper that the possession of wealth encourages people to invest in becoming more patient: By implication, therefore, poverty makes people (permanently) more impatient.[1]

One of the great virtues of the recent movement, among microcredit enthusiasts and others, to recognize the nascent capitalist inside every poor man and woman is that it moves us away from this view of the poor as either carefree or totally incompetent. In Chapter 6 on risk and insurance, we saw that the poor are in fact constantly worrying about the future (particularly about looming disasters) and take all sorts of ingenious or costly preventive measures to limit the risks they are subject to. Poor people show the same kind of ingenuity when managing their finances. They rarely have an account in a formal savings institution. In our eighteen-country data set, in the median country (Indonesia), 7 percent of the rural poor and 8 percent of the urban poor have formal savings accounts. In Brazil, Panama, and Peru, that number is less than 1 percent. But they save, nevertheless. Stuart

Rutherford, the founder of SafeSave, a microfinance institution in Bangladesh that focuses on helping the poor to save, tells about how they do this in two wonderful books, *The Poor and Their Money* and *Portfolios of the Poor*.[2] As background for that book, 250 poor families in Bangladesh, India, and South Africa described every single one of their financial transactions to survey researchers who visited them every two weeks for an entire year. One of their main findings is that the poor find many ingenious ways to save. They form savings "clubs" with other savers, in which each member is supposed to make sure that the others achieve their savings goals. Self-help groups (SHGs), popular in parts of India and found in many other countries as well, are savings clubs that also give loans to their members out of the accumulated savings of the group. In Africa, the most popular instruments are rotating savings and credit associations (ROSCAs)—more commonly known as "merry-go-rounds" in English-speaking Africa and as *tontines* in Francophone countries. ROSCA members meet at regular intervals, and all deposit the same amount of money into a common pot at every meeting. Each time, on a rotating basis, one member gets the whole pot. Other savings arrangements include paying deposit collectors to take their deposits and put them in a bank, depositing savings with local moneylenders, leaving them with "money guards" (acquaintances who take care of small sums of money for a little fee, or for free), and, as we saw, slowly building a house. Similar institutions also exist in the United States, mostly within recent immigrant communities.

Jennifer Auma, a market vendor in the small town of Bumala in western Kenya, embodies this sophistication. Auma sells maize, sorghum, and beans. During our entire conversation, she expertly sorted beans, the red ones to one side, the white ones to the other. When we met her, she belonged to no fewer than six ROSCAs, which differed in size and frequency of meeting. In one of them, she contributed 1,000 Kenyan shillings, or KES ($17.50 USD PPP), per month, in another one 580 KES twice a month (500 for the pot, 50 to pay for the sugar for the tea, which is an essential part of the ceremony, and 30 for the welfare fund). In another, the contribution was 500 KES per month, plus 200 as extra savings. Then there was a weekly ROSCA (150 KES per week), one that met three times a week

(50 KES), and one that was daily (20 KES). Each ROSCA had a specific, separate purpose, she explained. The small ones were for her rent (this was before she built a house), the bigger ones for long-term projects (such as house improvements) or for school fees. Auma saw many advantages to ROSCAs over traditional savings accounts: They don't have fees, she could make small deposits, and on average she got access to the pot much faster than it would take her if she saved the same amount every week. Moreover, the ROSCA group was also a good place to ask for advice.

But her financial portfolio did not end with the six ROSCAs. She had taken a loan from one of her ROSCA savings pools in early May 2009 (a little over two months before we met her) to buy maize worth 6,000 KES ($105 USD PPP). She was also a member of the village savings bank, where she had a savings account, though it was currently almost empty. She had used that money to buy shares in the village bank worth 12,000 KES ($210 USD PPP). Along with some shares she already had (each share entitled the borrower to borrow up to 4 KES from the village bank), this allowed her to borrow 70,000 KES ($1,222 USD PPP) and build herself a house. She also had little stashes of money hidden in various parts of her house to deal with small emergencies such as health needs, although as she pointed out, sometimes the health money was used for feeding visitors. Finally, she was owed money by a variety of people, including 1,200 KES by her clients and 4,000 KES by a former member of her joint liability group in the village savings bank. He had defaulted on the loan when he still owed the bank 60,000 KES ($1,050 USD PPP), obliging the group members to cover for him, and he was only now slowly paying them back.

As a market vendor married to a farmer, Jennifer Auma probably lived on much less than $2 a day. Yet she had an array of finely tuned financial instruments. We see this kind of financial ingenuity time and time again.

Yet all the ingenuity the poor employ to save may simply be a symptom of the fact that they don't have access to the more conventional and simpler alternatives. Banks don't like managing small accounts, largely because of the administrative costs of running them. Deposit-taking institutions are heavily regulated, for good reason—the government is worried about fly-by-night operators running away with people's savings—but this means that managing each account requires bank employees to fill out some amount of paperwork, which can quickly become too burdensome, relative to any money that the bank can hope to make from these tiny accounts. Jennifer Auma explained to us that her savings account at the village savings bank was not a good place to save small amounts, because the withdrawal fees were too high. The fees were 30 KES for withdrawals less than 500 KES, 50 KES for withdrawals between 500 KES and 1,000 KES, and 100 KES for a larger withdrawal. As a result of such administrative fees, most of the poor may not want a bank account even when they are entitled to one.

The fact that the poor have to substitute for lack of access to proper bank accounts by adopting complicated and costly alternative strategies to save might also mean that they save less than they would if they had a bank account. To find out whether this was the case, Pascaline Dupas and Jonathan Robinson paid the opening fees for a savings account at a local village bank, on behalf of a random sample of small business owners (bicycle taxi drivers, market vendors, carpenters, and the like) in Bumala. The bank had an office in the main marketplace where all these people operated their businesses. The accounts didn't pay any interest. Instead, they charged a fee for each withdrawal.[3]

Few men ended up using the accounts that were offered to them, but about two-thirds of the women deposited money at least once. And these women saved more than comparable women who were not offered an account, invested more in their businesses, and were less likely to draw on their working capital when ill. After six months, they were able to purchase on average 10 percent more food for themselves and their family, day in and day out.

Although the poor do find sophisticated ways to put some money aside, these results show that they would be better off if it were much cheaper to start a bank account. As it is, each account in Kenya costs 450 KES to open, and on average about 5,000 KES got deposited in any account that was used at least once. This means that if Dupas and Robinson had not paid the fee for them, these poor clients would have had to pay a "tax" of nearly 10 percent for the privilege of having an account, not counting the withdrawal fees. To this, we have to add the cost for the poor of going to the bank, usually in a town center, far from where they live. The cost to the bank of managing small amounts of savings has to go down a lot before savings accounts for the poor can be economically viable.

The "self-help groups" popular in India and elsewhere represent one way to reduce costs, leveraging the idea that if members pool their savings and coordinate their withdrawals and deposits, the total amount in the account will be larger, and the bank will be happy to take it. Technology can also play a role. In Kenya, M-PESA allows users to deposit money into an account linked to their cell phones and then use the cell phone to send money to other people's accounts and to make payments. Someone like Jennifer Auma, for example, could deposit cash at one of the many local grocery shops that happens to be an M-PESA correspondent. This would credit her M-PESA account. She could then send a text message to her cousin in Lamu, who would be able to present the text message to his local correspondent to get his money. Once he gets the cash, the money would be deducted from her M-PESA account. Once M-PESA is linked to banks, people will be able to wire money in and out of their savings accounts using a local M-PESA correspondent, without having to trek all the way to the bank.

Of course, no technology would remove the need for regulation of bank accounts. A part of the problem, however, comes from the fact that under the current regulations only highly paid bank employees are generally allowed to handle depositors' money. This is probably unnecessary. Instead, the bank could use a local shopkeeper to take deposits. As long as the local shopkeeper issues the depositor a receipt for the money that the bank is *legally obligated to honor*, the depositor is protected. Then it is the bank's problem to make sure that the shopkeeper doesn't run away with the saver's money. If the bank is willing to take that risk—and many banks would be happy to—then why should the regulator care? This realization has been percolating through the system in recent years, and a number of countries have passed new laws permitting this kind of deposit taking (in India, for example, this is called the Banking Correspondent Act). This might eventually revolutionize the whole business of savings.

There is currently an important international effort, led in particular by the Bill & Melinda Gates Foundation, to increase access to savings accounts for the poor. Microsaving is poised to become the next microfinance revolution. But is the lack of access to formal saving accounts the only issue? Should we concentrate exclusively on making it easy and safe to save? Dupas and Robinson's results suggest that this is not the whole story. First, there was the disturbing fact that most men did not use their (free) accounts. Many women did not use them either, or used them very little. Forty percent of women did not make a single deposit, and less than half made more than one; many who had started to use the account stopped after a while. In Busia, Kenya, in another study,[4] only 25 percent of the couples who were offered up to three accounts for free (one for each member of the couple and a joint account) deposited any money in any of the accounts. This went up to only 31 percent among those who also received a free ATM card to make withdrawals and deposits easier and cheaper. Savings accounts clearly help some people. However, their absence is not the only thing that stops the poor from saving.

We have already seen, in the previous chapter, another example of people who had lucrative opportunities to save but did not use them: the fruit vendors from Chennai, who borrowed about 1,000 rupees ($45.75 USD PPP) each morning at the rate of 4.69 percent per day. Suppose that the vendors decided to drink two fewer cups of tea for three days. This would save them 5 rupees a day, which could be used to cut down on the amount they would have to borrow. After the first day with less tea, they would have to borrow 5 rupees less. This means that at the end of the second day, they would have to repay 5.23 rupees less (the 5 rupees they did not borrow, plus 23 paisas in interest), which, when added to the 5 rupees they saved that second day by again drinking less tea, would allow them to borrow 10.23 rupees less. By the same logic, by the fourth day, they would have 15.71 rupees that they could use for buying fruit instead of borrowing. Now, say they go back to drinking their two cups more tea but continue to plough the 15.71 rupees they had saved from three days of not drinking so much tea back into the business (that is, borrowing that much less). That accumulated amount continues to grow (just as the 10 rupees had turned into 10.71 after two days) and after exactly ninety days, they would be completely debt-free. They would save 40 rupees *a day*, which is the equivalent of about half a day's wages. All just for the price of six cups of tea!

The point is that these vendors are sitting under what appears to be as close to a money tree as we are likely to find anywhere. Why don't they shake it a bit more? How can we square this with the sophisticated financial planning that we encountered with Jennifer Auma?

THE PSYCHOLOGY OF SAVINGS

Understanding the way people think about the future can help resolve these apparent contradictions. Andrei Shleifer, probably the best exponent of the theory that many people sometimes do silly things (he coined, or at least popularized, the term "noise traders" to characterize the behavior of naïve stock traders who are ruthlessly exploited by sophisticated traders), who had just returned from Kenya, shared with us something that he had noticed there: a huge difference between the farms run by a group of nuns, which were lush and vibrant, and those run by their neighbors, which were much less impressive. The nuns were using fertilizer and hybrid seeds. Why, he asked us, were the farmers not able to do what the nuns were doing? Could it be a sign that they were much more impatient (the nuns' profession presumably inclines them to patience because the rewards are mainly in the afterlife)?

He had hit on something that had long been a puzzle for us. In surveys conducted over several years, Michael Kremer, Jonathan Robinson, and Esther found that only about 40 percent of the farmers in the Busia region in western Kenya (not far from Sauri, the village where Jeffrey Sachs and Angelina Jolie met Kennedy, the young farmer who had not been using fertilizer before the project gave it to him) had ever used fertilizer, and just 25 percent used fertilizer in any given year.[5] Conservative estimates, based on offering a random group of farmers free fertilizer to use on a small part of their fields and then comparing the harvest on that plot to that on a similar plot of land belonging to the same farmer, suggest that the average annual return to using fertilizer exceeds 70 percent: For $1 paid in fertilizer, the average farmer would get $1.70 worth of extra maize. Not quite the returns the fruit vendors could make, but seemingly well worth the effort of saving a little. Why were they not doing it more? It may be that farmers do not know exactly how to use fertilizer. Or they could underestimate the returns. But if that were true, then at least the farmers who got the offer of free fertilizer (and a demonstration of how best to use it) and earned the high returns should be hugely enthusiastic about using it in subsequent seasons. In fact, Esther, Kremer, and Robinson found that the farmers who were given free fertilizer one season were 10 percentage points more likely on average to use fertilizer in the very next season after the study, but that still meant that a majority had gone back to not using fertilizer. It was not that they were unimpressed with what they saw: The vast majority claimed to be convinced and initially said they would surely use fertilizer.

When we asked some farmers why they did not end up using fertilizer, most replied that they did not have enough money on hand to buy fertilizer when it was time to plant and use it. What is surprising is that fertilizer can be purchased (and used) in small quantities, so this is an investment opportunity that seems easily accessible to farmers with even a small amount of savings. It suggests that the issue, once again, is that farmers find it difficult to hold on to even very small sums of money for the period from harvest to planting. As Michael and Anna Modimba, a couple who farm maize near Budalengi in western Kenya, explained, saving is hard. On their farm, they had used fertilizer in the last growing season, but not the one before, because they had had no money left to buy it then. Saving at home is difficult, they explained, because there is always something that comes up that requires money (someone is sick, someone needs clothes, a guest has to be fed), and it is hard to say no.

Another farmer we met the same day, Wycliffe Otieno, had found a way to solve this problem. He always made the decision about whether or not to buy fertilizer just after the harvest. If the harvest was sufficient to pay for school fees and provide food for the family, he immediately sold the rest of his crop and used the money to purchase hybrid seeds, and if he had any leftover money, fertilizer. He stored the seeds and the fertilizer until the next planting season. He explained to us that he always bought the fertilizer in advance, because, like the Modimbas, he knew that money kept in the house would not be saved: When there is money in the house, things always happen, he said, and the money disappears.

We asked him what he did when he had already purchased fertilizer (but not yet used it) and someone got sick. Wasn't he tempted to resell it at a loss? His answer was that he never found the need to resell the fertilizer. Instead, he tended to reevaluate the true urgency of any need when there was no money lying around. And if something really needed to be paid for, he would kill a chicken or work a bit harder as a bicycle taxi driver (a job he did on the side when he was not too busy with farming). Although they had never purchased fertilizer in advance, the Modimbas had the same view. If a problem came up but they had no money (say, because they had purchased fertilizer), they would figure something out—perhaps borrow from friends or, as they put it, "suspend the issue"; but they would not resell the fertilizer. It was their opinion that it would be a good thing for them to be forced to find an alternative solution, instead of using the cash at home.

So to help people like the Modimbas, Esther, Kremer, and Robinson designed the Savings and Fertilizer Initiative (SAFI) program. Right after the harvest—when farmers have money in hand—they are given the opportunity to purchase a voucher entitling them to fertilizer at sowing time.[6] ICS Africa, an NGO working in the area, implemented the program. Fertilizer was sold at market price, but an ICS field officer visited the farmers at home to sell the vouchers, and the fertilizer was delivered to their homes when they wanted it. The program increased the fraction of farmers who used fertilizer by at least 50 percent. To put this in perspective, the effect of this program was greater than the effect of a 50 percent reduction in the price of fertilizer. Just as Michael and Anna Modimba and Wycliffe Otieno had predicted, as long as it was brought to their door at the right time, farmers were very happy to buy fertilizer.

But that didn't explain why the farmers did not buy the fertilizer in advance on their own. A huge majority of the farmers who bought the vouchers went for immediate delivery, then stored the fertilizer and used it later on. In other words, just as Wycliffe Otieno had told us, once they had fertilizer, they didn't resell it. But if they really want fertilizer, why don't they go ahead and buy it themselves? We asked the Modimbas. Their answer was that the fertilizer shops did not always have fertilizer available immediately after harvest—they only got it later, just before planting. As Michael Modimba said: "When we have money, they don't have fertilizer. When they have fertilizer, we don't have money." For Wycliffe Otieno, this was not such a problem: Because his job as a bicycle taxi driver brought him into town all the time, he was able to regularly check whether fertilizer had come in, and then buy it from whatever shop happened to have it. But for farmers like the Modimbas, who lived about an hour's walk from the market town and had few reasons to go there, checking the stores was more difficult. It was this small inconvenience of keeping an eye out for fertilizer delivery (asking a friend to check, calling the store) that was holding back their savings and productivity. All our intervention really did was to remove this minor bottleneck.

Savings and Self-Control

The experience of the Indian fruit sellers and the Kenyan farmers suggests that a lot of people fail to save even when they have access to good saving opportunities. This suggests that barriers to savings are not all externally imposed. Part of the problem comes from human psychology. Most of us have some memory of trying to explain to an irate parent that we were just sitting next to the cookie jar and the cookies somehow vanished. We knew eating the cookies would mean trouble, but the temptation was too strong.

As we discussed in Chapter 3 on preventive health, the human brain processes the present and the future very differently. In essence, we seem to have a vision of how we should act in the future that is often inconsistent with the way we act today and will act in the future. One form that this "time inconsistency" takes is to spend now, at the same time as we *plan* to save in the future. In other words, we hope that our "tomorrow's self" will be more patient than "today's self" is prepared to be.

Another manifestation of time inconsistency is to buy what we want today (alcohol, sugary or fatty foods, trinkets) but to plan on spending money in more responsible ways tomorrow (school fees, bed nets, roof repairs). In other words, the things we take pride or pleasure in imagining buying in the future are not always what we end up buying today. Knowing that we will have one drink too many again tomorrow gives most of us no pleasure—indeed, it probably makes us unhappy—yet when tomorrow comes along many of us cannot resist it. Alcohol, in this sense, is a *temptation good* for many people, something that makes immediate claims on us without giving us anticipatory pleasure. In contrast, a television is probably not a temptation good: Many poor people plan and save for months or even years to buy one.

A group of economists, psychologists, and neuroscientists worked together to establish that there is in fact a physical basis for such disjunction in decisionmaking.[7] They gave participants a choice of various rewards that would be enjoyed at different points in time, using time-dated gift cards. Each participant thus had a set of decisions to make. For example: receive $20 *now* or $30 in two weeks (present vs. future); receive $20 in two weeks or $30 in four weeks (future vs. more distant future); or receive $20 in four weeks or $30 in six weeks (more distant future vs. even more distant future). The twist was that the subjects made these decisions inside an fMRI scanner, so the researchers could look at what zones of their brains were activated. They found that the parts of the brain corresponding to the limbic system (thought to respond only to more visceral, immediate rewards) were activated only when the decision involved comparing a reward today with one in the future. In contrast, the lateral prefrontal cortex (a more "calculating" part of the brain) responded with a similar intensity to all decisions, regardless of the timing of the options.

Brains that work like this would produce a lot of failed good intentions. And indeed, we do see a lot of those, from New Year's resolutions to gym memberships that lie unused. However, many people, such as the Modimbas or Wycliffe Otieno, seem fully aware of such inconsistency. They talked about freezing their money in the form of fertilizer as a way to get around it. They also seemed to be convinced that some of the "emergencies" they faced were in effect a kind of temptation good, because it was easier in the moment to spend money rather than just "suspend the issue" (Michael Modimba's phrase), or to stay at home rather than go out to earn something extra.

In Hyderabad, we explicitly asked slum dwellers to tell us whether there were any goods they would like to cut back on. They readily came up with tea, snacks, alcohol, and tobacco. And indeed it was clear from what they told us and from the data we collected that significant parts of their budgets ended up getting spent on these items. The same self-knowledge was apparent when Esther, Kremer, and Robinson asked a group of participants in the Kenyan fertilizer program, in advance of the harvest, to choose the day when they would come to sell the vouchers. A large fraction asked them to come early. The farmers knew that right after harvest was when they would have money available, but that it would soon disappear.

Given this self-awareness, it is no surprise that many of the ways the poor save seem to be not only intended to keep the money safe from others, but also to guard it from themselves. For example, if you want to reach a goal (buy a cow, a refrigerator, a roof), joining a ROSCA where the total pot size is exactly enough to achieve that goal is a great option, because once you join, you are committed to contributing a certain amount every week or month, and when you get the pot, you have just enough to buy that thing you have been looking forward to buying, and you can do it right away before the money slips through your fingers. Building a house brick by brick may be another way to make sure your savings remain focused toward a concrete goal.

Indeed, if the lack of self-control is sufficiently serious, it would be worth *paying* someone to force us to save. For example, we might prefer to run the risk that the mortar on our freshly built walls might get washed away by the rain so that we wouldn't have to keep the cash on hand and risk that we might, on a whim, use it all for a party. And somewhat paradoxically, some MFI clients may borrow in order to save. A woman we met in a slum in Hyderabad told us that she had borrowed 10,000 rupees ($621 USD PPP) from Spandana and had immediately deposited the proceeds of the loan in a savings account. Thus, she was paying a 24 percent annual interest rate to Spandana, while earning about 4 percent on her savings account. When we asked her why this made sense, she explained that her daughter, now sixteen, would need to get married in about two years. That 10,000 rupees was the beginning of her dowry. When we asked her why she had not opted to simply put the money she was paying to Spandana for the loan into her savings account directly every week, she explained that it was simply not possible: Other things kept coming up.

We were still a bit bothered by this rather unusual arrangement and kept asking questions. This attracted a group of other women, who were patently amused by our ignorance. Didn't we know that this was a perfectly normal thing to do? The point, as we eventually figured out, is that the obligation to pay what you owe to Spandana—which is well enforced—imposes a discipline that the borrowers might not manage on their own.

However, it is clear that people should not have to pay 20 percent or more per year in order to save. Designing financial products that share the commitment features of the microfinance contracts, without the interest that comes with them, could clearly be of great help to many people. A group of researchers teamed up with a bank that works with poor people in the Philippines to design such a product,[8] a new kind of account that would be tied to each client's own savings targets. This target could be either an amount (the client would commit not to withdraw the funds until the amount was reached) or a date (the client would commit to leave the money in the account until that date). The client chose the type of commitment and the specific target. However, once those targets were set, they were binding, and the bank would en-force them. The interest rate was no higher than on a regular account. These accounts were proposed to a randomly selected set of clients. Of the clients they approached, about one in four agreed to open such an account. Out of those takers, a little over two-thirds chose the date goal, and the remaining one-third, the amount goal. After a year, the balances in the savings accounts of those who were *offered* the account were on average 81 percent higher than those of a comparable group of people who were not offered the account, *despite the fact that only one in four of the clients who had been offered the account actually signed on.* And the effects were probably smaller than they could have been, because even though there was a commitment not to withdraw any money, there was no positive force pushing the client to actually save, and many of the accounts that were opened remained dormant.

Yet most people preferred not to take up the offer of such an account. They were clearly worried about committing themselves to not withdrawing until the goal was reached. Dupas and Robinson ran into the same problem in Kenya—many people did not end up using the accounts they were offering, some of them because the withdrawal fees were too high and they did not want to have their money tied up in the account. This highlights an interesting paradox: There are ways to get around self-control problems, but to make use of them usually requires an initial act of self-control. Pascaline Dupas and Jonathan Robinson demonstrated this nicely in another study with the vendors of Bumala market, in Kenya.[9] They had noticed that many small businesses lose sales when their owner (or someone in his family) gets sick and has to buy medicine. So they thought of helping people earmark some of their savings specifically for such contingencies, or for buying preventive health products (such as chlorine or a bed net). They contacted members of ROSCAs and offered them a lockbox, which could be used to save specifically for health contingencies. Some people (randomly selected) were given the key to the box, whereas for others, the NGO field officer kept the key: She would come and open the box when the people needed the money because of a health problem. Giving people a health box did help them to spend more on preventive health. But giving them a *locked* health box, to Dupas and Robinson's surprise, did not: They simply did not put much money in it. People reported not using it, or using it only for very small amounts, for fear that they would need the money for something else and would not be able to access it.

Awareness of our problems thus does not necessarily mean that they get solved. It may just mean that we are able to perfectly anticipate where we will fail.

POVERTY AND THE LOGIC OF SELF-CONTROL

Because self-control is hard to buy, self-aware decisionmakers take other defensive actions against the possibility of being tempted in the future.

An obvious strategy is not to save as much, because we know that we will just waste the money tomorrow: We might as well give in to the temptation today, if all we are going to do is give in to it tomorrow. This perverse logic of temptations operates in the same way for the poor as it does for the rich, but there are good reasons that the consequences may be much more serious for the poor than for the rich.

Temptations tend to be an expression of visceral needs (things like sex, sugar, fatty foods, cigarettes, not necessarily in that order). In that case, it is much easier for the rich to be at the point where they have already satiated their "tempted selves." When deciding whether to save or not, they can assume that any extra money that is allocated for the future will be used for long-term purposes. So if sugary tea is the archetype of a temptation good, as it seemed to be for the women in Hyderabad, then the rich are unlikely to be troubled by it—not because they are not tempted but because they can already afford so much tea (or other substitutes for tea) that they do not have to worry about their hard-earned savings being frittered away on extra cups of tea.

This effect is reinforced by the fact that a lot of the goods that the poor might really look forward to having, such as a refrigerator or bicycle or admission to a better school for their child, are relatively expensive, with the result that when they have a little bit of money in hand, the temptation goods are in an excellent position to stake their claim (*You'll never really save enough for that refrigerator,* the voice in your ear insists. *Have a cup of tea instead . . .*). The result is a vicious circle: Saving is less attractive for the poor, because for them the goal tends to be very far away, and they know that there will be lots of temptations along the way. But of course, if they do not save they remain poor.[10]

Self-control may also be more difficult for the poor for another reason: Decisions about how much should be saved are difficult decisions for anyone, rich and poor alike. These decisions require thinking about the future (a future probably unpleasant to contemplate, for many of the poor), carefully laying out a number of contingencies, negotiating with a spouse or a child. The richer we are, the more these decisions are made for us. Salaried workers contribute to Social Security, and their employers often contribute something more to a provident fund or a pension plan. If they want to save more, they have to decide just once, and the money is then automatically deducted from their bank accounts. The poor have access to none of these props: Even the savings accounts that are supposed to make it easier for them to commit to a goal still require an active step of depositing money. To be able to save every week or every month, they have to surmount self-control problems over and over again. The problem is that self-control is like a muscle: It gets tired as we use it, and therefore it would not be a surprise if the poor find it harder to save.[11] This is compounded by the fact, which we discussed in Chapter 6 on risk, that the poor live under considerable stress, and stress-induced cortisol makes us choose more impulsive decisions. The poor thus have to do a harder job on fewer resources.

For both reasons, we would expect the rich to save a higher fraction of their current net worth (think of wealth plus income). And because saving today is one ingredient of net worth tomorrow, this will have the tendency to create an S-shaped relationship between net worth today and net worth tomorrow. The poor save relatively little and therefore their future resources tend to be low. Then as people get richer, they start saving a higher fraction of their resources, which means that they will have, relatively, a lot more resources in the future than the poor. Finally, when people get rich enough, they don't have to save as much of their wealth to meet their aspirations for the future, unlike middle-class people (for whom this may be the only way, for example, to buy a house).

We do see this S-shape between net worth today and net worth in the future in the real world. Figure 1 plots the relationship between resources the households had in 1999 and what they had five years later in Thailand.[12] The curve has a flat, elongated S-shape (admittedly, we are torturing the S a little bit). People who are richer today (more resources) are, on average, richer tomorrow, which is of course not surprising. What is more distinctive is the way in which the relation is fairly flat at very low levels of resources but then turns up sharply before flattening off.

This S-shape, as we saw before, generates a poverty trap. Those who start just to the left of the point where the wealth curve just touches the 45°

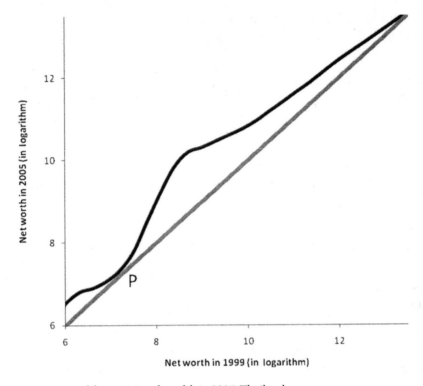

Figure 1: Wealth in 1999 and wealth in 2005, Thailand

line will not get richer than that point: They won't accumulate more— they are in the trap. Those just to the right of this point, P, on the other hand, are saving more than they need to stay in the same place and are getting richer. The poor stay poor here because they do not save enough.

Getting out of the Trap

Saving behavior crucially depends on what people expect will happen in the future. Poor people who feel that they will have opportunities to realize their aspirations will have strong reasons to cut down on their "frivolous" consumption and invest in that future. Those who feel that they have nothing to lose, by contrast, will tend to make decisions that reflect that desperation. This may explain not only the differences between rich and poor but also the differences among different poor people.

The fruit vendors are a good illustration. Dean Karlan and Sendhil Mullainathan fully repaid the loans of a random subset of these vendors (in India, and in the Philippines).[13] For a while, many of the vendors managed to stay debt-free: After ten weeks, 40 percent were still debt-free in the Philippines. So these fruit vendors seem to have enough patience to stay out of debt for a while. On the other hand, almost all of them eventually fell back into debt. It was usually a shock (an illness, an emergency need) that pushed them back into debt, and once that happened, they did not manage to pay the debt back on their own. This asymmetry between managing to stay free of debt and not managing to get *out* of debt shows the role of discouragement in making it harder to impose self-discipline.

Conversely, optimism and hope can make all the difference. Hope can be as simple as knowing that you will be able to buy the television you are looking forward to having. When we were working on the evaluation of Spandana's microfinance program, Padmaja Reddy once took us on a tour to meet her clients in the slums of Guntur, the birthplace of the organization. It was about 10:30 AM when we walked into a small clearing in the slum, where a dozen or so women were assembled. When Padmaja, whom they evidently knew, asked them what they were up to, they giggled. There was an awkward moment when we could see the women nudging each other, but then it came out—tea was being made. Padmaja joined in laughing with the women, but then, still smiling, went into a brief harangue about how they could improve their futures by cutting back on tea and snacks.

Most microcredit institutions disapprove of borrowing to buy consumption goods—some actually put a lot of effort into making sure that their money gets spent on some income-earning asset. Padmaja, on the other hand, is happy as long as the clients use the money to realize any of their long-term goals. Thinking about long-term goals and getting used to making short-term sacrifices in order to get there are the first steps, she thinks, toward liberation from one of the most frustrating aspects of poverty.

It was because of Padmaja's insistence on the ill effects of wanton tea drinking that, as reported above, we actually asked the women what things they would want to spend less money on, before our evaluation of Spandana's program. When we started the study, Padmaja confidently predicted that once people knew that there was a way to turn their tea money into stuff that really matters to them, they would have little trouble cutting back on these "wasteful expenditures." We saw no point in reminding her that this went diametrically against the view that we heard from so many people, that the worst thing about easy credit for the poor is precisely that it makes it too easy for them to indulge their momentary whims, but it was clearly on our minds when we started to look at the data, some eighteen months after the first round of loans. We needn't have worried. Padmaja, as she often says, knows how her clients think. As we saw in Chapter 7 on credit, one of the clearest impacts of getting access to microcredit was to reduce exactly the items that the women had told us they would like to give up—tea, snacks, cigarettes, alcohol. Total monthly spending on these goods went down by about 100 rupees ($5 USD PPP) per family for those that took an extra microcredit loan as a result of the program, or about 85 percent of what the average household spends. By itself, the cut in this kind of spending could pay for about one-tenth of the monthly repayment on a 10,000 rupee ($450 USD PPP) loan with a 20 percent interest rate. Later, we found very similar results for the clients of the MFI Al Amana in rural Morocco: They cut on social expenditures (and for some of them, on all expenditures), and built up their savings.[14]

Microcredit, of course, is just one of many ways in which we can help the poor think in terms of a future where some of their long-term goals can become attainable. Better education for their children would probably have the same effect. So would a steady and secure job, a theme to which we will return in the next chapter. Or insurance against health or weather disasters, so that they don't worry that any nest egg that they manage to accumulate will just get wiped out. Or even a social safety net: a minimum income support that people would be entitled to if their income fell below a certain range that would free them from having to worry about finding money to survive. The sense of security that any of these would provide would encourage savings for two reasons: by creating a sense that the future holds promises, and by lowering the stress level, which directly impedes decisionmaking ability.

The bigger point is that a little bit of hope and some reassurance and comfort can be a powerful incentive. It is easy for those of us who have enough, living a secure life, structured by goals that we can reasonably confidently aspire to achieve (that new sofa, the 50-inch flat screen, that second car) and institutions designed to help us get there (savings accounts, pension programs, home-equity loans) to assume, like the Victorians, that motivation and discipline are intrinsic. As a result, there are always worries about being overindulgent to the slothful poor. Our contention is that for the most part, the problem is the opposite: It is too hard to stay motivated when everything you want looks impossibly far away. Moving the goalposts closer may be just what the poor need to start running toward them.

9

Reluctant Entrepreneurs

A businessman sitting next to us on a plane many years ago described how, when he returned to India in the mid-1970s after completing his MBA in the United States, his uncle had taken him out for a lesson in true entrepreneurship. It was early one morning when he and his uncle headed for the Bombay (as Mumbai was then called) Stock Exchange. But instead of going into the modern tower that houses the exchange, his uncle wanted him to observe four women who were sitting on the sidewalk, facing the road in front of the exchange. The aspiring businessman and his uncle stood for a few moments watching them. The women mostly did nothing. But occasionally, when the traffic stopped, they would get up, scrape something off the road, and put it in plastic carrier bags next to them, before returning to their seats. After this happened several times, the uncle asked him if he understood their business model. He confessed to be baffled. So the uncle had to explain: Every morning before dawn the women went to the beach, where they collected wet sea sand. They then laid it evenly on the street before the real traffic began. When the cars started driving over the sand, the heat from their wheels dried it. All they had to do then was occasionally to scrape off the top layer of sand, now dry. By nine or ten, they had a quantity of dry sand, which they brought back to the slum to sell in small packets made from discarded newspapers: The local women used the dry sand to scrub their dishes. This, the uncle reckoned, was true entrepreneurship: If you have very little, use your ingenuity to create something out of nothing.

Women from slums who manage to make a living, quite literally, from the wheels of Bombay's commerce epitomize the incredible spirit of innovation and entrepreneurship the poor often display. This book could easily be filled with stories of creativity and resilience among owners of small-scale enterprises. Such images have been a powerful motivation for the recent microfinance and "social business" movement, which starts from the premise that the poor are natural-born entrepreneurs, and we can eradicate poverty by giving them the right environment and a little bit of help getting started. In the words of John Hatch, the CEO of FINCA, one of the largest microfinance institutions in the world: "Give poor communities the opportunities, and get out of the way."

Yet there are some perhaps surprising instances when, after you have gotten out of the way, the poor do not seem so ready to roll. Since 2007, we have been working with Al Amana, one of Morocco's largest MFIs, to evaluate the impact of access to microcredit in rural communities that had previously been completely excluded from formal financial sources. After about two years, it became evident that Al Amana was not getting as many clients in the villages as had been anticipated. Despite the lack of alternatives, less than one in six eligible families was interested in a loan. To try to understand why, we went with some Al Amana staff to interview a few families in a village called Hafret Ben Tayeb, where no one had borrowed. We were received by Allal Ben Sedan, the father of three sons and two daughters, all adults. He had four cows, one donkey, and eighty olive trees. One of his sons worked in the army; another tended to the animals; the third was mostly idle (his main activity was harvesting snails when they were in season). We asked Ben Sedan whether he would want to take a loan to buy some more cows, which his idle son could take care of. He explained that his field was too small—if he bought more cows they would have nowhere to graze. Before leaving, we asked him if there was anything else he could do with a loan. He replied, "No, nothing. We have enough. We have cows, we sell them, we sell the olives. That is enough for our family."

A few days later, we met Fouad Abdelmoumni, the founder (and then CEO) of Al Amana, a man of great warmth and intelligence, who in a previous life as an activist had spent years in jail as a political prisoner and was entirely devoted to improving the lives of the poor. We discussed the surprisingly low demand for microcredit. In particular, we went back to the story of Ben Sedan, who was convinced that he had no use for more money. Fouad drew up a clearly feasible business plan for him. He could take a loan, build a stable, and buy four young cows. They would not need to graze in a field: They could be fed in the stable. Within eight months, he could sell the cows for a hefty profit. Fouad was persuaded that if someone explained this to him, Ben Sedan would see the wisdom of this plan and take out a loan.

We were struck by the contrast between Fouad's enthusiasm and Ben Sedan's insistence that his family did not need anything. Yet Ben Sedan was not at all resigned to remaining poor: He was very proud of his son, who had been trained as a nurse and worked as a paramedic in the army. His son, he thought, had a real chance at a better life. So was Fouad right that Ben Sedan just needed to be led to a business plan? Or was Ben Sedan, who, after all, had been in the business of raising cows for most of his adult life, telling us something important?

Muhammad Yunus, founder of the world-famous Grameen Bank, often describes the poor as natural entrepreneurs. Combined with the late business guru C. K. Prahalad's exhortation to businessmen to focus more on what he called the "bottom of the pyramid,"[1] the idea of the entrepreneurial poor is helping to secure a space within the overall anti-poverty policy discourse where big business and high finance feel comfortable getting involved. The traditional strategies of public action are being supplemented by private actions, often taken by some of the leaders of the corporate world (for example, Pierre Omidyar of eBay), directed at helping the poor realize their true potential as entrepreneurs.

The basic premise of Yunus's view of the world, shared by many in the microfinance movement, is that everyone has a shot at being a successful entrepreneur. More specifically, there are two distinct reasons the poor may be particularly likely to find amazing opportunities. First, they haven't been given a chance, so their ideas are probably fresher and less likely to have been tried already. Second, the market so far has mostly ignored the bottom of the pyramid. As a result, it is argued, innovations that better the lives of the poor have to be the low-hanging fruit, and who better than the poor themselves to think of what they could be?

CAPITALISTS WITHOUT CAPITAL

Indeed, every self-respecting MFI has a Web site with a number of stories of successful microfinance clients who took advantage of an unusual opportunity to make a fortune. They are real: We have met several of those clients. In Guntur, in Andhra Pradesh, we met a client of Spandana who had built a very successful business collecting trash and sorting it. She started as a trash collector, which is pretty much as low as you can go in the Indian social and economic hierarchy. With her first loan from Spandana, she just paid back the loan she had from a moneylender, with its crippling interest rate. She knew that the businesses that bought the trash from her sorted it before selling it to recyclers—there would be bits of metal and tungsten from the filaments of used lightbulbs, plastics, organic matter for composting, and so forth, each of which went to a different recycler. With the breathing space that the first loan bought her, she decided to do the sorting herself to make some extra money. With her second loan and the savings from the first, she bought a cart, which helped her collect more trash, and because there was now more sorting to be done, she somehow managed to get her husband, who used to spend most of his time drinking, to start working with her. Together they were making significantly more money, and after receiving the third loan, they started buying trash from others. By the time we met her, she was at the helm of a large network of trash collectors, no longer a collector herself but an organizer of trash collection. Her husband, too, was working full-time by then: We saw him pounding away on a piece of metal, looking sober but a trifle glum.

MFIs advertise the stories of their most successful borrowers, but there are also entrepreneurs who succeed even when they have no access to microfinance. In 1982, Xu Aihua was one of the best middle-school students in her village, in the Shaoxing region of Zhejiang Province in China. Her parents were peasants and, like almost everyone else, had very little disposable cash. She was so bright, however, that the village decided to send her for a year to the local school of fashion design (whatever that meant, exactly, since everyone still wore Mao suits). The idea was that she would eventually take a leadership role in the local town and village enterprise that had just been set up (these were the early years of Chinese liberalization). But when she came back after her training, the local elders got cold feet—she was a girl, after all, not yet twenty. So she was sent unceremoniously home, jobless.

Xu Aihua had no intention of sitting idle. She decided that she had to do something, but her parents were too poor to help. So she borrowed a megaphone and went around the village offering to teach young girls how to make garments for a fee of 15 yuan ($13 USD PPP). She recruited 100 students, and with the money that she had just collected, she bought a secondhand sewing machine and some surplus fabric from the local state-owned factories, and started teaching. At the end of the course, she kept her eight best students and launched a business. The women would arrive every morning with their sewing machines on their back (they each got their parents to buy them one), then start cutting and sewing. They made uniforms for the local factory workers. At first they worked at Xu Aihua's home, but as the business expanded and Xu Aihua trained and hired more people, they moved to a building that she rented from the village government.

By 1991, she had saved so much from the profits of her business that she could afford to buy sixty automatic sewing machines for 54,000 yuan ($27,600 USD PPP). Her total fixed capital had grown more than a hundredfold in eight years. That is 80 percent per year. Even if we allow for an inflation rate of 10 percent per year, a real growth rate, net of inflation, of more than 70 percent a year is impressive. By this time, she was an established entrepreneur. Export contracts arrived soon after, and she now sells to Macy's, Benetton, JC Penney, and other major retailers. In 2008, she made her first investment in real estate of 20 million yuan ($4.4 million USD), because, as she says, she had some cash sitting around, and most other people did not.

Xu Aihua is not a typical case, of course: She was especially bright, and her village sent her to school. However, there is no dearth of success stories of entrepreneurship among the poor. And there is certainly no shortage of entrepreneurs. On average in our eighteen-country data set, 50 percent of the extremely poor in urban areas (those who live on under 99 cents a day) operate a nonagricultural business. Even among the rural extremely poor, many—from 7 percent in Udaipur to up to 50 percent in Ecuador (and 20 percent on average)—operate a non-agricultural business, in addition to the large number who run a farm. The number of entrepreneurs is roughly the same among the somewhat less poor in the same countries. Compare this to the Organization for Economic Co-operation and Development (OECD) average: 12 percent of those in the workforce describe themselves as self-employed. Purely in terms of stated occupations, most income groups in poor countries seem to be more entrepreneurial than their counterparts in the developed world—the poor no less so than others, an observation that inspired Harvard Business School professor Tarun Khanna's book, *Billions of Entrepreneurs.*[2]

The sheer number of business owners among the poor is impressive. After all, everything seems to militate against the poor being entrepreneurs. They have less capital of their own (almost by definition) and, as we saw in Chapters 6 and 7, little access to formal insurance, banks, and other sources of inexpensive finance. Moneylenders, who are the main source of untied financing (trade credit is an example of tied financing because it is tied to buying something and therefore cannot be used for paying wages) for those who cannot borrow enough from friends or family, charge interest rates of 4 percent a month or more. As a result, the poor are less able to make the investments needed to run a proper business and are more vulnerable to any additional risk that comes from the business itself. The very fact that they are still about as likely to go into business as their richer counterparts is often interpreted as a sign of their entrepreneurial spirit.

The fact that even after paying very high interest rates, the poor still manage to make enough money to repay their loans (we have seen that it is very rare for them to default) must mean that they are earning even more money per rupee invested. Otherwise, they would not borrow. This implies that the rate of return on the cash invested in their businesses is remarkably high. Fifty percent a year, which is what many of them pay, is quite a bit more than you can get by investing in the Dow Jones (especially these days, but even the long-term average return is about 9 percent a year).

Of course, not everyone borrows. Perhaps only the few entrepreneurs who have high returns in their businesses borrow, and everyone else has very low returns. However, a project conducted in Sri Lanka suggests otherwise. A number of owners of tiny businesses—retail shops, repair shops, lace makers, and the like—were invited to participate in a lottery. The winners (two-thirds of them) would get a grant for their business, worth either 10,000 rupees ($250 USD PPP) or 20,000 rupees ($500 USD PPP).[3]

The grants were tiny by global standards but were reasonably large as far as these businesses were concerned; for many, $250 was the entire capital stock they had started from. The lottery winners of the grants had no trouble putting the money to good use. The return on the first $250 was over 60 percent a year for the average business. Subsequently, the same exercise was repeated with small businesses in Mexico.[4] The returns found in that experiment were even higher, reaching 10–15 percent per month.

Another program, conceived by BRAC, a large MFI in Bangladesh, and now imitated in a number of developing countries, shows that when given the right kind of help, even the poorest of the poor have the ability to succeed in running small businesses, and these small businesses can change their lives. The program targets those identified by their fellow villagers as the poorest among them: Many of them live purely on others' generosity. MFIs typically do not lend to these clients, who are deemed incapable of running a business and regularly reimbursing their loan. To get them started, BRAC designed a program in which they would be given an asset (a pair of cows, a few goats, a sewing machine, and so on), a small financial allowance for a few months (to serve as working capital and to ensure they would not be tempted to liquidate the asset), and a lot of hand-holding: regular meetings, literacy classes, encouragement to save a little bit every week. Variants of this program are currently being evaluated in six countries, using randomized control trials (RCTs). We were involved in one of these studies, in partnership with Bandhan, an MFI in West Bengal. We visited households before the program was started and heard, from each of the families that were selected for the program, stories of crisis and desperation: A husband was a drunkard and regularly beat his wife; another died in an accident, leaving a young family behind; a widow was abandoned by her children; and so forth. But after two years, the difference is impressive: Compared to other extremely poor households that were not selected to participate, the beneficiaries have more animals and other business assets; they earn more from livestock and other animals, but they also work longer hours and earn more from working for others. Their total monthly spending is up by 10 percent; food expenditure is what increases the most, and they are less likely to complain that they do not have enough to eat. Even more impressive, their outlook on life seems to have changed. The way they describe their own health, happiness, and economic status is much more positive. They save more and are also more likely to say they are willing to borrow—they are now eligible to borrow from the MFI—and they feel confident managing assets.

Of course, this has not made them rich by any standards—they are only 10 percent richer after two years in terms of consumption, which means they are still poor. But the initial gift and support seem to have started a virtuous circle: Given the chance, it seems that even people who had been hit by extreme hardship were able to take charge of their lives and start their exit out of extreme poverty.[5]

THE BUSINESSES OF THE POOR

Seeing results like these, it is not difficult to share the enthusiasm of Muhammad Yunus or Fouad Abdelmoumni for the potential of investing in the poor: So many have managed to be entrepreneurs in the face of so much adversity, and have made so much out of so little. There are, however, two troubling shadows in this otherwise sunny picture. First, while many of the poor operate businesses, they mainly operate *tiny* businesses. And second, these tiny businesses are, for the most part, making very little money.

Very Small and Unprofitable Businesses

In our eighteen-country data set, the majority of businesses operated by the poor have no paid staff, with the average number of paid employees ranging from essentially zero in rural Morocco to 0.57 in urban Mexico. The assets of these businesses also tend to be very limited. In Hyderabad, only 20 percent of the businesses have a dedicated room of their own. Very few have any machines or a vehicle. The most common assets are tables, scales, and pushcarts.

Obviously, if these people had large and successful businesses, they wouldn't be poor any longer. The problem is, notwithstanding the exceptional stories of the trash collector or Xu Aihua, the vast majority of the businesses run by the poor never grow to the point where they start having any employees or much in the way of assets. In Mexico, for example, 15 percent of those living on less than 99 cents per day had a business in 2002. Three years later, when the same families were visited again, only 41 percent of these businesses were still in operation. Out of those that were observed in both periods, one in five of the businesses that had zero employees in 2002 had one by 2005. But almost one-half of those that had one in 2002 had none by 2005. Similarly, in Indonesia, only two-thirds of the businesses of the poor survived five years. And out of those that did, the fraction that had one employee or more did not increase over the five-year period.

Another characteristic of the businesses of the poor and the near-poor is that, on average, they are not making much money. We calculated profits and sales of small businesses in Hyderabad: The average sales figure was 11,751 rupees ($730 USD PPP) per month, and the median, 3,600 rupees. The average monthly profit after deducting any rent paid but not including the unpaid time spent by household members was 1,859 rupees ($115 USD PPP) and the median, 1,035 rupees:

It is as if the median businesses were generating just enough money to pay one member about 34 rupees per day, or about $2 USD PPP. In our Hyderabad data set, 15 percent of businesses had lost money in the last month, after subtracting rents. When we valued the hours spent by household members, even at the low rate of 8 rupees an hour (which would give someone close to the minimum wage for an eight-hour day), the average profits turned mildly negative. In Thailand, the median *annual* profit from a business of this scale was 5,000 baht ($305 at USD PPP) after deducting business costs but without accounting for family labor time. Seven percent of the household-run businesses had lost money in the last year, once again *before deducting the value of family labor.*[6]

The low profitability of businesses run by the poor also explains why, as we saw in Chapter 7 (in our RCT of the Spandana program, for example), microcredit does not seem to lead to a radical transformation in the clients' lives. If the businesses run by the poor are generally unprofitable, this may well explain why giving them a loan to start a new business does not lead to a drastic improvement in their welfare.

The Marginal and the Average

But wait. Didn't we start off making the point that the return on investment in these small businesses is very high?

What is confusing here are the two possible uses of the word *return*. Economists (for once, probably usefully) distinguish between the *marginal* return on a dollar and the *overall* return from a business. The marginal return on a dollar is the answer to the question "What would happen to your revenue net of all operating costs (but not interest costs) if you were to invest $1 less, or $1 more?" The marginal return is what is relevant when you ask whether you should cut your investment a little (or grow it a little): If investing $1 less allows you to borrow $1 less and therefore repay 4 cents less in principal and interest, you would want to do so if the marginal return is less than 4 percent and not otherwise. So when people borrow at a rate of interest of 4 percent a month, it must mean that their *marginal* return is at least 4 percent a month. The ability of the poor to borrow and repay and the high extra profits made thanks to the extra $250 in the Sri Lanka experiment show us that the businesses of the poor have high marginal return: Growing them a little would be worthwhile.

The overall return on a business, on the other hand, is the *total* revenue net of *operating* expenses (the costs of materials, any wages you pay to your workers, and so on). This is what you can take home at the end of the day. You should look at the overall return to decide whether you should be in that business in the first place. If it is not high enough to cover the value of the time you are putting in the business, plus what it cost you to set up the business, and if you don't expect things to improve dramatically, then you should shut it down.

The paradox is explained by the fact that marginal returns can be high even though overall returns are low. In Figure 1 below, the curve OP represents the relation between the amount of investment in the firm (measured along the horizontal axis, OI) and its overall returns (measured along the vertical axis, OR), or what economists call the *production technology*. The overall return, for any invested capital of size K, is the height of the curve, whereas the marginal return is the change in height when you go from K to K+1. It tells us by how much the overall return increases when we increase the investment in the firm just a little bit.

The curve in Figure 1 looks like the inverted L-curve we discussed in Chapter 1: The returns are first high, and then lower. OP is steepest when the investment is small (nearest to O) and slowly flattens out (as it gets closer to P)—which means that increasing the amount invested increases returns the most when the initial investment is small, and this increase eventually tapers off. In other words, the marginal return is high when investment is small.

To see how this works, think of someone who has just started a shop in her home. She spends some money building shelves and a counter, but then she runs out of money and has nothing to sell. The overall return on her business is zero: not high enough to cover the cost of the shelves. Then her mother lends her 100,000 rupiahs ($18 USD PPP), and she buys a few packages of cookies to put on her empty shelves. The kids from the neighborhood notice that she has the brand of cookies they like and come and buy all of them. She makes 150,000

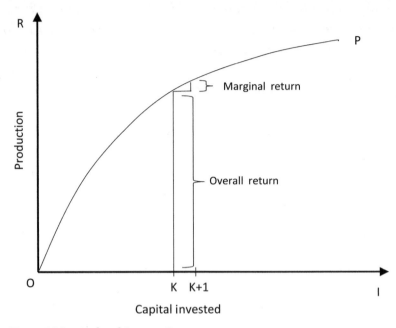

Figure 1: Marginal and Average Return

rupiahs. The marginal return is 1.5 rupiahs per rupiah of her mother's loan, or 50 percent net, which is not bad at all for a week. But the overall return is nonetheless just 50,000 rupiahs—and that doesn't cover the cost of her time and building the shelves and the counter.

Then our shopkeeper gets a loan of 3 million rupiahs and buys enough cookies and candy to fill up her shelves. The kids now tell their other friends and she sells a lot of her stock, but by the time all of the new customers get there, some of the cookies have gotten stale and can't be sold. Still, she makes 3.6 million rupiahs in a week. The marginal return is now much lower than 50 percent—her investment was thirty times larger (3 million versus 100,000) but her revenues are only twelve times as much. Her overall return, though, is now a respectable 600,000 rupiahs ($107 USD PPP), enough to make staying in business a real possibility.

This is exactly how it looks for many of the poor. The empty shelves, in particular, are not a figment of our imagination. The entire stock of a shop we visited in the outskirts of the town of Gulbarga in northern Karnataka, about a five-hour drive from Hyderabad, consisted of largely empty plastic jars in a dimly lit room. It did not take long to take inventory:

**Inventory of a General Store in a Village in
Rural Karnataka, India**

1 jar of savory snacks

3 jars of soft candies

1 jar and 1 small bag of wrapped hard candies

2 jars of chickpeas

1 jar of Magimix instant stock

1 packet of bread (5 pieces)

1 packet of *papadum* (a snack made from lentils)

1 packet of crispbread (20 pieces)

2 packets of cookies

36 incense sticks

20 bars of Lux soap

180 individual portions of *pan parag* (a combination of betel nuts
  and chewing tobacco)

20 tea bags

40 individual packets of *haldi* powder (turmeric)

5 small bottles of talcum powder

3 packs of cigarettes

55 small packets of *bidis* (thin, flavored cigarettes)

35 larger packets of *bidis*

3 packs of washing powder (500 grams each)

15 small packs of Parle-G biscuits (cookies)

6 individual-size packets of shampoo

During the two hours we spent with this household, we saw two customers. One bought a single cigarette, the other a few sticks of incense. Clearly, the marginal return of increasing the size of the inventory a little was potentially extremely high, especially if the family could try to buy something that the other shops in the same village did not supply. But the overall return of the activity was very low: With this volume of sales, it was not really worth the time spent sitting in the shop all day.

There are countless such shops in developing countries, several in every village, thousands in alleys of big cities, all selling the same very limited inventory. And the same is true of the fruit vendors, the coconut sellers, and the snack stalls. Walking down the main street of the biggest slum in the town of Guntur at 9:00 AM, it is hard to miss the long line of women selling *dosas,* the rice-and-lentil pancakes that are South India's answer to the morning croissant. Smeared with a spicy sauce, and wrapped in a piece of newspaper or a banana leaf, these sell for 1 rupee (roughly 5 cents, at PPP). By our count, one particular morning, there was one *dosa* seller for every six houses. The result was that at any particular time, many of these women were just waiting around for customers. It seemed obvious that if they could have merged three of the businesses together, and sent the others on some other endeavor, they could have made more money.

This is the paradox of the poor and their businesses: They are energetic and resourceful and manage to make a lot out of very little. But most of this energy is spent on businesses that are too small and utterly undifferentiated from the many others around them. As a result, their operators have no chance to earn a reasonable living. The creative sand-driers of Mumbai had spotted an opportunity to make a profitable use of the resources available to them: some free time and the sand on the beach. But what the businessman's uncle had failed to point out was that, for all their ingenuity, the profits from this activity were almost surely negligible.

The very small scale of many of these businesses explains why their overall returns are often so low, despite the high marginal return. But it brings to light a new puzzle. The fact that marginal returns are high means that it is easy to grow the overall returns—just put more money into the business. So why aren't all the small businesses growing really fast?

One part of that answer we already know—most of these businesses cannot borrow very much, and what they can borrow is very expensive. But this is not the whole answer. First, as we saw, although there are millions of microcredit borrowers, there are many more who have the opportunity to borrow but choose not to. Ben Sedan was one of them. He had a business raising cows and could have grown it with a microcredit loan, but he decided against it. Even in Hyderabad, where there are several competing MFIs, the sign-up rate for any microcredit loan among families who were eligible to borrow was only 27 percent, and only 21 percent of those who had a small business had taken a microcredit loan.

Moreover, even those who cannot borrow can save: Consider the shopkeeper family in Gulbarga. They lived on about $2 per day per person. In nearby Hyderabad, our data show that those with this level of consumption spend about 10 percent of their total monthly expenditures on health care, whereas those living on less than 99 cents a day spend about 6.3 percent. If, instead of spending an extra 3.7 percent of his budget on health care, our shopkeeper had used it to build up his inventory, he could have doubled his inventory in a year. Alternatively, the family could cut down completely on cigarettes and alcohol and save about 3 percent of their daily expenditure per capita: This would allow them to double their inventory in about fifteen months. Why don't they?

The experiment in Sri Lanka provides another striking illustration of the fact that financing is not the only barrier to expansion. Recall that entrepreneurs who got $250 made a lot of money—far more, per dollar invested, than most successful firms in the United States. But here is the catch: The profits of micro-entrepreneurs who received the $500 grant *did not increase any more than the profits of those who received the $250 grant, in absolute terms.* In part, it is because those who received the $500 grant did not choose to invest all of it in their business: They invested about half of it, and used the rest to buy things for their home.

What is going on? Could the owners really have something better to do with this free money, given how high the marginal return is?

The notable fact is that the Sri Lankan micro-entrepreneurs did invest the first tranche of dollars. If they chose not to invest the second tranche, it is perhaps because they thought that their businesses would not be able to absorb it: Investing the entire amount would have meant tripling the capital stock of the average business, and a step like that

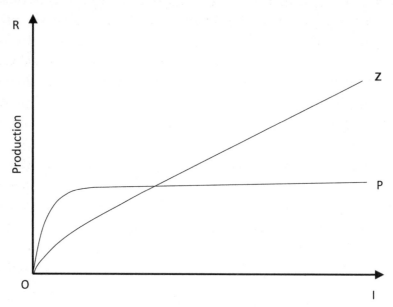

Figure 2: Two Technologies

might well require hiring a new employee or finding more storage space, which then would cost much more money.

So part of the reason the businesses of the poor don't grow, it seems to us, goes back to the nature of the businesses they operate. Recall the inverted L-shape in Figure 1, showing that overall returns could be low even when the marginal returns are high. Figure 2 shows two versions of the curve in Figure 1: One, denoted OP, is very steep when it starts out and then flattens very quickly. The other, OZ, goes up less quickly to start with but keeps going up a long way.

If, in the real world, the profits of poor businesses look like the curve OP, then it is easy for a very small firm to grow, but the growth potential tapers off quite fast. This is similar to the shopkeeper example: Once you have set aside some room in your home for a shop and have committed to working there a few hours a day, your profits will be much higher if you have enough goods to fill up the shelves and keep you busy than if you have next to nothing (as many shops seem to). But once your shelves are full, any further expansion probably would not have enough marginal return to pay off the very high interest rates on the loan you might use to make it happen. So all the businesses will stay small. If the shape is more like OZ, on the other hand, there is much more scope for growing the business. Our reading of the evidence is that for most poor people, the world is more like OP.

Of course, we know that it can't all be like OP—otherwise there would be no large firms anywhere. Perhaps the businesses of shopkeepers, tailors, and sari sellers look like OP, but it must be possible for some other kinds of businesses to use more productive capital. It is clearly possible to run large retail chains or textile factories if one can buy the right equipment, but doing so must require either some special skill or a much larger up-front investment. You can start Microsoft in a garage somewhere and keep scaling up, but to do so you need to be the kind of person who is at the absolute cutting edge of some new product. For most people, that is not really an option. The alternative is to invest enough to get a production technology that allows your business to operate on a large scale. Recall Xu Aihua, the Chinese woman who started her business with one sewing machine and built a garment empire. Her big break came once she got an export order. Without that, she would have soon hit the limits of the local market. However, in order to be considered for the export order she needed to have a modern factory with automatic sewing machines. This required her to invest more than 100 times the initial capital in the firm.

Figure 3 represents the idea of these two production technologies. There is OP on the left, but way over on the right there is a new production technology, QR, which generates no returns whatsoever until a minimum investment is made, but high returns thereafter. Notice also the way we have marked parts of OP and QR in bold to make one connected line, OR—this represents the actual return on investing a given amount. When you invest just a little, you invest in OP; you have no reason to invest in QR because QR produces no return at first. When you invest more, OP becomes a bad deal, so for a while, the marginal returns are quite low. However, once you have enough money, you may switch to QR. This represents Xu Aihua's history: She started with OP with her secondhand sewing machines and at some point managed to switch to QR and the automatic machines.

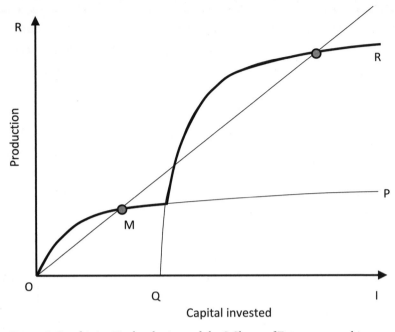

Figure 3: Combining Technologies and the S-Shape of Entrepreneurship

What does OR look like? Kind of like the S-shape, right? There is a big hump in the middle, which is the point you need to reach to make serious money. OR brings back the usual S-shape dilemma: Invest little, make little money, and remain too poor to invest much more, or invest enough to cross the hump and then become rich and invest even more and get even richer. The point is that for most people, crossing that hump is not an option. Although small loans may be available, no one (not even the MFIs, which, as we have seen, like playing it safe) will lend these small entrepreneurs enough money. Moreover, getting there might also need some management and other skills that they don't have and cannot afford to buy. Therefore, they are stuck staying small. Sometimes, the initial flattening off of returns comes so soon that the same person ends up running three different businesses rather than trying to grow any one of them, for instance, selling *dosas* in the morning, trading saris during the day, threading beads to make necklaces in the evening.

But then how did Xu Aihua do it? Remember that she increased her stock of machines by 70 percent a year for eight years through reinvesting her profits. Therefore, her profits must have been at least 70 percent of the value of her machines, *after paying her workers,* and her overall returns must have been even higher. That is unusually profitable—the average small business in the Hyderabad survey, we noted, would actually lose money if it were to pay even minimum wages. We suspect that this reflects in part that Xu Aihua is an especially talented woman, and in part the fact that in those early days of China's opening up, there was very little competition and lots of demand, so she was at the right place at the right time.

Entrepreneurship Is Too Hard

If our diagnosis is correct, the reason that the poor do not grow their businesses is that, for most of them, it is too hard: They cannot borrow to cross the hump, and saving up to get there will take too long unless their businesses have extremely high overall returns. For example, imagine that you start a business with $100 and, like Xu Aihua, you need to invest 100 times as much ($10,000) to buy the new machine. Suppose that you make a very attractive 25 percent profit per dollar invested and reinvest it all. After one year, you would have $125 to invest. After two years, $156. After three years, $195. It would take you twenty-one years before you could cross the hump and buy the new machine. If you needed some money to live on in the meanwhile and saved only half of your profits, forty years would be barely enough. And this does not take into account the stress from all the risk that doing business entails, the hard work, and the long days.

Furthermore, once a micro-entrepreneur realizes that she is probably stuck in the low part of the S-shaped curve and will never be able to make that much money, it may be difficult for her to be fully committed to her business. Imagine an entrepreneur who is below point M in Figure 3. It could be the shopkeeper we met in Gulbarga. She could increase her profits by saving some money and acquiring a slightly more exciting inventory. But even if she does that, she will not be able to go much further than point M. Is it worth it? Most likely, even if that was everything she ever hoped for, it would not change her life in any meaningful way. Given that her business is destined to remain small and never make much money, she may decide to devote her attention and her resources to other things.

In the same way that the poor may save less than the middle class because they know that their savings will not be enough to reach a consumption goal they are really looking forward to, they may not invest as much (not only money but also emotions and intellectual energy) in their businesses because they already know that they can't make a real difference. This may explain the gulf between the outlook of Ben Sedan, the Moroccan farmer, and that of Fouad Abdelmoumni: Fouad may well be right that Ben Sedan hadn't thought about the possibility of raising cattle in a barn. Or he may have thought about it, but concluded that going through the whole process of getting a loan, building a whole new stable for just four cows, and eventually selling them wasn't worth it—after all, his family would still be quite poor. So in a sense they were both right: Fouad because his business model could work, and Ben Sedan because it was not worth his while to make it work.

The fact that most micro-entrepreneurs may not be fully committed to making every penny count may also explain the disappointing effects of the business training programs that many MFIs have now started proposing to their clients as an added service. At weekly meetings, clients are told about how to keep better accounts, manage their inventories, understand interest rates, and so forth. Programs of this kind were evaluated in studies in Peru and India.[7] The research results in both countries found some improvement in business knowledge but no changes in profits, sales, or assets. These programs are motivated by a sense that these businesses are not particularly well run, but if the businesses are run that way because of a lack of enthusiasm rather than a lack of knowledge, it is not particularly surprising that the training does very little to help. In the Dominican Republic, another training program tried, alongside the regular training module, a simplified curriculum, suggesting the entrepreneurs focus on simple "rules of thumb" (such as keeping the business and household expenses separate, and paying oneself a fixed salary).[8] Here again, the regular training was ineffective, but giving the entrepreneurs the simplified tips did lead to an increase in profit. This is probably because people were willing to adopt these rules of thumb, and they actually simplified their lives rather than demanding even more intellectual resources from them.

Taken together, this evidence makes us seriously doubt the idea that the average small business owner is a natural "entrepreneur," in the way we generally understand the term, meaning someone whose business has the potential to grow and who is able to take risks, work hard, and keep trying to make it happen even in the face of multiple hardships. We are, of course, not saying that there are no genuine entrepreneurs among the poor—we have met many such people. But there are also many of them who run a business that is doomed to remain small and unprofitable.

Buying a Job

This naturally begs the question: Why do so many poor people run a business in the first place? We got an answer to this question from Pak Awan and his wife, a young couple from Cica Das, the slum in Bandung, Indonesia. They owned a small shop that they were running out of one room in his parents' house. Pak Awan worked as a casual construction laborer, but more often than not, he could not find employment. When we met the couple in summer 2008, Pak Awan had not had a job for two months. With two young children, the family needed some extra income, so his wife needed to find work. She would have liked a factory job, but she was not qualified: Factories wanted people who were young or unmarried or who had experience. She had no such experience, because after high school she studied to be a secretary, but she couldn't get through the tests that are required to get the jobs and eventually gave up on this career. Starting a small business was the only option they had. Her first venture was to cook snacks and sell them in the city, but she wanted something she could do from home, so she could mind the children. So they started a shop with a loan Pak Awan got from a cooperative he belonged to, even though there were already two other shops within 50 yards.

Pak Awan and his wife did not enjoy running the business. They were eligible for a second loan from the cooperative, which would have allowed them to expand their shop, but had decided that they didn't want it. Unfortunately for them, a fourth shop opened in the neighborhood and threatened their livelihood by offering a more diverse array of goods, and when we met them, they were in the process of taking out a new loan to buy more stock. Their hope for their children was that they would each grow up to get a salaried job, preferably in a government office.

The enterprises of the poor often seem more a way to buy a job when a more conventional employment opportunity is not available than a reflection of a particular entrepreneurial urge. Many of the businesses are run because someone in the family has (or is believed to have) some time on hand and every little bit helps. This person is often a woman, and she typically does it in addition to her housework; indeed it is not clear that she always has much of a choice when the opportunity to start a business comes up. It is only recently that men in the West have learned to at least pay lip service to the many things that their wife who "does not work" does for them; it would not be astonishing if their developing-country counterparts ascribed more leisure to their spouses than they actually enjoy. It is entirely possible, therefore, that many business owners, and especially female business owners, do not particularly enjoy running a business, and indeed, dread the thought of expanding it. This may be why, when women business owners in Sri Lanka were offered $250 nominally for investing in their business, many of them did something else with it, unlike the male business owners we encountered above who invested the money and got high returns from it.[9] Perhaps the many businesses of the poor are less a testimony to their entrepreneurial spirit than a symptom of the dramatic failure of the economies in which they live to provide them with something better.

GOOD JOBS

We have started including the question "What are your ambitions for your children?" in surveys given to poor people around the world. The results are striking. Everywhere we have asked, the most common dream of the poor is that their children become government workers.

Among very poor households in Udaipur, for example, 34 percent of the parents would like to see their son become a government teacher and another 41 percent want him to have a nonteaching government job; 18 percent more want him to be a salaried employee in a private firm. For girls, 31 percent would like her to be a teacher, 31 percent would want her to have another kind of government job, and 19 percent want her to be a nurse. The poor don't see becoming an entrepreneur as something to aspire to.

The emphasis on government jobs, in particular, suggests a desire for stability, as these jobs tend to be very secure even when they are not very exciting. And in fact, stability of employment appears to be the one thing that distinguishes the middle classes from the poor. In our eighteen-country data set, middle-class people are much more likely to have jobs that pay them weekly or monthly, rather than daily, which is a crude way to separate temporary and more permanent jobs. In Pakistan, for example, in urban areas, 74 percent of those who are employed and who live on 99 cents or less per day work for a weekly or monthly wage, but 90 percent of those earning $6 to $10 a day do. In rural areas, 44 percent of the very poor who are employed work for a regular wage, and 64 percent of the middle class do.

The availability of secure jobs can have a transformational effect. In much of rural Udaipur District, most families live on less than $2 a day. But we once visited one village that superficially appeared to be not unlike many other villages we visited in the area, yet was in fact quite different. Signs of relative prosperity were apparent: an iron roof, two motorcycles in a courtyard, a neatly combed teenager in a starched school uniform. It turned out that a zinc factory had been set up near the village and at least one person in every family we met in the village had worked in the factory. In one of the families, the father of the current head of the household (a man in his late fifties) somehow got a job in the factory kitchen and parlayed that into a job on the factory floor. His son was part of the first batch of (eight) boys from the village to complete high school. Then he, too, went to work in the zinc factory, where he retired as a foreman. Both of his own sons finished high school. One of them works in the same zinc factory; the other has a job in Ahmedabad, the capital of the neighboring state of Gujarat. He also has two daughters, who completed high school before getting married. For this family, the fact that the zinc factory was established in this location was an initial stroke of good luck, which started a virtuous circle of human capital investment, and the progression up the employment ladder.

A study by Andrew Foster and Mark Rosenzweig shows that the role of factory employment in promoting wage growth in Indian villages goes beyond this particular anecdote.[10] Over the period 1960–1999, India experienced fast growth in the productivity of agriculture but also a very rapid increase in the number of individuals employed in factories located in or near villages, in part due to a pro-rural investment policy. Rural factory employment increased tenfold from the early 1980s to 1999. In 1999, about half of the villages Foster and Rosenzweig studied, which were initially all rural, were located near a factory, and in those villages, 10 percent of the male labor was employed at a factory. The factory was typically located in a village that had low wages to start with, and in those villages, the growth of factory employment did much more for wage growth than agricultural productivity growth resulting from the famed Green Revolution. Furthermore, the poor gained disproportionately from industrial growth, because higher-paid employment became available even to those with low skills.

Once such a job does materialize, it can make a tremendous difference in the lives of the people who get it. The middle class spends much more on health and education than the poor. Of course, in principle, it may be that patient, industrious people, inclined to invest in the future of their children, are better able to hang on to good jobs. But we suspect that this is not the entire explanation, and that this spending pattern has something to do with the fact that parents in better-off households have steady jobs: A stable job can, by itself, change people's outlook on life in decisive ways. A study of the height of Mexican children whose mothers worked in maquiladoras (export factories) in Mexico dramatically illustrates the power of a good job.[11] Maquiladoras generally have the reputation of being exploitative and paying poor wages. However, for many women without a high school education, the establishment of the maquiladoras offers the prospect of a better job than the jobs in retail, food services, or transportation that would otherwise be their lot—the hourly wages are not much higher, but they work longer hours and with more regularity. David Atkin, from Yale University, compared the height of children born to mothers who lived in a town where a maquiladora opened when the woman was sixteen years old to that of children of mothers who did not have this opportunity. The children whose mother's town had a maquiladora were much taller than those born to similar women in different towns. This effect is so large that it can bridge the *entire* gap in height between a poor Mexican child and the "norm" for a well-fed American child.

Furthermore, Atkin shows that the effect of a job in a maquilladora on the *level* of family income is nowhere near large enough to explain the entire increase in height. Perhaps the sense of control over the future that people get from knowing there will be an income coming in every month—and not just the income itself—is what allows these women to focus on building their own careers and those of their children. Perhaps this idea that there is a future is what makes the difference between the poor and the middle class. The title of Atkin's study, "Working for the Future," sums it up nicely.

In Chapter 6, we gave several examples of the effects of risk on household behavior: Poor families take preventive actions to limit risk even at the cost of higher levels of income. Here we see another consequence, possibly even deeper: A sense of stability may be necessary for people to be able to take the long view. It is possible that people who don't envision substantial improvements in their future quality of life opt to stop trying and therefore end up staying where they are. You will recall that many parents think (perhaps mistakenly) that the benefits of education have an S-shape. This means that there is no point for them to start investing in education if they do not think they will be able to continue to invest. If they are worried about their ability to afford schooling for their children in the future—say, because they think their business might fail—they may decide that it is not even worth trying.

A steady and predictable income makes it possible to commit to future expenditure and also makes it much easier and cheaper to borrow now. So, if a member of a family has a steady job, schools will accept their children more readily; hospitals will give more expensive treatments, knowing they will be paid; and other members of the family may be able to make the investments in their own businesses that are necessary to allow them to grow.

This is why a "good job" is important. A good job is a steady, well-paid job, a job that allows a person the mental space needed to do all those things the middle class does well. This is an idea that economists have often resisted, on the reasonable grounds that good jobs may be expensive jobs, and expensive jobs might mean fewer jobs. But if good jobs mean that children grow up in an environment where they are able to make the most of their talents, it may well be worth the sacrifice of creating somewhat fewer of them.

Because most good jobs are in the city, moving can be the first step to changing a family's trajectory. In summer 2009, we were in a slum of the Indian city of Hyderabad, talking to a woman in her fifties. She told us that she had never been to school and her daughter, who was born when this woman was sixteen, had started school but dropped out after third grade and had gotten married soon after. But her second son, she added almost in passing, was studying for his MCA. We had never heard of an MCA, and asked her what it was (our presumption was that it was a vocational degree of some kind). She didn't know, but her son appeared and explained it was a Master in Computer Applications. Before that, he had gotten his bachelor's degree in computer science. His elder brother had also graduated from college and had an office job in a private company, and the youngest, still in high school, was applying for college. They were hoping to send him to Australia to study, if they could get one of the preferential loans for Muslims.

What had happened to this family, somewhere between the time the first daughter dropped out of school and the first son graduated from high school, to transform the prospects for the younger children? The father retired from the army, and through his army connections had found a job as a guard in a public-sector firm in Hyderabad. Because he now had a job that did not involve frequent transfers, he moved his entire family to the city (except for his daughter, who was already married). Hyderabad has a number of affordable and relatively high-quality schools for Muslim children, a legacy of the fact that it was a semi-independent Muslim kingdom until 1948. The sons were sent to these schools, and they prospered.

Why aren't many more people adopting this strategy? After all, schools are better in most cities, even those that don't have Hyderabad's particular history. And the poor (particularly poor young men) are always moving in search of a job. In rural Udaipur for example, 60 percent of the families we interviewed had at least one member who had worked in some city over the last year. But very few of them migrate for long periods of time—the median duration of a trip is one month, and only 10 percent of the trips are longer than three months. And when they go on these trips, they mostly leave their families behind. The usual pattern is a few weeks at work, a few weeks at home. Permanent migration, even within the country, is relatively rare: In our eighteen-country data set, the share of extremely poor households that had one member who was born elsewhere and had migrated for work reasons was just 4 percent in Pakistan, 6 percent in Côte d'Ivoire, 6 percent in Nicaragua, and almost 10 percent in Peru. One of the consequences of temporary migration is that these workers never become indispensable enough to the employer to be made permanent or given any kind of special training; they remain casual laborers all their lives. Their families therefore never move to the city, and never benefit from the better city schools and peace of mind that come from a permanent job.

We asked a migrant construction worker from Orissa, on a visit back home, why he didn't stay longer in the city. He explained that he could not take his family there: The housing conditions were too insalubrious. On the other hand, he did not want to stay away from them for too long. Most cities in the developing world have very little planned housing for the very poor. The result is that the poor have had to squeeze themselves into every piece of land they can somehow grab from the city, often in a swamp or even a garbage dump. By comparison, the places where even the poorest live in villages are greener, airier, quieter; the houses are bigger; there is space for children to play. Life may be unexciting, but for those who grew up in the village, that is where their friends live. Moreover, a single male, going to the city for a few weeks or even a few months, does not need to actually find housing; he can sleep under a bridge or under some awning somewhere, or in the shop or construction site where he works. He can save the money he would have paid as rent and just go home more often. But he doesn't want this life for his family.

There is also the risk: Suppose you pay the cost of setting up a home in the city and moving your family there, only to lose your job. Indeed if you haven't already had a decent job before and saved up, how do you pay for the move? And what happens if someone gets very sick? It is true that health care is better in the city, but who will come with you to the hospital or have some cash handy if you need it? As long as your family is still in the village, even if you get sick in the city and end up in the hospital, you can rely on your connections in the village. But what if you actually pull up your roots and move?

This is why it is much easier to move if you know people in the city. They can house you and your family when you first arrive, help you out if someone suddenly gets sick, and help you find a job—by giving you a reference or hiring you themselves. Kaivan Munshi, for example, found that Mexican villagers migrate to cities where people from their village have already migrated, even if the original round of migration was purely accidental.[12] It is obviously also easier to move if you already have a steady job or some other source of steady income. The Muslim family from Hyderabad had both—an army pension and a job—which in turn was the product of having the right connections. In South Africa, when elderly parents get a pension, the most productive of their children permanently leave the household to move to the city.[13] The pension must be what gives them this sense of security, and it allows them to pay for the cost of their own move.

How then can more "good jobs" be created? Clearly, it would help if it were easier to migrate to cities, so policies on urban land use and low-income housing are obviously vital. Less obviously, effective social safety nets, consisting of both public assistance and market insurance, can make migration easier by reducing dependence on social networks.

But because not everyone will be able to move to the city, it is also important that more good jobs be created not just in the largest cities but in smaller towns all over the country. For this to be possible, there must be substantial improvements both in urban and in industrial infrastructure in towns of this sort. The regulatory environment is also important for creating jobs: Labor laws play a role in ensuring job security, but if they are so stringent that no one wants to hire, then they are counterproductive. Credit remains perhaps an even bigger problem, given the S-shaped nature of the production technologies: To set up businesses that create lots of jobs (rather than one job for the entrepreneur alone) takes more money than the average business owner in the developing world has access to, and as noted in Chapter 7 on credit, it is not clear how to get the financial sector to lend more to these people.

It follows, therefore (though it is not a particularly fashionable idea among economists), that there may be a case for using some governmental resources to help create enough large businesses by providing loan guarantees to medium-size ventures, for example. Something like that happened in China, where state businesses, or at least part of their equipment, land, and buildings, were quietly handed over to their employees. This was also, more explicitly, part of the Korean industrial policy. This may set off some virtuous circle: Stable and higher wages would give workers the financial resources, the mental space, and the necessary optimism both to invest in their children and save more. With those savings, and the access to easier credit that a steady job brings, the most talented among them would eventually be able to start businesses large enough to, in turn, hire other people.

So are there really a billion barefoot entrepreneurs, as the leaders of MFIs and the socially minded business gurus seem to believe? Or is this just an illusion, stemming from a confusion about what we call an "entrepreneur"? There are more than a billion people who run their own farm or business, but most of them do this because they have no other options. Most of them manage to do this well enough to survive, but without the talent, the skills, or the appetite for risk needed to turn these small businesses into really successful enterprises. For every Xu Aihua, who started a clothing empire with nothing but a little training and a huge amount of talent, there are millions of Ben Sedans, who know that the way out of poverty is not one more shed with some cows in it, but a son with a secure job in the army. Microcredit and other ways to help tiny businesses still have an important role to play in the lives of the poor, because these tiny businesses will remain, perhaps for the foreseeable future, the only way many of the poor can manage to survive. But we are kidding ourselves if we think that they can pave the way for a mass exit from poverty.

10

Policies, Politics

Even the most well-intended and well-thought-out policies may not have an impact if they are not implemented properly. Unfortunately, the gap between intention and implementation can be quite wide. The many failings of governments are often given as the reason good policies cannot really be made to work. Government inadequacy is also one of the older arguments advanced by some of the aid skeptics to explain why foreign aid and other attempts by outsiders to influence social policy are likely to make things worse in poor countries rather than better.[1]

The Ugandan government gives per-student grants to schools to maintain their buildings, buy textbooks, and fund any extra programs that their students might need (teacher salaries are paid directly out of the budget). In 1996, Ritva Reinikka and Jakob Svensson set out to answer a simple question: How much of these funds allocated to schools by the central government actually made it to the schools?[2] It was a relatively straightforward exercise. They just sent survey teams to the schools and asked them how much they had received. Then they compared the numbers to computer records of how much had been sent. The answer they got was nothing short of stunning: Only 13 percent of the funds ever reached the schools. More than half the schools got nothing at all. Inquiries suggested that a lot of the money most likely ended up in the pockets of district officials.

It is easy to get depressed by such findings (which have been corroborated by similar studies in several other countries). We are often asked why we do what we do: "Why bother?" These are the "small" questions. William Easterly, for one, criticized randomized control trials (RCTs) on his blog in these terms: "RCTs are infeasible for many of the big questions in development, like the economy-wide effects of good institutions or good macroeconomic policies." Then, he concluded that "embracing RCTs has led development researchers to lower their ambitions."[3]

This statement was a good reflection of an institutionalist view that has strong currency in development economics today. The real problem of development, in this view, is not one of figuring out good policies: It is to sort out the political process. If the politics are right, good policies will eventually emerge. And conversely, without good politics, it is impossible to design or implement good policies, at least not on any scale. There is no point to figuring out the best way to spend a dollar on schools, if 87 cents will never reach the school anyway. It follows (or so it is assumed) that "big questions" require "big answers"—social revolutions, such as a transition to effective democracy.

At the other extreme, Jeffrey Sachs sees corruption, perhaps not surprisingly, as a poverty trap: Poverty causes corruption, and corruption causes poverty. His suggestion is to break the trap by focusing on making people in developing countries less poor: Aid should be given for specific goals (such as malaria control, food production, safe drinking water, and sanitation) that can easily be monitored. Raising living standards, Sachs argues, would empower civil society and governments to maintain the rule of law.[4]

This presumes that it is possible to successfully implement such programs on a large scale in poor, corrupt countries. According to Transparency International in 2010, Uganda ranked 127th out of 178 countries in terms of how corrupt it was (better than Nigeria, at the same level as Nicaragua and Syria, worse than Eritrea). Can we expect any progress on education until Uganda solves the bigger problem of corruption?

However, there was an interesting coda to Reinikka and Svensson's story. When their results were released in Uganda, there was something of an uproar, with the result that the Ministry of Finance started giving the main national newspapers (and their local-language editions) month-by-month information about how much money had been sent to the districts for the schools. By 2001, when Reinikka and Svensson repeated their school survey, they found the schools were getting, on average, 80 percent of the discretionary money that they were entitled to. About half of the headmasters of schools that had received less than they were supposed to had initiated a formal complaint, and eventually most of them received their money. There were no reports of reprisals against them, or against the newspapers that had run the story. It seems that the district officials had been happy to embezzle the money when no one was watching but stopped when that became more difficult. A generalized theft of government funds was possible, it seems, mainly because no one had bothered to worry about it.

The Ugandan headmasters suggest an exciting possibility: If rural school headmasters could fight corruption, perhaps it is not necessary to wait for the overthrow of the government or the profound transformation of society before better policies can be implemented. Careful thinking and rigorous evaluations can help us design systems to keep corruption and inefficiency in check. We are not "lowering our ambitions": Incremental progress and the accumulation of these small changes, we believe, can sometimes end in a quiet revolution.

POLITICAL ECONOMY

Corruption, or the simple dereliction of duty, creates massive inefficiencies. If teachers or nurses do not come to work, no education or health policy can really be implemented. If truck drivers can pay a small bribe to drive massively overloaded trucks, billions of dollars will be wasted in building roads that will be destroyed under their wheels.

Our colleague Daron Acemoglu and his long-term coauthor, Harvard's James Robinson, are two of the most thoughtful exponents of the rather melancholy view, active in economics today, that until political institutions are fixed, countries cannot really develop, but institutions are hard to fix. Acemoglu and Robinson define institutions as follows: "Economic institutions shape economic incentives, the incentives to become educated, to save and invest, to innovate and adopt new technologies, and so on. Political institutions determine the ability of citizens to control politicians."[5]

Both political scientists and economists typically think of institutions at a very high level. They have in mind, if you like, institutions in capital letters—economic INSTITUTIONS like property rights or tax systems; political INSTITUTIONS like democracy or autocracy, centralized or decentralized power, universal or limited suffrage. The argument in Acemoglu and Robinson's book *Why Nations Fail,*[6] which reflects a widely shared view among scholars[7] of political economy, is that these (broad) institutions are the prime drivers of the success or failure of a society. Good economic institutions will encourage citizens to invest, accumulate, and develop new technologies, as a result of which society will prosper. Bad economic institutions will have the opposite effects. One problem is that rulers, who have the power to shape economic institutions, do not necessarily find it in their interest to allow their citizens to thrive and prosper. They may personally be better off with an economy that imposes lots of restrictions on who can do what (that they selectively relax to their advantage), and weakening competition may actually help them stay in power. This is why political institutions matter—they exist to prevent leaders from organizing the economy for their private benefit. When they work well, political institutions put enough constraints on rulers to ensure that they cannot deviate too far from the public interest.

Unfortunately, bad institutions tend to perpetuate bad institutions, creating a vicious circle, sometimes called the "iron law of oligarchy." Those who have power under the current political institutions get to make sure that the economic institutions work toward making them rich, and once they are rich enough they can usually use their wealth to forestall any attempts to move them out of power.

The long shadow of bad political institutions, for Acemoglu and Robinson, is the main reason many countries in the developing world have failed to grow. Those countries inherited from the colonial period a set of institutions that were put in place by colonial rulers not for the development of the country but to maximize the extraction of resources for the benefit of the colonial powers. After decolonization, the new rulers found it convenient to hold on to the same extractive institutions and use them for their own benefit, thereby setting off a vicious cycle. For example, in an article that has become a classic, Acemoglu, Robinson, and Simon Johnson showed that former colonies where the disease environment prevented large-scale settlements by Europeans tended to have worse institutions during colonial times (because they were naturally picked for being exploited from afar), and these bad institutions continued after decolonization.[8]

Abhijit and Lakshmi Iyer found a striking example of the long shadow of political institutions in India.[9] During British colonization, different districts got different systems of land-revenue collection, for largely accidental reasons (mainly, which institution was chosen depended on the ideology of the British servant in charge of the districts and the views prevalent in Britain at the time of conquest). In the *zamindari* system, the local landlord was given the responsibility for collecting land taxes: This served to reinforce his power and strengthen feudal relationships. In the *rayatwari* system, farmers were individually responsible for their own taxes: These regions developed more cooperative and horizontal social relationships. Strikingly, the areas that were placed under elite domination still have tenser social relationships, lower agricultural yield, and fewer schools and hospitals than those placed under village control today, 150 years later and long after all land-revenue collection has stopped.

Acemoglu and Robinson do not think it is impossible for former colonies to escape the vicious circle of bad political and bad economic institutions. But they say that it will take the right alignment of forces, combined with a fair amount of luck. The examples they emphasize are the Glorious Revolution in England and the French Revolution. The fact that they are both major upheavals from at least 200 years ago is not entirely encouraging. Acemoglu and Robinson do end their book with some suggestions about what *may* help to bring about this change, but they are very cautious.

There are two other influential points of view that share Acemoglu and Robinson's basic stance about the primacy of institutions, but not their essential pessimism. The two groups want to take us in radically opposed directions: In one view, if countries are stuck because they have bad institutions, it is incumbent on the rich countries of the world to help them get better institutions, by force, if need be. In the other view, any attempt at manipulating institutions *or policies* from the top down is doomed to fail, and changes can only come from within.

One possible way to break the vicious cycle of bad institutions is to import change from the outside. Paul Romer, known for his pioneering work on economic growth a couple of decades ago, came up with what seems like a brilliant solution: If you cannot run your country, subcontract it to someone who can.[10] Still, running an entire country may be difficult. So he proposes starting with cities, small enough to be manageable but large enough to make a difference. Inspired by the example of Hong Kong, developed with great success by the British and then handed back to China, he developed the concept of "charter cities." Countries would hand over an empty strip of territory to a foreign power, who would then take the responsibility for developing a new city with good institutions. Starting from scratch, it is possible to establish a set of good ground rules (his examples range from traffic congestion charges to marginal cost pricing for electricity, and of course include legal protection of property rights). Because no one was forced to move there and all new arrivals are voluntary—the strip was empty to start with—people would not have any reason to complain about the new rules.

One minor drawback with this scheme is that it is unclear that leaders in poorly run countries would willingly enter into an agreement of this sort. Moreover, even if they did, it is not clear they could find a buyer: Committing not to take over the strip of land once it is actually successful would be quite difficult. So some development experts go further. In his books *The Bottom Billion: Why the Poorest Countries Are Failing and What Can Be Done About It* and *Wars, Guns, and Votes: Democracy in Dangerous Places,* Paul Collier, an Oxford University professor and former World Bank economist, argues that there are sixty "basket case" countries (think Chad, Congo, and so forth) in which about 1 billion people live.[11] These countries are stuck in a vicious circle of bad economic and bad political institutions, and it is the duty of the Western world to get them out, if necessary through military interventions. As an example of a successful intervention of this type, Collier cites British support for Sierra Leone's fledgling effort at democratization.

One of the most vocal critics of Collier's proposal is, predictably, William Easterly.[12] The central problem, he rightly points out, is that it is easier to take over a country than to know how to make it run well. The disastrous effort of the United States to institute a market-friendly democracy in Iraq is just one recent example.[13] But more generally, one size does not fit all. Institutions need to be tailored to the local environment, and therefore any top-down attempt to change them would probably backfire. Reform, if possible at all, must be gradual, and must recognize that existing institutions are most likely there for a reason.[14]

This mistrust of outside experts leads Easterly to be very skeptical not only of foreign takeovers but of foreign aid in general, in part because aid typically comes with an attempt to influence policies often at the cost of actually worsening the politics by continuing to spend aid even when leaders are corrupt.[15]

Easterly is not pessimistic, though. He believes that countries can find their own way to success, but they need to be left alone to do so. Despite his aversion to experts and his claims that there are no "one-size-fits-all" solutions, Easterly has one piece of expert advice—freedom. Freedom means both as much political freedom as possible and economic freedom, "the most underrated of human inventions," that is, free markets.[16] This is part of his notion that we need to let the "7 billion experts" take charge of their destiny.[17] Free markets will give would-be entrepreneurs opportunities to start their ventures and create wealth if they are successful. As a committed demand wallah, Easterly also wants governments to stop pushing education and health care on an indifferent populace but rather allow them the freedom to find ways to get themselves educated and healthy, through their own collective action.

Of course, there are many instances where people within the society may feel that the complete free market outcome may not be the ideal one. First, as Easterly points out,[18] the poor may not be able to participate in the market, and they need to be helped until the market finds a way to reach them. Second, some rules are necessary for markets and society to function. For example, people who don't know how to drive may nevertheless want to drive their car. But society feels that it is better if they don't, because of what it means for the rest of us. A free market in driver's licenses obviously cannot solve this problem. The problem is that if the state is weak or corrupt, the free market will tend to naturally reemerge via bribes and corruption. A study of the allocation of driver's licenses in Delhi showed that knowing how to drive did not really make it more likely that someone would actually get a driver's license, but being willing to pay more to get it fast did.[19] Delhi effectively has a free market in driver's licenses, and that's exactly what we do not want. The challenge is how to get the state to do the job when avoiding the free market outcome is precisely the goal.

So governments are necessary, to provide basic common goods and enforce the rules and norms that the market requires to function. According to Easterly, democracy will help provide the bottom-up feedback to hold governments accountable. The next question, then, is how will free market institutions and democracy emerge? Easterly is consistent: He points out that freedom cannot be imposed from outside, otherwise it would not be freedom. These institutions, then, have to be homegrown and emanate from the bottom up. All that can be done is to campaign for the ideals of individual equality and rights.[20]

The main lesson from Acemoglu and Robinson's historical analysis, however, is that bad institutions are very persistent, and there may be no natural process to eliminate them. We share their skepticism both about the danger of a strategy to impose institutional change wholesale from outside and about the hope that things will eventually fix themselves if we leave people alone. Where we part with them is in continuing to be optimistic: In practice, we do see a lot of significant institutional changes happening, at the margin, in the absence of an outside invasion or a full-scale social revolution.

Indeed, we feel that this entire debate is missing something basic about the definition of institutions: Institutions define the rules of engagement. This certainly includes the INSTITUTIONS that have been the focus of much of the analysis, at least by economists and political scientists, and still dominate the debate: democracy, decentralization, property rights, the caste system, and so on. But every INSTITU-TION at this level is realized, on the ground, through many specific local *institutions*. Property rights, for example, are constituted by a combination of a whole range of laws—about who can own what (Switzerland, for example, restricts foreign ownership of chalets), what ownership means (in Sweden people have the right to walk everywhere, including on other people's private land), how the combination of the legal system and the police acts to enforce those laws (jury trials are common in the United States, but not in France or Spain), and much more. Democracies have rules about who is eligible to run for what office, who can vote, how campaigns should be run, and legal protection systems that make it more or less easy to buy votes or intimidate citizens. For that matter, even autocratic regimes sometimes leave some limited space for citizen participation. We have seen it over and over in this book: Details matter. Institutions are no exception. To really understand the effect of institutions on the lives of the poor, what is needed is a shift in perspective from INSTITUTIONS in capital letters to institutions in lower case—the "view from below."[21]

CHANGES AT THE MARGIN

Acemoglu and Robinson's pessimism comes in part from the fact that we rarely see successful drastic regime change from authoritarian and corrupt to well-functioning democracy. The first thing the view from below allows us to see is that it is not always necessary to fundamentally change institutions to improve accountability and reduce corruption.

Although wholesale democratic reforms are few and far between, there are many instances where democracy has been introduced, to a limited extent and at the local level, within an authoritarian regime. Electoral reforms have even taken place in otherwise authoritarian states such as Indonesia under Suharto, Brazil during the military dictatorship, and Mexico under the Institutional Revolutionary Party (PRI). More recently, local elections have been introduced in Vietnam in 1998, Saudi Arabia in 2005, and Yemen in 2001. The reforms have typically been met with skepticism in the West: The elections are often rigged, and the elected officials have very limited powers. Yet there is compelling evidence that even very imperfect local elections can make a substantial difference in how local governments are run. In the early 1980s, village-level elections were progressively introduced in rural China. Early on, the Communist Party still decided who was allowed to run. The Communist Party branch continued to operate in the village, with its appointed secretary. Ballots were not always anonymous, and the ballot boxes were reportedly often stuffed. Despite these shortcomings, a study[22] found a surprisingly large effect of this reform, suggesting greater accountability to villagers. After a village starts holding elections, the village chiefs are more likely to relax unpopular central policies, such as the one-child policy. The reallocation of farmland, which happens from time to time in Chinese villages, is more likely to benefit "middle-class" farmers. Public expenditures are more likely to reflect villagers' needs.

Similarly, fighting corruption appears to be to some extent possible even without fixing the larger institutions. Relatively straightforward interventions, such as the newspaper campaign successfully implemented by the Ugandan government, have shown impressive success. Another interesting story comes from Indonesia, which remains quite corrupt even after the fall of Suharto. In 2010, it ranked 110th out of 178 countries in Transparency International's corruption perception index. Corruption was evident in a government program, funded by the World Bank, that provided money to villages to build local infrastructure, including roads. The easiest way for the community leader to skim some of these funds is to over-invoice for materials and to report wage payments that have never been made. Our colleague Benjamin Olken hired teams of engineers to excavate a tiny bit of road in 600 or so villages to figure out how much material had actually gone into the road's construction. The cost estimate was then compared with what was reported. Another team interviewed some of the people who were reported to have worked on the project about how much they had actually been paid. Theft was rife: 27 percent of the wages reported to have been paid had somehow vanished, and so had 20 percent of the materials. To make matters worse, the money was only one part of the waste. The roads that were built were still the same length (otherwise the theft would be too obvious) but the missing materials meant that they were built less well, and therefore more liable to be washed away by the next rains.[23]

In an effort to fight corruption, government officials in charge of the program told the village leaders that the building programs would be audited, and the results would be made public. The government did not hire especially honest auditors—they worked within the existing system. Yet, Olken showed that the threat of audits reduced the theft of wages and materials by one-third, compared to the villages where audits were not conducted (the villages where audits were conducted were randomly selected).

In the Indian state of Rajasthan, we worked with the police department and sent "mystery shoppers," or "decoys," to police stations with instructions to try to get the police to register some made-up petty cases—stolen cell phones, a case of "Eve-teasing" (the expression that Indians use to describe harassing women in the streets), and such similar cases.[24] Indian police stations are evaluated on the basis of the number of unsolved cases, that is, the more unresolved cases, the worse the evaluation. Therefore, an easy way to get better evaluations is to register as few cases as possible. In our first set of decoy visits, only 40 percent of the cases actually got to the point where the police were willing to register them (at which point our decoys were required to reveal that it was just a test). It is therefore no surprise that the poor rarely attempt to report any petty crimes to the police.

The police in India represent a near-perfect example of a persistent colonial institution. Despite the fact that they were originally designed to protect the interests of the colonists, there was no attempt to reform the Indian police after Independence. The Police Act of 1861 is still in effect! Since 1977, a succession of Police Reform Commissions have recommended wide-ranging changes, but implementation, so far, has been very limited. Yet the system is nowhere near as sclerotic as this history would suggest.

At the end of each decoy visit where the case was about to get registered, the decoys revealed their ploy: The police therefore figured out that there were these decoys running around, trying to register petty cases. Despite the fact that the data from the visits were explicitly not shared with their bosses, and not linked to any sanction, the registration rate went from 40 percent at the first visit to 70 percent by the fourth. They had no way to identify the decoys (they were just a set of local people who had been fed the stories), so registration rates must have increased for all such cases: The fear of decoys was sufficient to lead the police to do their job better.

Top-down monitoring is not a particularly new idea. But audits and decoys seem to be effective, presumably because once the information is out there, there is some chance that it will be used to punish the offenders. A few people within the system who believe in fighting corruption may be enough.

Information technology could help. Led by Nandan Nilekani, who used to run Infosys, one of the country's largest software companies, India is in the midst of an unprecedented effort to give each resident a "unique ID" number, linked to people's fingerprints and a picture of their irises. The idea is that any person registered in the system will be able to identify himself at any place equipped with the right fingerprint-recognition equipment. Once this is done, it will be possible, for example, to require people to scan their fingerprints to take delivery of any subsidized grains from the government fair-price shops. This will make it much harder for the shop owners to sell off the grains at market prices and claim that they have sold to the poor. The fundamental flaws in the Indian institutional frame will remain. Despite that, there is a chance that this "technical fix" can actually contribute to making life significantly better for the poor (although we do not have evidence yet, as the system is still being put in place).

DECENTRALIZATION AND DEMOCRACY IN PRACTICE

Although there is scope for improvement in accountability and corruption even within the framework of generally "bad" INSTITUTIONS, there is, conversely, no guarantee that good INSTITUTIONS necessarily work well in practice. Once again, it depends on how they operate on the ground. At some level, this is a rather obvious point, and one that institutional pessimists agree with. What is not recognized as often, however, is how important the effect of seemingly very small modifications in the rules can be.

There was a striking example of the impact of such a small change in Brazil. Brazil used to have a complex paper ballot. Voters had to choose one candidate from a long list, then write in the name (or the number) of the candidate they wanted to vote for on their ballot. In a country where roughly one-fourth of adults are not functionally literate, this led to the de facto disenfranchisement of a large number of voters. In the average election, almost 25 percent of the votes were invalid and not counted. In the late 1990s, electronic voting was introduced, at first in the largest municipalities, and then in all of them. A simple interface allowed voters to select the number of their candidate, and a picture of the candidate appeared on the screen before the voters validated their vote. This reform, introduced primarily to make it easier to tally the election results, had an unintended consequence: The number of invalid votes was 11 percent lower in the municipalities that introduced electronic voting than in very similar municipalities that had not yet converted to the new system. The newly enfranchised voters were poorer and less educated; the politicians they elected were themselves poorer and less educated; and the policies they chose were more likely to be targeted to the poor: In particular, there was an increase in public health expenditures and a reduction in the number of low-birth-weight babies among less educated mothers. A seemingly minor technical fix, involving no major political battle, changed the way in which the voice of the poor was taken into account in Brazil's political process.[25]

Power to the People

Another example of the surprising power of small changes comes from the rules governing local political processes. The new ideology in a lot of international institutions is that we should hand the beneficiaries the responsibility for making sure that schools, clinics, and local roads work well. This is usually done without asking the poor whether they really want to take on this responsibility.

In the face of the state's clear failure to deliver public services to the poor, as documented in various chapters of this book, the logic of handing anti-poverty policy back to the poor is superficially irresistible.

The beneficiaries are directly hurt by bad services, and they should therefore care the most; moreover, they have better information, both on what they want and on what is happening on the ground. Giving them the power to control the service providers (teachers, doctors, engineers)—either the ability to hire and fire them or, at least, the power to complain about them—ensures that those who have the right incentives and the right information are the ones making the decisions. "If the stakes are high enough," the World Bank wrote in its 2004 World Development Report, devoted to the delivery of social services, "communities tackle the problem."[26] Moreover, the very act of working together on a collective project may help communities rebuild their social ties after a major civil conflict. The so-called Community Driven Development projects, in which the communities choose and manage collective projects, are quite the rage in post-conflict environments like those in Sierra Leone, Rwanda, Liberia, and Indonesia.

However, in practice, the implementation of community participation and decentralization matters quite a lot. How exactly does the community express its preferences, given that different people often have different views? How can we ensure that the interests of the underprivileged groups (women, ethnic minorities, lower castes, the landless) are represented?

The fairness and the outcomes of the decision process in such environments crucially depend on such details as project selection rules (a meeting? a vote?), who is invited to the meetings, who speaks, who is in charge of implementing the project on a day-to-day basis, how these project leaders are selected, and much more. If the rules operate to exclude minorities or the poor, it is not clear that this kind of decentralization will help them or that handing power to the locality will help maintain communal harmony. On the contrary, groups that now discover they are disenfranchised by their own neighbors may in fact become angrier.

Take the example of the village meeting, an essential institution of local governance. This is where grievances are discussed, budgets are voted on, and projects are suggested and approved. The idea of a village meeting perhaps evokes quaint images of the yearly Town Meeting in Vermont, full of bonhomie and salty humor. But the reality of local government meetings in developing countries is much less attractive. The meetings of the Kecamatan Development Project (KDP) in Indonesia (a World Bank–funded project in which communities were given money to build or repair village infrastructure such as local roads or irrigation canals) had an attendance of about fifty, out of the several hundred adults in the village, and half of those were members of the local elite. Most people who attend do not speak: In the KDP meetings, an average of eight people actually said something, of whom seven were from the elite.

It would be tempting to conclude that the iron law of oligarchy was reasserting itself at the village level. But a small change in the rules changed everything. In Indonesia, in some randomly selected villages, people were formally *invited* to meetings through letters. This made a big difference in attendance: Turnout increased to almost sixty-five attendees on average, including about thirty-eight not from the elite. More villagers spoke, and the meetings were more animated. Moreover, some of the invitation letters included comment forms that asked about the way the KDP was being conducted, and in a randomly chosen fraction of villages, these were distributed to all schoolchildren to take home. In the rest of the villages, letters were given to the village head to distribute. When the comment forms were distributed through the schools, the average comments were significantly more critical than when they were distributed by the village heads.

If the rules make such a difference, then it becomes very important who gets to make them. If the village is left to its own devices, it seems likely that rule making would be captured by the elite. It might therefore be better for the decentralization to be designed by a centralized authority, with the interest of the less advantaged or less powerful in mind. Power to the people, but not all the power.

One specific example of such top-down intervention is to restrict whom villagers can elect as representatives. These restrictions may be needed in order to ensure adequate representation of the minorities, and they make a difference.

India's system of village government, or *gram panchayat* (the GP, or village council), has such restrictions. Elected every five years at the local level, the GP administers the local collective infrastructure, such as wells, school buildings, local roads, and so on. To protect underrepresented groups, the rules reserve leadership positions in a fraction of GPs for women and for members of various minorities (including the lower castes). If the elites had completely captured the *panchayat*, however, mandated representation of women or minorities would make no difference. The real bosses of the villages would continue to rule, presumably fronted by their wives, or by their lower-caste servants, whenever the bosses themselves are prevented from running for office. Indeed, when Raghabendra Chattopadhyay, of the Indian Institute of Management in Kolkata, and Esther embarked on a *panchayat* survey in 2000 to find out whether women leaders invested in different types of local infrastructure, they were warned by everyone, from the minister of rural development in Kolkata to their survey staff (and including many local academics), that this was a futile quest. The show, everyone claimed, was run by *pradhanpatis* (the husband of the *pradhan,* or chief of the GP), and the shy, often illiterate women, many of them with their heads covered, were certainly not making any decisions on their own.

The survey, however, revealed the opposite. In the state of West Bengal, under the quota system, one-third of the GPs were randomly selected every five years to be "reserved" for women to be the village head: In these villages, only women can run for office. Chattopadhyay and Esther compared the local infrastructure available in reserved and unreserved villages, just two years after the reservation system was first put in place.[27] They found that women invested much more of their (fixed) budget in the local infrastructure that women wanted—in West Bengal, that meant roads and drinking water—and less in schools. They then replicated these findings in Rajasthan, reputed to be one of India's most male chauvinist states. There, they found that women wanted closer sources of drinking water above all, and men wanted roads. And sure enough, women leaders invested more in drinking water, less on roads.

Further studies elsewhere in India have made it clear that women leaders almost always make a difference. Furthermore, over time, women also appear to be doing more than men with the same limited budget and are reported to be less inclined to take bribes. Yet whenever we present these results in India, there is someone who will tell us this has to be wrong: They have gone personally to a village and have talked to a woman *pradhan*, under her husband's supervision; they have seen political posters where the picture of the candidate's husband figured more prominently than the candidate herself. They are right: We, too, have had those conversations and seen those posters. Forcing women to run as political leaders is not the instant revolution that it is sometimes made out to be, with powerful women aggressively taking charge and reforming their villages. The women who are elected are often related to someone who was in politics before. They are less likely to chair the village meetings, and they speak less at them. They are less educated and less politically experienced. But despite all this, and despite the evident prejudice they face, many women are quietly taking charge.

Papering over the Ethnic Divide

Our final example looks at the role of ethnicity in voting. There is reason to be concerned that voting is often based on ethnic loyalties, which means that the candidate from the largest ethnic group often wins, whatever his intrinsic merit.

To measure the extent of political advantage from ethnic prejudice, Leonard Wantchekon, a political scientist at New York University and former student leader from Benin, convinced candidates for the presidential election (whom he knew well from his student days, when they were all part of the pro-democracy movement) to give very different speeches in different villages where they ran political meetings.[28] In the "clientelist" villages, the speech stressed the ethnic origin of the candidate and promised to bring schools and hospitals to the region and government jobs to his people. In the "national unity" villages, the same candidate promised to work for a national reform of the health and education sector and to work for peace among all the ethnic groups of Benin. The villages were randomly chosen to get different speeches, but all of them were in the candidate's political stronghold. The clientelist speech was a clear winner: On average, the clientelist candidate got 80 percent of the votes, as opposed to 70 percent in the national unity villages.

Ethnic politics is damaging for many reasons. One of them is that if voters choose based on ethnicity rather than on merit, the quality of candidates representing the majority group will suffer: These candidates don't need to make much of an effort because the fact that they are from the "right" caste or ethnic group is sufficient to ensure that they are elected. The Indian state of Uttar Pradesh, where politics became increasingly caste-based in the 1980s and 1990s, provides a clear illustration of this. Over time, there was a very large increase in the level of corruption among winning politicians from the numerically dominant caste group in all areas.[29] It did not matter whether that area was dominated by the lower caste or by the upper caste: The winners from the dominant group were more likely to be corrupt. By the 1990s, one-fourth of the members of the Legislative Assembly had a criminal case lodged against them.

Is it inevitable that voting in developing countries will end up being dominated by ethnicity? There is a long tradition of scholars who think so. Their view is that ethnic loyalties are the basis of traditional societies and are bound to dominate political attitudes until the society modernizes.[30] Yet the evidence suggests that ethnic voting is not as entrenched as is often believed. In one experiment in Uttar Pradesh during the 2007 state elections, Abhijit, Donald Green, Jennifer Green, and Rohini Pande worked with an NGO that ran a nonpartisan campaign (using street plays and puppet shows) around a simple slogan, "Don't vote on caste, vote on development issues," in randomly selected villages. This simple message reduced the probability that voters would choose a candidate from their own caste from 25 percent to 18 percent.[31]

Why do some people vote based on caste but readily change their minds when an NGO asks them to rethink? One answer is that, often, voters actually know very little about what they are choosing—they have typically never met the candidate except at election time, when everyone shows up and makes more or less the same promises. There is no obvious mechanism for finding out, for example, who is corrupt and who is not, and there is a tendency to assume that everyone is equally corrupt. Nor do voters know very much about the actual powers of the legislators: In India, we have often heard urban dwellers blaming the state legislator for the condition of the drains in their slums, when in fact it is their local legislator who is supposed to take care of such problems, with the result that legislators feel that they will be blamed for whatever goes wrong, which does not create a strong incentive to perform.

Given that all the candidates look more or less the same to voters (and perhaps equally bad), the voters may feel that they might as well vote on caste: There is a small chance that caste loyalty will pay off and the politician will help, and in any case, what do they have to lose? But many of them probably don't feel particularly strongly about it, which is why they are also easily swayed.

Brazil is one country that has tried to provide voters with useful information about candidates. Since 2003, every month, sixty municipalities are drawn at random in a televised lottery, and their accounts are audited. These audit results are made public through the Internet and the local media. Being audited hurts corrupt incumbents. In the 2004 election, they were 12 percentage points less likely to be elected if their audit was revealed before the election. Honest incumbents, on the other hand, were 13 percentage points more likely to be elected if their audit results were revealed just before an election. Similar results were found in the slums of Delhi: Voters who were informed about the performance of their incumbents voted against incumbents when they had done poorly.[32]

So politics is not very different from policy: It can (and must) be improved at the margin, and seemingly minor interventions can make a significant difference. The same kind of philosophy we have advocated throughout this book—attend to the details, understand how people decide, and be willing to experiment—applies as much to politics as it does to everything else.

AGAINST POLITICAL ECONOMY

Political economy is the view (embraced, as we have seen, by a number of development scholars) that politics has primacy over economics: Institutions define and limit the scope of economic policy.

However, as we have just shown, there is scope for improving the functioning of institutions, even in relatively hostile environments. Obviously, not all the problems will be solved in this way. The fact that there are powerful people who stand to lose from the reforms does impose limits on how far you can take things, but there is a lot that remains possible: The politicians in Brazil who were going to be exposed by the audit did not manage to stop the legislation, nor did the newspapers in Delhi balk at publishing the records of the legislators. In Indonesia and China, the autocratic regimes themselves decided to allow a measure of democracy. The important lesson is to take advantage of whatever slack there is. The same is true for policies. Policies are not completely determined by politics. Good policies (sometimes) happen in bad political environments. And, perhaps more important, bad policies (often) happen in quite good ones.

Suharto's Indonesia is an example of the first point. Suharto was a dictator and was known for being particularly corrupt. Whenever he fell seriously ill, the stock market values of the companies owned by his relatives fell, which clearly shows that being connected to him was valuable.[33] Despite this, as discussed in Chapter 4, it was in Suharto's Indonesia that oil money was used to build schools. Suharto thought that education was a powerful way to diffuse an ideology, impose a unified language, and create a sense of unity in the country. The policy, as we have reported, led to an increase in education and, for the generations that benefited from this schooling, an increase in wages. The education expansion was accompanied by a massive program promoting better nutritional practices for children, in part by training 1 million village volunteers who were supposed to bring the message to their villages. Perhaps in part because of this intervention, malnutrition in children was halved in Indonesia over the 1973–1993 period. The point is obviously not to claim that Suharto's regime was good for the Indonesian poor, but merely to underscore that the motivations of the political elites are complex enough that it may be in their interest, at a particular time and place, to implement some policies that happen to be good for the poor.

And, once again, the converse holds as well. Good intentions are probably a necessary ingredient for good policies, but they only go so far. Very bad policies are sometimes born out of the best of intentions, because of a misreading of what the real problem is: Public school systems fail the majority because everyone believes that only the elite can learn. Nurses never come to work because no one tried to make sure that there was demand for their services and because of unrealistic expectations about what they can do. Poor people have no safe place to save because the regulatory standards that governments set for institutions that are allowed to legally accept their savings are absurdly high.

Part of the problem is that even when governments are well intentioned, what they are trying to do is fundamentally difficult. Governments exist to a large extent to solve problems that markets cannot solve—we have already seen that in many instances government intervention is necessary precisely when, for some reason, the free market cannot do the job. For example, many parents may not end up immunizing their children or giving them deworming pills, both because they do not take into account the benefit this would have for others and because of the time inconsistency problems we discussed in Chapter 3. They may not choose the right level of education for their children, in part because they are not sure the children will be able to repay them after they have grown up. Firms would rather not operate their effluent treatment plant, partly because it costs money and partly because they don't really care if the water is polluted. At an intersection, we would rather go than stop at the red light. And so on. As a result, the agents of the government (the bureaucrats, the pollution inspectors, the policemen, the doctors) cannot be paid directly for the value they are delivering to the rest of us—when a policeman gives us a ticket, we complain, but we don't offer him a reward for doing his job well and keeping the roads safe for everyone. Contrast this with the grocery store owner: She delivers value by selling us eggs, and when we pay her for the eggs, we know we are paying for the social value she is delivering.

This simple observation has two very important implications: First, there is no easy way of assessing the performance of most people who work for the government. This is why there are so many rules for what bureaucrats (or policemen, or judges) should and shouldn't do. Second, the temptation to break the rules is ever present, both for the bureaucrat and for us, which is what leads to corruption and dereliction of duty.

The risk of corruption and neglect is thus endemic in any government, but it is likely to be more severe in three circumstances: First, in cases when the government is trying to get people to do things whose value they don't appreciate, such as wearing a helmet on a motorcycle, or immunizing a child. Second, when what people are getting is worth a lot more than they are paying for it; for example, a hospital bed provided free to those who need it, regardless of income, invites a bribe from richer people who want to jump the queue. Third, when bureaucrats are underpaid, overworked, and not well monitored, and have little to lose by getting fired anyway.

The evidence of many of the previous chapters suggests that these problems are likely to be more serious in poor countries. Lack of the right kind of information and a history of government failures make people trust the government's diktats less. Extreme poverty makes it necessary to give away a lot of services at well below market prices. And people don't know what their exact rights are, so they cannot effectively demand or monitor performance; governments have limited resources to pay bureaucrats, and so on.

This is one important reason why government programs (and similar programs run by NGOs and international organizations) often do not work. The problem is inherently difficult and the details need a lot of attention. Failures are often not the result of sabotage by a specific group, as a lot of political economists would have it, but come about because the whole system was badly conceived to start with and no one has taken the trouble to fix it. In such cases, change can be a matter of figuring out what will work and leading the charge.

Absenteeism among health workers is a perfect, if tragic, illustration. You may remember, from Chapter 3 on health, the nurses in Udaipur District who were upset with us because we were part of a project that was trying to get them to come to work. As it turned out, they got the last laugh: The program we were working on with the local government and the NGO Seva Mandir was an utter disaster.

The program had started when, after seeing data we had collected with Seva Mandir, which showed that nurses were absent at least half the time, the head of the district administration decided to tighten up the rules for nurse attendance. Under the new regime, the main nurse was supposed to be at the center for the entire day for one day a week, on Monday. On this day, she was not allowed to make home visits to her patients (often a convenient excuse to avoid coming to work). Seva Mandir was charged with monitoring attendance: Each nurse was given a time-and-date stamp and was asked to stamp a register affixed to the wall of the center several times a day on Mondays to prove her presence. Those who didn't show up at least 50 percent of the time would get their wages docked.

To see whether this new policy made a difference, we sent independent survey researchers to record absence both in the centers that Seva Mandir was monitoring and in the other centers (where the same rules applied in principle but where there was no monitoring).[34] Initially, everything went according to plan. Nurse attendance, which was around 30 percent before the launch of the program, jumped to 60 percent by August 2006 in centers where Seva Mandir was monitoring, but it remained unchanged elsewhere. Everyone (except the nurses, as they clearly let us know on the day we met them) was quite elated. Then, sometime in the month of November, the tide turned. Nurse attendance in the monitored centers started to drop, and kept dropping. By April 2007, the monitored and unmonitored centers were performing exactly the same—equally badly.

When we looked into what happened, the striking fact was that *recorded* absence remained low even after the program fell apart. What went up sharply were "exempt days"—days when there was some reason, the nurses claimed, that excused them from coming in (training and meetings were the most common reasons cited). We tried to figure out why the exempt days suddenly exploded; we could find no record of meetings or training on the claimed dates. The only possible interpretation was that everyone in charge of supervising the nurses must have decided to look the other way when the nurses suddenly started reporting 30 percent more exempt days. Indeed, the nurses in the monitored centers ended up getting a bonus from the whole episode—they discovered just how little their bosses cared about whether they came to work and, based on that, figured that they had actually been coming in *too often*. At some point, attendance in the monitored centers actually fell below that in the unmonitored ones and remained lower until the end of the study. By the end, the nurses in monitored centers came to work only 25 percent of the time. No one complained. Villagers were so used to the centers not working that they had lost interest in the system altogether. In our visits to the village, we could hardly find anyone to acknowledge that the nurses were absent. Everyone had entirely given up on the system and did not find it worth their while to find out what the nurse was doing, let alone complain about it.

Neelima Khetan, the head of Seva Mandir, offered an interesting interpretation of what happened. Khetan is someone who leads by example. She sets a high standard of behavior in her own professional life and expects others to follow. The nurses troubled her because they seemed so unconcerned about their own dereliction. She had discovered, though, that what they were supposed to do was crazy: Come to work six days a week. Sign in, then take your medicine bag and head out to one of the hamlets to do the rounds. Walk anywhere up to 3 miles to reach the hamlet, even if it is 100°F in the shade. Go from house to house checking on the health status of women of childbearing age and their children. Try to convince a few uninterested women to be sterilized. After five or six hours of doing this, walk back to the center. Sign out. Take a bus to go home, two hours away.

It is clear that no one could do this day in, day out. What had happened was that everyone accepted that the nurses were not really expected to do the job as described. But given that, what should they actually do? The nurses got to set their own rules. In the course of our meeting with them, they very clearly told us that we could not possibly expect them to come to work before 10:00 AM. The center opening hour, clearly posted on the wall outside, was 8:00 AM.

The rules were (obviously) not designed with the objective of undermining the effectiveness of the entire health-care system in India. On the contrary, they were probably put on paper by a well-meaning bureaucrat, who had his own views of what the system should do and did not pay too much attention to what that demanded on the ground. This is what we call, for short, the "three Is" problem: ideology, ignorance, inertia. This problem plagues many efforts to supposedly help the poor.

The nurses' workload was based on an *ideology* that wants to see nurses as dedicated social workers, designed in *ignorance* of the conditions on the ground, that lives on, mostly just on paper, because of *inertia*. Altering the rules to make the jobs doable might not be sufficient to get the nurses to come to work regularly, but it has to be a necessary first step.

The same three Is problem has similarly undermined India's effort to make schools accountable to parents and students. The government of India's last major education reform introduced the idea of parental participation in the oversight of primary schools. Under the Sarva Siksha Aviyan (SSA), a massive, federally funded effort to improve the quality of education, each village was supposed to form a "village education committee" (or VEC, the local equivalent to the American Parent-Teacher Association) to help run the school, find ways to improve the quality of teaching, and report on any problems. In particular, the VEC had the option to petition for funds for an extra teacher's help for the school, and if it was granted the necessary funds, it had the authority to hire and, later, if need be, fire this extra teacher. This is a significant power, given that teachers are not cheap. But in a survey we conducted in the district of Jaunpur, in Uttar Pradesh (India's most populous state), nearly five years after the program was launched, we found that 92 percent of parents had never heard of the VEC. Furthermore, when we interviewed the parents who were members of the VEC, one in four did not know that they were members; of those who knew they were members, roughly two-thirds were unaware of the Sarva Siksha Aviyan program and their right to hire teachers.

This program suffered from the classic three Is problem. Inspired by an ideology—people's power is good—and designed in ignorance of what people want and how the village works, it was, by the time we were studying it, entirely sustained by inertia. No one had paid any attention to it for many years, except for some bureaucrat somewhere who was making sure that all the boxes had been checked.

Working with Pratham, the Indian education NGO responsible for the Annual State of Education Report (ASER) and the Read India program we discussed in Chapter 4 on education, we thought that making parents more aware of their rights could breathe new life into the VEC. Teams of Pratham field staff were sent to sixty-five randomly chosen villages to inform and mobilize parents around their rights under Sarva Siksha Aviyan.[35] Because the Pratham team was somewhat doubtful that just telling people what they can do would have any effect without also telling them *why* they ought to do something, in another set of sixty-five villages a Pratham team taught interested villagers how to conduct the "dipstick" reading and math tests that are at the core of ASER and to prepare a report card for their village. The discussion of the report cards (which revealed that the number of children who could read and write was pathetically low in most villages) formed the starting point of the discussion on the potential role of parents and the VEC.

But neither of these interventions made any difference in parental involvement in the VEC, VEC activism, or child learning (what we ultimately care about) after a year. It was not that the community was not ready to mobilize. The Pratham team had also asked the community to come up with some volunteers who would be trained in Pratham's Read India techniques for teaching children how to read, and thereafter run after-school reading classes for the children. Volunteers did come forward, and they taught several classes each. As we saw in Chapter 4, children's reading levels improved dramatically in these villages.

The difference was explained by the fact that the villagers had been given a clear, concrete task: Identify volunteers and send the children in need of help to the remedial classes. This was much better defined than the probably overambitious target to convince people to go lobby the administration for extra teachers, or to force teachers to come to school, as the SSA would have it. In Kenya, a study that gave parents' school committees a narrow assignment was successful in getting them to act. The committees were given a sum of money and asked to hire extra teachers with it, and in some of the schools, they were given the additional responsibility of paying close attention to what this extra teacher was doing and making sure the school was not misusing the new teacher. The program was well implemented in all the schools, and its effects were even stronger in schools where the school committee was asked to pay close attention to how it worked.[36] Thus, parent participation in school can work, but it requires some thinking about what parents are asked to do.

What these two examples (the nurses and the school committees) illustrate is that large-scale waste and policy failure often happen not because of any deep structural problem but because of lazy thinking at the stage of policy design. Good politics may or may not be necessary for good policies; it is certainly not sufficient.

So there is no reason to believe, as the political economy view would have it, that politics always trumps policies. We can now go one step further and invert the hierarchy between policies and politics. Can good policies be a first step to good politics?

Voters adjust their views based on what they see happening on the ground, even when they are initially biased. The female policy makers in India are an example. Whereas the Delhi elite remained convinced that women could not be empowered by legal fiat, citizens on the ground were much more open to the opposite view. Before the policy of setting aside one-third of the seats of *panchayat* leaders to women, very few women were ever elected to a position of power. In West Bengal, in GPs that had never been reserved for women leaders, 10 percent of the *pradhans* in 2008 were women. Not surprisingly, the share jumped to 100 percent when the seats were reserved for women. But, once a seat that had been reserved went back to being open, women were more likely to be elected again: The share of women elected increased to 13 percent for currently unreserved seats that had been reserved once in the past and to 17 percent if they had been reserved twice. The same thing applied to city government representatives in Mumbai.[37] One reason for this is that voters' attitudes toward women changed. In West Bengal,[38] to measure prejudices about competence, villagers were asked to listen to a recording of a leader's speech. All villagers heard the same speech, but some heard it spoken in a male voice, and others in a female voice. After they heard the recording, they were asked to judge its quality. In villages that had never had reserved seats for women, and therefore had no experience of a woman leader, men who heard the "male" speech gave higher approval ratings than those who heard the "female" speech. On the other hand, in villages that had been reserved for women before, men tended to like the "female" speech better. Men did recognize that women were capable of implementing good policies and changed their opinion of women leaders. The temporary reservation of one-third of the seats for women could thus lead not only to some additional drinking water sources but also to a permanent transformation of the role of women in politics.

Good policies can also help break the vicious cycle of low expectations: If the government starts to deliver, people will start taking politics more seriously and put pressure on the government to deliver more, rather than opting out or voting unthinkingly for their co-ethnics or taking up arms against the government.

A study in Mexico[39] compared the voting behavior at the 2000 presidential election in villages that had received the social welfare program PROGRESA—which gave poor households cash transfers as long as their children attended school and they visited health-care centers—for six months and in others that had received it for twenty-one months. Both the poll turnout and votes in favor of the PRI (the party that brought them PROGRESA) were higher in villages that had received the benefits for longer. It cannot be because the households were "bought" by the program, since by that time, all of them had received the benefits and knew the rules. But because the program was successful in improving health and education and the households that had received the program for longer had started to see some of these benefits in their lives, they responded by being more engaged (higher turnout) and rewarding the party that had initiated the program (higher vote for the PRI). In a context where all too many electoral promises are made and broken, tangible achievements provide useful information to voters about what the candidates may do in the future.

Lack of trust can explain why in the 2001 experiment in Benin, Wantchekon found that the clientelist message was more successful than an appeal to general interest. When politicians talked in broad terms about the "public interest," no one took them seriously. At least, voters could more or less trust a clientelist message. If the "general interest" message had been clearer, more focused on some specific proposals, and had proposed an agenda that voters could hold the candidates accountable to if elected, they might have been more swayed.

A follow-up experiment that Wantchekon conducted before the 2006 election suggests that voters are indeed prepared to support those politicians who take seriously the job to design and explain social policies.[40] Wantchekon and other civil society leaders in Benin started by organizing a broad consultation: "Election 2006: What Policy Alternative?" There were four panels on education, public health, governance, and urban planning, and four experts (two from Benin and two from neighboring Niger and Nigeria) provided a white paper with policy recommendations. These were all broad proposals, without clientelist appeal. All the parties represented in the National Assembly, as well as representatives from various NGOs, attended the conference. After the conference, several parties volunteered to use the proposals made at the conference as electoral platforms on an experimental basis. They did this in randomly selected villages, in town meetings, where the proposals were presented in detail and participants had a chance to respond and react. In the comparison villages, the usual festive political meeting took place, with the usual mix of clientelist messages, and broad but vague policy proposals. This time, the results were reversed: Instead of showing support for the clientelist message, the turnout and support for the party running the campaign were higher in villages where the town meetings were held and specific policy proposals were discussed.

This result suggests that a credible message can convince the voters to vote in favor of general-interest policies. Once the trust is there, the individual politician's incentives also change. He can start to feel that if he does something good he will be appreciated and reelected. Many people in positions of power have mixed motives—they want to be loved or do good, both because they care and because it secures their position, even when they are corrupt. These individuals will do things to promote change, as long as they are not entirely inconsistent with their economic objectives. Once the government proves that it is trying to deliver, and wins the people's trust, a further possibility arises. The government can now afford to be less concerned with the short term, less keen to win the voters' approval at all costs, less compelled to indulge in giveaways. This is its chance to design better and more farsighted policies. As we saw in Chapter 4, the demonstrated success of PROGRESA encouraged Vicente Fox, who took over as president after the PRI lost power in Mexico, to expand the program, instead of canceling it. What's more, programs of this kind have expanded all over Latin America, and from there to the rest of the world. These programs may initially be less popular than simple giveaways, because to get the money, the family has to do something it may not otherwise want to do, but it is believed (although, as we saw, perhaps incorrectly) that the conditionality is an integral part of "breaking the cycle of poverty." It is encouraging that parties, both on the left and on the right, now feel that they should run on platforms that put this long-term view at the center of the agenda.

Many Western scholars and policy makers are extremely pessimistic about political institutions in the developing world. Depending on their political leanings, they may blame old agrarian institutions, or the original sin from the West—colonization and its extractive political institutions—or just the unfortunate culture that countries are stuck with. Whatever the reason, this viewpoint holds that bad political institutions are in large part responsible for keeping poor countries poor, and getting out of that state is difficult. Some feel this is a reason to give up; others want to impose institutional change from outside.

Easterly and Sachs are both somewhat impatient with these arguments, for different reasons. Easterly sees no reason for "experts" from the West to judge whether a set of political institutions in another place is necessarily good or bad in that specific context. Sachs believes that poor institutions are a disease of poor countries: We can successfully address poverty, perhaps in a limited way, even in bad institutional environments, by focusing on concrete, measurable programs; and making people richer and more educated can start a virtuous circle where good institutions will emerge.

We agree with both of them: The focus on the broad INSTITUTIONS as a necessary and sufficient condition for anything good to happen is somewhat misplaced. The political constraints are real, and they make it difficult to find big solutions to big problems. But there is considerable slack to improve institutions and policy at the margin.

Careful understanding of the motivations and the constraints of everyone (poor people, civil servants, taxpayers, elected politicians, and so on) can lead to policies and institutions that are better designed, and less likely to be perverted by corruption or dereliction of duty. These changes will be incremental, but they will sustain and build on themselves. They can be the start of a quiet revolution.

In Place of a Sweeping Conclusion

Economists (and other experts) seem to have very little useful to say about why some countries grow and others do not. Basket cases, such as Bangladesh or Cambodia, turn into small miracles. Poster children, such as Côte d'Ivoire, fall into the "bottom billion." In retrospect, it is always possible to construct a rationale for what happened in each place. But the truth is, we are largely incapable of predicting where growth will happen, and we don't understand very well why things suddenly fire up.

Given that economic growth requires manpower and brainpower, it seems plausible, however, that whenever that spark occurs, it is more likely to catch fire if women and men are properly educated, well fed, and healthy, and if citizens feel secure and confident enough to invest in their children, and to let them leave home to get the new jobs in the city.

It is also probably true that until that happens, something needs to be done to make that wait for the spark more bearable. If misery and frustration are allowed to have their way, and anger and violence take over, it is not clear that the spark will ever arrive. A social policy that works, that keeps people from striking out because they feel that they have nothing to lose, may be a crucial step toward preserving the country's date with that elusive takeoff.

Even if all this is not correct—if social policy has nothing to do with growth—the case for doing everything possible in order to improve the lives of the poor now, and not waiting for the growth spark, remains overwhelming. We made the moral case in our opening chapter: To the extent that we know how to remedy poverty, there is no reason to tolerate the waste of lives and talent that poverty brings with it. As this book has shown, although we have no magic bullets to eradicate poverty, no one-shot cure-all, we *do* know a number of things about how to improve the lives of the poor. In particular, five key lessons emerge.

First, the poor often lack critical pieces of information and believe things that are not true. They are unsure about the benefits of immunizing children; they think there is little value in what is learned during the first few years of education; they don't know how much fertilizer they need to use; they don't know which is the easiest way to get infected with HIV; they don't know what their politicians do when in office. When their firmly held beliefs turn out to be incorrect, they end up making the wrong decision, sometimes with drastic consequences—think of the girls who have unprotected sex with older men or the farmers who use twice as much fertilizer as they should. Even when they know that they don't know, the resulting uncertainty can be damaging. For example, the uncertainty about the benefits of immunization combines with the universal tendency to procrastinate, with the result that a lot of children don't get immunized. Citizens who vote in the dark are more likely to vote for someone of their ethnic group, at the cost of increasing bigotry and corruption.

We saw many instances in which a simple piece of information makes a big difference. However, not every information campaign is effective. It seems that in order to work, an information campaign must have several features: It must say something that people don't already know (general exhortations like "No sex before marriage" seem to be less effective); it must do so in an attractive and simple way (a film, a play, a TV show, a well-designed report card); and it must come from a credible source (interestingly, the press seems to be viewed as credible). One of the corollaries of this view is that governments pay a huge cost in terms of lost credibility when they say things that are misleading, confusing, or false.

Second, the poor bear responsibility for too many aspects of their lives. The richer you are, the more the "right" decisions are made for you. The poor have no piped water, and therefore do not benefit from the chlorine that the city government puts into the water supply. If they want clean drinking water, they have to purify it themselves. They cannot afford ready-made fortified breakfast cereals and therefore have to make sure that they and their children get enough nutrients. They have no automatic way to save, such as a retirement plan or a contribution to Social Security, so they have to find a way to make sure that they save. These decisions are difficult for everyone because they require some thinking now or some other small cost today, and the benefits are usually reaped in the distant future. As such, procrastination very easily gets in the way. For the poor, this is compounded by the fact that their lives are already much more demanding than ours: Many of them run small businesses in highly competitive industries; most of the rest work as casual laborers and need to constantly worry about where their next job will come from. This means that their lives could be significantly improved by making it as easy as possible to do the right thing—based on everything else we know—using the power of default options and small nudges: Salt fortified with iron and iodine could be made cheap enough that everyone buys it. Savings accounts, the kind that make it easy to put in money and somewhat costlier to take it out, can be made easily available to everyone, if need be, by subsidizing the cost for the bank that offers them. Chlorine could be made available next to every source where piping water is too expensive. There are many similar examples.

Third, there are good reasons that some markets are missing for the poor, or that the poor face unfavorable prices in them. The poor get a negative interest rate from their savings accounts (if they are lucky enough to have an account) and pay exorbitant rates on their loans (if they can get one) because handling even a small quantity of money entails a fixed cost. The market for health insurance for the poor has not developed, despite the devastating effects of serious health problems in their lives because the limited insurance options that can be sustained in the market (catastrophic health insurance, formulaic weather insurance) are not what the poor want.

In some cases, a technological or an institutional innovation may allow a market to develop where it was missing. This happened in the case of microcredit, which made small loans at more affordable rates available to millions of poor people, although perhaps not the poorest. Electronic money transfer systems (using cell phones and the like) and unique identification for individuals may radically cut the cost of providing savings and remittance services to the poor over the next few years. But we also have to recognize that in some cases, the conditions for a market to emerge on its own are simply not there. In such cases, governments should step in to support the market to provide the necessary conditions, or failing that, consider providing the service themselves.

We should recognize that this may entail giving away goods or services (such as bed nets or visits to a preventive care center) for free or even rewarding people, strange as it might sound, for doing things that are good for them. The mistrust of free distribution of goods and services among various experts has probably gone too far, even from a pure cost-benefit point of view. It often ends up being cheaper, per person served, to distribute a service for free than to try to extract a nominal fee. In some cases, it may involve ensuring that the price of a product sold by the market is attractive enough to allow the market to develop. For example, governments could subsidize insurance premiums, or distribute vouchers that parents can take to any school, private or public, or force banks to offer free "no frills" savings accounts to everyone for a nominal fee. It is important to keep in mind that these subsidized markets need to be carefully regulated to ensure they function well. For example, school vouchers work well when all parents have a way of figuring out the right school for their child; otherwise, they can turn into a way of giving even more of an advantage to savvy parents.

Fourth, poor countries are not doomed to failure because they are poor, or because they have had an unfortunate history. It is true that things often do not work in these countries: Programs intended to help the poor end up in the wrong hands, teachers teach desultorily or not at all, roads weakened by theft of materials collapse under the weight of overburdened trucks, and so forth. But many of these failures have less to do with some grand conspiracy of the elites to maintain their hold on the economy and more to do with some avoidable flaw in the detailed design of policies, and the ubiquitous three Is: ignorance, ideology, and inertia. Nurses are expected to carry out jobs that no ordinary human being would be able to complete, and yet no one feels compelled to change their job description. The fad of the moment (be it dams, barefoot doctors, microcredit, or whatever) is turned into a policy without any attention to the reality within which it is supposed to function. We were once told by a senior government official in India that the village education committees always include the parent of the best student in the school and the parent of the worst student in the school. When we asked how they decided who were the best and worst children, given that there are no tests until fourth grade, she quickly changed subjects. And yet even these absurd rules, once in place, keep going out of sheer inertia.

The good news, if that is the right expression, is that it is possible to improve governance and policy without changing the existing social and political structures. There is tremendous scope for improvement even in "good" institutional environments, and some margin for action even in bad ones. A small revolution can be achieved by making sure that everyone is invited to village meetings; by monitoring government workers and holding them accountable for failures in performing their duties; by monitoring politicians at all levels and sharing this information with voters; and by making clear to users of public services what they should expect—what the exact health center hours are, how much money (or how many bags of rice) they are entitled to.

Finally, expectations about what people are able or unable to do all too often end up turning into self-fulfilling prophecies. Children give up on school when their teachers (and sometimes their parents) signal to them that they are not smart enough to master the curriculum; fruit sellers don't make the effort to repay their debt because they expect that they will fall back into debt very quickly; nurses stop coming to work because nobody expects them to be there; politicians whom no one expects to perform have no incentive to try improving people's lives. Changing expectations is not easy, but it is not impossible: After seeing a female *pradhan* in their village, villagers not only lost their prejudice against women politicians but even started thinking that their daughter might become one, too; teachers who are told that their job is simply to make sure that all the children can read can accomplish that task within the duration of a summer camp. Most important, the role of expectations means that success often feeds on itself. When a situation starts to improve, the improvement itself affects beliefs and behavior. This is one more reason one should not necessarily be afraid of handing things out (including cash) when needed to get a virtuous cycle started.

Despite these five lessons, we are very far from knowing everything we can and need to know. This book is, in a sense, just an invitation to look more closely. If we resist the kind of lazy, formulaic thinking that reduces every problem to the same set of general principles; if we listen to poor people themselves and force ourselves to understand the logic of their choices; if we accept the possibility of error and subject every idea, including the most apparently commonsensical ones, to rigorous empirical testing, then we will be able not only to construct a toolbox of effective policies but also to better understand why the poor live the way they do. Armed with this patient understanding, we can identify the poverty traps where they really are and know which tools we need to give the poor to help them get out of them.

We may not have much to say about macroeconomic policies or institutional reform, but don't let the apparent modesty of the enterprise fool you: Small changes can have big effects. Intestinal worms might be the last subject you want to bring up on a hot date, but kids in Kenya who were treated for their worms at school for two years, rather than one (at the cost of $1.36 USD PPP per child and per year, all included), earned 20 percent more as adults every year, meaning $3,269 USD PPP over a lifetime. The effect might be lower if deworming became universal: The children lucky enough to have been dewormed may have been in part taking the jobs of others. But to scale this number, note that Kenya's highest sustained per capita growth rate in modern memory was about 4.5 percent in 2006–2008. If we could press a macroeconomic policy lever that could make that kind of unprecedented growth happen again, it would still take four years to raise average incomes by the same 20 percent. And, as it turns out, no one has such a lever.

We also have no lever guaranteed to eradicate poverty, but once we accept that, time is on our side. Poverty has been with us for many thousands of years; if we have to wait another fifty or hundred years for the end of poverty, so be it. At least we can stop pretending that there is some solution at hand and instead join hands with millions of well-intentioned people across the world—elected officials and bureaucrats, teachers and NGO workers, academics and entrepreneurs—in the quest for the many ideas, big and small, that will eventually take us to that world where no one has to live on 99 cents per day.

Acknowledgments

We became development economists because of our mothers, Nirmala Banerjee and Violaine Duflo. In their lives and their work they each constantly express an unwillingness to live with the injustice that they see in the world. We would have had to be deaf and blind to escape their influence.

Our fathers, Dipak Banerjee and Michel Duflo, taught us the importance of getting the argument right. We do not always measure up to the exacting standard of precision they set for themselves, but we came to understand why it is the right standard.

The genesis of this book was a conversation in 2005 with Andrei Shleifer, who was then editing the *Journal of Economic Perspectives*. He asked us to write something about the poor. While we were writing that piece, which was eventually called "The Economic Lives of the Poor," we realized that this could be a way to bring together the many disparate facts and ideas that we have spent our lives trying to fathom. Max Brockman, our agent, then persuaded us that there might be interest in publishing a book stemming from this piece.

Many of those facts and ideas came from others: From those who taught us, mentored us, challenged us; from our coauthors, coeditors, students, and friends; from our colleagues in the Abdul Latif Jameel Poverty Action Lab; and from the many people we have worked with in governments and development organizations around the world. Any list of more specific influences is necessarily going to be incomplete, even unfair. However, we would still like to acknowledge Josh Angrist, Rukmini Banerji, Annie Duflo, Neelima Khetan, Michael Kremer, Andreu Mas Colell, Eric Maskin, Sendhil Mullainathan, Andy Newman, Rohini Pande, Thomas Piketty, and Emmanuel Saez, who, in their own individual ways, did more to shape the thoughts that went into this book than they probably realize. We hope that they are not entirely put off by the result.

We benefited immensely from the comments of a number of people on earlier drafts of the book: Daniel Cohen, Angus Deaton, Pascaline Dupas, Nicholas Kristof, Greg Lewis, Patrick McNeal, Rohini Pande, Ian Parker, Somini Sengupta, Andrei Shleifer, and Kudzai Takavarasha. Emily Breza and Dominic Leggett read through every chapter several times and came up with important ways to improve the book. The book is immensely better for that, though probably not as good as they could have made it if we had been less impatient to get it done. Our editor at PublicAffairs, Clive Priddle, was wonderful to work with: The book came to life when he took charge.

Notes

Foreword

1. Throughout the book, we use the collective "we" whenever at least one of us was present in an interview.

2. The key reference we follow for our definition of poverty is Angus Deaton and Olivier Dupriez, "Purchasing Power Parity for the Global Poor," *American Economic Journal: Applied Economics,* forthcoming. How do we know how much prices need to be adjusted to reflect the cost of living? The ICP project, led by the World Bank, has collected a comprehensive set of price data in 2005. Deaton and Dupriez have used those to calculate the cost of a basket of goods typically consumed by the poor in all the poor countries for which they have data. They do the exercise using the Indian rupee as the benchmark and use a price index in India compared to the United States to convert this poverty line into dollars, adjusted for the purchasing power parity. They propose the 16-rupee poverty line as the average of the poverty line of fifty countries where the vast majority of the poor live, weighted by the number of poor in those countries. They then use the exchange rate, adjusted for the price index between India and the United States, to convert the 16 rupees into a figure in dollars, which comes to 99 cents. Throughout this book, we present all prices in local currency and in 2005 Purchasing Power Parity–adjusted dollars (which we will note as "USD PPP"), using Deaton and Dupriez's numbers. In this way, the price of anything mentioned in the book is directly scalable to the standard of living of the poor (for example, if something costs 3 USD PPP, it is roughly three times the poverty line).

Chapter 1

1. United Nations, Department of Economic and Social Affairs, *The Millennium Development Goals Report* (2010).

2. Pratham Annual Status of Education Report 2005: Final Edition, available at http://scripts.mit.edu/~varun_ag/readinggroup/images/1/14/ASER.pdf.

3. Deborah Small, George Loewenstein, and Paul Slovic, "Sympathy and Callousness: The Impact of Deliberative Thought on Donations to Identifiable and Statistical Victims," *Organizational Behavior and Human Decision Processes* 102 (2007): 143–153.

4. Jeffrey Sachs, *The End of Poverty: Economic Possibilities for Our Time* (New York: Penguin Press, 2005).

5. William Easterly, *The White Man's Burden: Why the West's Efforts to Aid the Rest Have Done So Much Ill and So Little Good* (Oxford: Oxford University Press, 2006); and William Easterly, *The Elusive Quest for Growth: Economists' Adventures and Misadventures in the Tropics* (Cambridge: MIT Press, 2001).

6. Dambisa Moyo, *Dead Aid: Why Aid Is Not Working and How There Is a Better Way for Africa* (London: Allen Lane, 2009).

7. Everywhere in the book, whenever we present an amount in a country's local currency, we give the equivalent amount in dollars, adjusted for the cost of living (see Endnote 1 in the Foreword). This is denoted by USD PPP (USD at purchasing power parity).

8. Todd Moss, Gunilla Pettersson, and Nicolas van de Walle, "An Aid-Institutions Paradox? A Review Essay on Aid Dependency and State Building in Sub-Saharan Africa," Working Paper No. 74, Center for Global Development (January 2006). Still, eleven countries out of forty-six received more than 10 percent of their budget in aid, and eleven got more than 20 percent.

9. Peter Singer, "Famine, Affluence, and Morality," *Philosophy and Public Affairs* 1 (3) (1972): 229–243.

10. Amartya Sen, *Development as Freedom* (New York: Knopf, 1999).

11. Nicholas D. Kristof and Sheryl WuDunn, *Half the Sky: Turning Oppression into Opportunity for Women Worldwide* (New York: Knopf, 2009).

12. Peter Singer, *The Life You Can Save* (New York: Random House, 2009), available at http://www.thelifeyoucansave.com.

13. See the WHO fact sheet on malaria, available at http://www.who.int/mediacentre/factsheets/fs094/en/index.html. Note that here, as in many other places in the book, we cite the official international statistics. It is good to keep in mind that the numbers are not always accurate: On many issues, the data these numbers are based on are incomplete or of doubtful quality.

14. C. Lengeler, "Insecticide-Treated Bed Nets and Curtains for Preventing Malaria," *Cochrane Database of Systematic Reviews* 2 (2004), Art. No. CD000363.

15. William A. Hawley, Penelope A. Phillips-Howard, Feiko O. Ter Kuile, Dianne J. Terlouw, John M. Vulule, Maurice Ombok, Bernard L. Nahlen, John E. Gimnig, Simon K. Kariuki, Margarette S. Kolczak, and Allen W. Hightower, "Community-Wide Effects of Permethrin-Treated Bed Nets on Child Mortality and Malaria Morbidity in Western Kenya," *American Journal of Tropical Medicine and Hygiene* 68 (2003): 121–127.

16. World Malaria report, available at http://www.who.int/malaria/world_malaria_report_2009/factsheet/en/index.html.

17. Pascaline Dupas, "Short-Run Subsidies and Long-Run Adoption of New Health Products: Evidence from a Field Experiment," draft (2010); Jessica Cohen and Pascaline Dupas, "Free Distribution or Cost-Sharing? Evidence from a Randomized Malaria Prevention Experiment," *Quarterly Journal of Economics* 125 (1) (February 2010): 1–45; V. Hoffmann, "Demand, Retention, and Intra-Household Allocation of Free and Purchased Mosquito Nets," *American Economic Review: Papers and Proceedings* (May 2009); Paul Krezanoski, Alison Comfort, and Davidson Hamer, "Effect of Incentives on Insecticide-Treated Bed Net Use in Sub-Saharan Africa: A Cluster Randomized Trial in Madagascar," *Malaria Journal* 9 (186) (June 27, 2010).

18. Available at http://www.millenniumvillages.org/.

Chapter 2

1. Food and Agriculture Organization, "The State of Food Insecurity in the World, 2009: Economic Crises, Impact and Lessons Learned," available at http://www.fao.org/docrep/012/i0876e/i0876e00.htm.

2. World Bank, "Egypt's Food Subsidies: Benefit Incidence and Leakages," Report No. 57446 (September 2010).

3. A. Ganesh-Kumar, Ashok Gulati, and Ralph Cummings Jr., "Foodgrains Policy and Management in India: Responding to Today's Challenges and Opportunities," Indira Gandhi Institute of Development Research, Mumbai, and IFPRI, Washington, DC, PP-056 (2007).

4. It was part of a Ph.D. thesis by Dipak Mazumdar at the London School of Economics. In 1986, Partha Dasgupta and Debraj Ray, then both professors at Stanford, gave it an elegant exposition. See Partha Dasgupta and Debraj Ray, "Inequality as a Determinant of Malnutrition and Unemployment: Theory," *Economic Journal* 96 (384) (1986): 1011–1034.

5. These and other statistics based on the eighteen-country data set (and more details on the data) are available on the book's Web site, available at http://www.pooreconomics.com.

6. Shankar Subramanian and Angus Deaton, "The Demand for Food and Calories," *Journal of Political Economy* 104 (1) (1996): 133–162.

7. Robert Jensen and Nolan Miller, "Giffen Behavior and Subsistence Consumption," *American Economic Review* 98 (4) (2008): 1553–1577.

8. Alfred Marshall, one of the founders of modern economics, discusses this idea in his *Principles of Economics* (first published by McMillan, London, 1890), using the example that when the price of bread goes up, people "are forced to curtail their consumption of meat and the more expensive farinaceous foods: and, bread being still the cheapest food which they can get and will take, they consume more, and not less of it." Marshall attributed this observation to one Mr. Giffen, and goods whose consumption goes down when they become cheaper are called "Giffen goods." However, before the Jensen-Miller experiment, most economists were quite doubtful that the Giffen goods existed in real life. See Alfred Marshall, *Principles of Economics* (Amherst, NY: Prometheus Books, revised edition, May 1997).

9. Angus Deaton and Jean Dreze, "Food and Nutrition in India: Facts and Interpretations," *Economics and Political Weekly* 44 (7) (2009): 42–65.

10. "Food for All," *World Food Summit, November 1996,* Food and Agriculture Organization of the United Nations.

11. Nathan Nunn and Nancy Qian, "The Potato's Contribution to Population and Urbanization: Evidence from an Historical Experiment," NBER Working Paper W15157 (2009).

12. This is the case that Roger Thurow and Scott Kilman, two journalists at the *Wall Street Journal,* make in their book, aptly titled *Enough: Why the World's Poorest Starve in an Age of Plenty* (New York: Public Affairs, 2009).

13. John Strauss, "Does Better Nutrition Raise Farm Productivity?" *Journal of Political Economy* 94 (1986): 297–320.

14. Robert Fogel, *The Escape from Hunger and Premature Death, 1700–2100: Europe, America and the Third World* (Cambridge: Cambridge University Press, 2004).

15. Emily Oster, "Witchcraft, Weather and Economic Growth in Renaissance Europe," *Journal of Economic Perspectives* 18 (1) (Winter 2004): 215–228.

16. Elaina Rose, "Consumption Smoothing and Excess Female Mortality in Rural India," *Review of Economics and Statistics* 81 (1) (1999): 41–49.

17. Edward Miguel, "Poverty and Witch Killing," *Review of Economic Studies* 72 (4) (2005): 1153–1172.

18. Amartya Sen, "The Ingredients of Famine Analysis: Availability and Entitlements," *Quarterly Journal of Economics* 96 (3) (1981): 433–464.

19. "Intake of Calories and Selected Nutrients for the United States Population, 1999–2000," Centers for Disease Control, results from the NHANES survey.

20. Measure DHS Statcompiler, available at http://statcompiler.com, also cited in Angus Deaton and Jean Dreze, "Food and Nutrition in India: Facts and Interpretations," *Economics and Political Weekly* 44 (7) (2009): 42–65.

21. Ibid.

22. Anne Case and Christina Paxson, "Stature and Status: Height, Ability and Labor Market Outcomes," *Journal of Political Economy* 166 (3) (2008): 499–532.

23. See the story by Mark Borden on the reaction to the Case-Paxson article, available at http://www.newyorker.com/archive/2006/10/02/061002ta_talk_borden.

24. Sarah Baird, Joan Hamory Hicks, Michael Kremer, and Edward Miguel, "Worm at Work: Long-Run Impacts of Child Health Gains," University of California at Berkeley (2010), unpublished manuscript.

25. Cesar G. Victora, Linda Adair, Caroline Fall, Pedro C. Hallal, Reynaldo Martorell, Linda Richter, and Harshpal Singh Sachdev, "Maternal and Child Undernutrition: Consequences for Adult Health and Human Capital," *Lancet* 371 (9609) (2008): 340–357.

26. David Barker, "Maternal Nutrition, Female Nutrition, and Disease in Later Life," *Nutrition* 13 (1997): 807.

27. Erica Field, Omar Robles, and Maximo Torero, "Iodine Deficiency and Schooling Attainment in Tanzania," *American Economic Journal: Applied Economics* 1 (4) (2009): 140–169.

28. Duncan Thomas, Elizabeth Frankenberg, Jed Friedman, et al., "Causal Effect of Health on Labor Market Outcomes: Evidence from a Random Assignment Iron Supplementation Intervention" (2004), mimeo.

29. Michael Kremer and Edward Miguel, "The Illusion of Sustainability," *Quarterly Journal of Economics*, 122 (3) (2007): 1007-1065.

30. George Orwell, *The Road to Wigan Pier* (New York: Penguin, Modern Classic Edition, 2001), p. 88.

31. Anne Case and Alicia Menendez, "Requiescat in Pace? The Consequences of High Priced Funerals in South Africa," NBER Working Paper W14998 (2009).

32. "Funeral Feasts of the Swasi Menu," *BBC News,* 2002, available at http://news.bbc.co.uk/2/hi/africa/2082281.stm.

33. These statistics are from our eighteen-country data set and are available at http://www.pooreconomics.com.

34. Orwell, *The Road to Wigan Pier,* p. 81.

35. Available at http://www.harvestplus.org/.

Chapter 3

1. Available at http://www.povertyactionlab.org/policy-lessons/health/child-diarrhea.

2. Nava Ashraf, James Berry, and Jesse Shapiro, "Can Higher Prices Stimulate Product Use? Evidence from a Field Experiment in Zambia," NBER Working Paper W13247 (2007).

3. Available at http://www.unicef.org/infobycountry/india_statistics.html.

4. John Gallup and Jeffrey Sachs, "The Economic Burden of Malaria," *American Journal of Tropical Medicine and Hygiene* 64 (2001): 1, 85–96.

5. Available at http://www.cdc.gov/malaria/history/index.htm#eradicationus.

6. Hoyt Bleakley, "Malaria Eradication in the Americas: A Retrospective Analysis of Childhood Exposure," *American Economic Journal: Applied Economics* 2 (2) (2010): 1–45.

7. David Cutler, Winnie Fung, Michael Kremer, Monica Singhal, and Tom Vogl, "Early-Life Malaria Exposure and Adult Outcomes: Evidence from Malaria Eradication in India," *American Economic Journal: Applied Economics* 2 (2) (April 2010): 72–94.

8. Adrienne Lucas, "Malaria Eradication and Educational Attainment: Evidence from Paraguay and Sri Lanka," *American Economic Journal: Applied Economics* 2 (2) (2010): 46–71.

9. WHO and UNICEF, *Progress on Sanitation and Drinking Water,* 2010, available at http://whqlibdoc.who.int/publications/2010/9789241563956_eng_full_text.pdf.

10. David Cutler and Grant Miller, "The Role of Public Health Improvements in Health Advances: The Twentieth-Century United States," *Demography* 42 (1) (2005): 1–22; and J. Bryce, C. Boschi-Pinto, K. Shibuya, R. E. Black, and the WHO Child Health Epidemiology Reference Group, "WHO Estimates of the Causes of Death in Children," *Lancet* 365 (2005): 1147–1152.

11. Lorna Fewtrell and John M. Colford Jr., "Water, Sanitation and Hygiene: Interventions and Diarrhoea," HNP Discussion Paper (2004).

12. World Health Organization, "Water, Sanitation and Hygiene Links to Health: Facts and Figures," 2004.

13. Dale Whittington, W. Michael Hanemann, Claudia Sadoff, and Marc Jeuland, "Sanitation and Water," Copenhagen 2008 Challenge Paper, p. 21.

14. Available at http://www.who.int/features/factfiles/breastfeeding/en/index.html.

15. R. E. Quick, A. Kimura, A. Thevos, M. Tembo, I. Shamputa, L. Hutwagner, and E. Mintz, "Diarrhea Prevention Through Household-Level Water Disinfection and Safe Storage in Zambia," *American Journal of Tropical Medicine and Hygiene* 66 (5) (2002): 584–589.

16. Ashraf, Berry, and Shapiro, "Can Higher Prices Stimulate Product Use?"

17. Jessica Cohen and Pascaline Dupas, "Free Distribution or Cost-Sharing? Evidence from a Randomized Malaria Prevention Experiment," *Quarterly Journal of Economics* 125 (1) (2010): 1–45.

18. Pascaline Dupas, "What Matters (and What Does Not) in Households' Decision to Invest in Malaria Prevention?" *American Economic Review: Papers and Proceedings* 99 (2) (2009): 224–230.

19. Obinna Onwujekwe, Kara Hanson, and Julia Fox-Rushby, "Inequalities in Purchase of Mosquito Nets and Willingness to Pay for Insecticide-Treated Nets in Nigeria: Challenges for Malaria Control Interventions," *Malaria Journal* 3 (6) (March 16, 2004).

20. Anne Case and Angus Deaton, "Health and Well-Being in Udaipur and South Africa," chap. 9 in D. Wise, ed., *Developments in the Economics of Aging* (Chicago: University of Chicago Press, for NBER, 2006).

21. Abhijit Banerjee, Angus Deaton, and Esther Duflo, "Wealth, Health, and Health Services in Rural Rajasthan," *AER Papers and Proceedings* 94 (2) (2004): 326–330.

22. Abhijit Banerjee and Esther Duflo, "Improving Health Care Delivery in India," MIT (2009), mimeo.

23. Jishnu Das and Jeffrey Hammer, "Money for Nothing: The Dire Straits of Medical Practice in Delhi, India," *Journal of Development Economics* 83 (1) (2007): 1–36.

24. Jishnu Das and Jeffrey Hammer, "Which Doctor? Combining Vignettes and Item Response to Measure Clinical Competence," *Journal of Development Economics* 78 (2) (2005): 348–383.

25. Abhijit Banerjee, Angus Deaton, and Esther Duflo, "Wealth, Health, and Health Services in Rural Rajasthan," *AER Papers and Proceedings* 94 (2) (2004): 326–330.

26. World Health Organization, *WHO Report on Infectious Diseases 2000: Overcoming Antimicrobial Resistance* (Geneva: WHO/CDS, 2000), 2.

27. Ambrose Talisuna, Peter Bloland, and Umberto d'Alessandro, "History, Dynamics, and Public Health Importance of Malaria Parasite Resistance," *American Society for Microbiology* 17 (1) (2004): 235–254.

28. Nazmul Chaudhury et al., "Missing in Action: Teacher and Health Worker Absence in Developing Countries," *Journal of Economic Perspectives* 20 (1) (2006): 91–116.

29. Kenneth L. Leonard and Melkiory C. Masatu, "Variations in the Quality of Care Accessible to Rural Communities in Tanzania," *Health Affairs* 26 (3) (2007): 380–392; and Jishnu

Das, Jeffrey Hammer, and Kenneth Leonard, "The Quality of Medical Advice in Low-Income Countries," *Journal of Economic Perspectives* 22 (2) (2008): 93–114.

30. Abhijit Banerjee, Esther Duflo, and Rachel Glennerster, "Putting a Band-Aid on a Corpse: Incentives for Nurses in the Indian Public Health Care System," *Journal of the European Economic Association* 6 (2–3) (2008): 487–500.

31. William Easterly, *The White Man's Burden: Why the West's Efforts to Aid the Rest Have Done So Much Ill and So Little Good* (New York: Penguin Group, 2006).

32. See Michael Specter's analysis of this and other incidences of "irrational thinking" in his book *Denialism: How Irrational Thinking Hinders Scientific Progress, Harms the Planet and Threatens Our Lives* (New York: Penguin Press, 2010).

33. Jishnu Das and Saumya Das, "Trust, Learning and Vaccination: A Case Study of a North Indian Village," *Social Science and Medicine* 57 (1) (2003): 97–112.

34. Jishnu Das and Carolina Sanchez-Paramo, "Short but Not Sweet—New Evidence on Short Duration Morbidities from India," Policy Research Working Paper Series 2971, World Bank (2003).

35. Abhijit Banerjee, Esther Duflo, Rachel Glennerster, and Dhruva Kothari, "Improving Immunisation Coverage in Rural India: Clustered Randomised Controlled Immunisation Campaigns With and Without Incentives," *British Medical Journal* 340 (2010): c2220.

36. Mohammad Ali, Michael Emch, Lorenz von Seidlein, Mohammad Yunus, David A. Sack, Malla Rao, Jan Holmgren, and John D. Clemens, "Herd Immunity Conferred by Killed Oral Cholera Vaccines in Bangladesh: A Reanalysis," *Lancet* 366 (2005): 44–49.

37. The psychological research has found its way in economics thanks to researchers such as Dick Thaler from the University of Chicago, George Lowenstein from Carnegie-Mellon, Matthew Rabin from Berkeley, David Laibson from Harvard, and others, whose work we cite here.

38. Richard H. Thaler and Cass R. Sunstein, *Nudge: Improving Decisions About Health, Wealth, and Happiness* (New York: Penguin, 2008).

39. See a comparative cost-effectiveness analysis on the Web site of the Abdul Latif Jameel Poverty Action Lab, available at http://www.povertyactionlab.org/policy-lessons/health/child-diarrhea.

40. Abhijit Banerjee, Esther Duflo, and Rachel Glennerster, "Is Decentralized Iron Fortification a Feasible Option to Fight Anemia Among the Poorest?" chap. 10 in David Wise, ed., *Explorations in the Economics of Aging* (Chicago: University of Chicago Press, 2010).

41. Pascaline Dupas, "Short-Run Subsidies and Long-Run Adoption of New Health Products: Evidence from a Field Experiment," draft paper (2010).

Chapter 4

1. Esther Duflo, *Lutter contre la pauvreté: Volume 1, Le Développement humain* (Paris: Le Seuil, 2010). In our most recent survey, in Morocco, we found a lower absence rate.

2. Edward Miguel and Michael Kremer, "Worms: Identifying Impacts on Education and Health in the Presence of Treatment Externalities," *Econometrica* 72 (1) (January 2004): 159–217.

3. The Probe Team, *Public Report on Basic Education in India* (New Delhi: Oxford University Press, 1999).

4. See *Higher Education in Developing Countries: Perils and Promises,* World Bank, 2000, available at http://siteresources.worldbank.org/EDUCATION/Resources/278200-10990798 77269/547664-1099079956815/peril_promise_en.pdf; *State of the World's Children, Special Edition 2009,* UNICEF, available at http://www.unicef.org/rightsite/sowc/fullreport.php;

and Education for All Global Monitoring Report, Annex (Statistical Tables), United Nations Educational, Scientific and Cultural Organization, 2009.

5. Nazmul Chaudhury, Jeffrey Hammer, Michael Kremer, Karthik Muralidharan, and Halsey Rogers, "Missing in Action: Teacher and Health Worker Absence in Developing Countries," *Journal of Economic Perspectives* (Winter 2006): 91–116.

6. Pratham Annual Status of Education Report, 2005, Final Edition, available at http://scripts.mit.edu/~varun_ag/readinggroup/images/1/14/ASER.pdf.

7. "Kenya National Learning Assessment Report 2010," and "Uwezo Uganda: Are Our Children Learning?" both available at http://www.uwezo.net.

8. Tahir Andrabi, Jishnu Das, Asim Khwaja, Tara Vishwanath, and Tristan Zajonc, "Pakistan Learning and Educational Achievement in Punjab Schools (LEAPS): Insights to Inform the Education Policy Debate," World Bank, Washington, DC, 2009.

9. Andrew Foster and Mark Rosenzweig, "Technical Change and Human Capital Returns and Investments: Evidence from the Green Revolution," *American Economic Review* 86 (4) (1996): 931–953.

10. Robert Jensen, "Economic Opportunities and Gender Differences in Human Capital: Experimental Evidence for India," NBER Working Paper W16021 (2010).

11. Paul Schultz, "School Subsidies for the Poor: Evaluating the Mexican Progresa Poverty Program," *Journal of Development Economics* 74 (1) (2004): 199–250.

12. Sarah Baird, Craig McIntosh, and Berk Ozler, "Designing Cost-Effective Cash Transfer Programs to Boost Schooling Among Young Women in Sub-Saharan Africa," World Bank Policy Research Working Paper No. 5090 (2009).

13. Najy Benhassine, Florencia Devoto, Esther Duflo, Pascaline Dupas, and Victor Pouliquen, "The Impact of Conditional Cash Transfers on Schooling and Learning: Preliminary Evidence from the Tayssir Pilot in Morocco," MIT, mimeo (2010).

14. Esther Duflo, "Schooling and Labor Market Consequences of School Construction in Indonesia: Evidence from an Unusual Policy Experiment," *American Economic Review* 91 (4) (2001): 795–813.

15. David Card, "The Causal Effect of Education on Earnings," in Orley Ashenfelter and David Card, eds., *Handbook of Labor Economics*, vol. 3 (Amsterdam: Elsevier Science B.V., 2010), pp. 1801–1863.

16. Chris Spohr, "Formal Schooling and Workforce Participation in a Rapidly Developing Economy: Evidence from 'Compulsory' Junior High School in Taiwan," *Asian Development Bank* 70 (2003): 291–327.

17. Shin-Yi Chou, Jin-Tan Liu, Michael Grossman, and Theodore Joyce, "Parental Education and Child Health: Evidence from a Natural Experiment in Taiwan," NBER Working Paper 13466 (2007).

18. Owen Ozier, "The Impact of Secondary Schooling in Kenya: A Regression Discontinuity Analysis," University of California at Berkeley Working Paper (2010).

19. Tahir Andrabi, Jishnu Das, and Asim Khwaja, "Students Today, Teachers Tomorrow? The Rise of Affordable Private Schools," working paper (2010).

20. Sonalde Desai, Amaresh Dubey, Reeve Vanneman, and Rukmini Banerji, "Private Schooling in India: A New Educational Landscape," Indian Human Development Survey, Working Paper No. 11 (2010).

21. However, among applicants to a lottery for secondary school vouchers for private schools in the Colombian city of Bogotá, the difference persisted: The winners did better than the losers on standardized tests, were 10 percentage points more likely to graduate, and scored better on the graduation exam. See Joshua Angrist, Eric Bettinger, Erik Bloom, Elizabeth King, and Michael Kremer, "Vouchers for Private Schooling in Colombia: Evidence from a Randomized Natural Experiment," *American Economic Review* 92 (5) (2002): 1535–

1558; and Joshua Angrist, Eric Bettinger, and Michael Kremer, "Long-Term Educational Consequences of Secondary School Vouchers: Evidence from Administrative Records in Colombia," *American Economic Review* 96 (3) (2006): 847–862.

22. Desai, Dubey,Vanneman, and Banerji, "Private Schooling in India."

23. Abhijit Banerjee, Shawn Cole, Esther Duflo, and Leigh Linden, "Remedying Education: Evidence from Two Randomized Experiments in India," *Quarterly Journal of Economics* 122 (3) (August 2007): 1235–1264.

24. Abhijit Banerjee, Rukmini Banerji, Esther Duflo, Rachel Glennerster, and Stuti Khemani, "Pitfalls of Participatory Programs: Evidence from a Randomized Evaluation in Education in India," *American Economic Journal: Economic Policy* 2 (1) (February 2010): 1–30.

25. Trang Nguyen, "Information, Role Models, and Perceived Returns to Education: Experimental Evidence from Madagascar," MIT Working Paper (2008).

26. Abhijit Banerjee and Esther Duflo, "Growth Theory Through the Lens of Development Economics," in Steve Durlauf and Philippe Aghion, eds., *Handbook of Economic Growth,* vol. 1A (Amsterdam: Elsevier Science Ltd./North Holland, 2005), pp. 473–552.

27. A. D. Foster and M. R. Rosenzweig, "Technical Change and Human Capital Returns and Investments: Evidence from the Green Revolution," *American Economic Review* 86 (4) (September 1996): 931–953.

28. Richard Akresh, Emilie Bagby, Damien de Walque, and Harounan Kazianga, "Child Ability and Household Human Capital Investment Decisions in Burkina Faso," University of Illinois at Urbana–Champaign (2010), mimeo.

29. Felipe Barrera-Osorio, Marianne Bertrand, Leigh Linden, and Francisco Perez Calle, "Conditional Cash Transfers in Education: Design Features, Peer and Sibling Effects—Evidence from a Randomized Experiment in Colombia," NBER Working Paper W13890 (2008).

30. Esther Duflo, Pascaline Dupas, and Michael Kremer, "Peer Effects, Teacher Incentives, and the Impact of Tracking: Evidence from a Randomized Evaluation in Kenya," NBER Working Paper W14475 (2008).

31. The Probe Team, *Public Report on Basic Education in India* (New Delhi: Oxford University Press, 1999).

32. Rema Hanna and Leigh Linden, "Measuring Discrimination in Education," NBER Working Paper W15057 (2009).

33. Steven Spencer, Claude Steele, and Diane Quinn, "Stereotype Threat and Women's Math Performance," *Journal of Experimental Social Psychology* 35 (1999): 4–28; and Claude Steele and Joshua Aronson, "Stereotype Threat and the Test Performance of Academically Successful African Americans," *Journal of Personality and Social Psychology* 69 (5) (1995): 797–811.

34. Karla Hoff and Priyank Pandey, "Belief Systems and Durable Inequalities: An Experimental Investigation of Indian Caste,"World Bank Policy Research Working Paper No. 3351 (2004).

35. Paul Glewwe, Michael Kremer, and Sylvie Moulin, "Textbooks and Test Scores: Evidence from a Prospective Evaluation in Kenya," BREAD Working Paper (2000).

36. Eric Gould,Victor Lavy, and Daniele Paserman, "Fifty-Five Years After the Magic Carpet Ride: The Long-Run Effect of the Early Childhood Environment on Social and Economic Outcome," *Review of Economic Studies* (2010), forthcoming.

37. Joshua Angrist, Susan Dynarski, Thomas Kane, Parag Pathak, and Christopher Walters, "Who Benefits from KIPP?" NBER Working Paper 15740 (2010); Atila Abdulkadiroglu, Joshua Angrist, Susan Dynarski, Thomas Kane, and Parag Pathak, "Accountability and Flexibility in Public Schools: Evidence from Boston's Charters and Pilots," NBER Working Paper 15549 (2009);Will Dobbie and Roland Fryer, "Are High Quality Schools Enough to Close

the Achievement Gap? Evidence from a Social Experiment in Harlem," NBER Working Paper 15473 (2009).

38. C. Walters, "Urban Charter Schools and Racial Achievement Gaps," MIT (2010), mimeo.

39. Pascaline Dupas, Esther Duflo, and Michael Kremer, "Peer Effects, Teacher Incentives, and the Impact of Tracking: Evidence from a Randomized Evaluation in Kenya," *American Economic Review,* forthcoming.

40. Trang Nguyen, "Information, Role Models and Perceived Returns to Education: Experimental Evidence from Madagascar," MIT Working Paper (2008).

41. Robert Jensen, "The (Perceived) Returns to Education and the Demand for Schooling," *Quarterly Journal of Economics* 125 (2) (2010): 515–548.

42. Michael Kremer, Edward Miguel, and Rebecca Thornton, "Incentives to Learn," *Review of Economics and Statistics,* forthcoming.

43. Roland Fryer, "Financial Incentives and Student Achievement: Evidence from Randomized Trials," Harvard University, manuscript (2010).

44. Abhijit Banerjee, Shawn Cole, Esther Duflo, and Leigh Linden, "Remedying Education: Evidence from Two Randomized Experiments in India," *Quarterly Journal of Economics* 122 (3) (August 2007): 1235–1264.

45. This may be helped by making sure that money is never a factor in a student's decision to attend the best schools and that there is a way to make it happen. In Chile, in a largely voucher-based system, the poorest students are given an extra voucher, but any school that accepts voucher students (all but a handful of elite schools) must admit these students at no additional cost. To make this system fully operational, students and parents should, however, be better informed that they have this option, and the results of regular standardized assessments should be regularly examined to identify the most promising students everywhere in the country.

Chapter 5

1. Cited in Davidson R. Gwatkin, "Political Will and Family Planning: The Implications of India's Emergency Experience," *Population and Development Review* 5 (1): 29–59 (1979), which is the source of this account of the forced sterilization episode during the Emergency.

2. John Bongaarts, "Population Policy Options in the Developing World," *Science* 263 (5148) (1994): 771–776.

3. Jeffrey Sachs, *Common Wealth: Economics for a Crowded Planet* (New York: Allen Lane/Penguin, 2008).

4. World Health Organization, Water Scarcity Fact File, 2009, available at http://www.who.int/features/factfiles/water/en/.

5. Thomas Malthus, *Population: The First Essay* (Ann Arbor: University of Michigan Press, 1978).

6. Alywn Young, "The Gift of the Dying: The Tragedy of AIDS and the Welfare of Future African Generations," *Quarterly Journal of Economics* 120 (2) (2005): 243–266.

7. Jane Forston, "HIV/AIDS and Fertility," *American Economic Journal: Applied Economics* 1 (3) (July 2009): 170–194; and Sebnem Kalemli-Ozcan, "AIDS, 'Reversal' of the Demographic Transition and Economic Development: Evidence from Africa," NBER Working Paper W12181 (2006).

8. Michael Kremer, "Population Growth and Technological Change: One Million B.C. to 1990," *Quarterly Journal of Economics* 108 (3) (1993): 681–716.

9. Gary Becker, "An Economic Analysis of Fertility," *Demographic and Economic Change in Developed Countries* (Princeton: National Bureau of Economic Research, 1960).

10. Sachs, *Common Wealth.*

11. Vida Maralani, "Family Size and Educational Attainment in Indonesia: A Cohort Perspective," California Center for Population Research Working Paper CCPR-17-04 (2004).

12. Mark Montgomery, Aka Kouamle, and Raylynn Oliver, *The Tradeoff Between Number of Children and Child Schooling: Evidence from Côte d'Ivoire and Ghana* (Washington, DC: World Bank, 1995).

13. Joshua Angrist and William Evans, "Children and Their Parents' Labor Supply: Evidence from Exogenous Variation in Family Size," *American Economic Review* 88 (3) (1998): 450–477.

14. Joshua Angrist, Victor Lavy, and Analia Schlosser, "New Evidence on the Causal Link Between the Quantity and Quality of Children," NBER Working Paper W11835 (2005).

15. Nancy Qian, "Quantity-Quality and the One Child Policy: The Positive Effect of Family Size on School Enrollment in China," NBER Working Paper W14973 (2009).

16. T. Paul Schultz and Shareen Joshi, "Family Planning as an Investment in Female Human Capital: Evaluating the Long Term Consequences in Matlab, Bangladesh," Yale Center for Economic Growth Working Paper No. 951 (2007).

17. Grant Miller, "Contraception as Development? New Evidence from Family Planning in Colombia," *Economic Journal* 120 (545) (2010): 709–736.

18. Kristof and WuDunn, *Half the Sky.*

19. See, for example, Attila Ambrus and Erica Field, "Early Marriage, Age of Menarche, and Female Schooling Attainment in Bangladesh," *Journal of Political Economy* 116 (5) (2008): 881–930; and Esther Duflo, Pascaline Dupas, Michael Kremer, and Samuel Sinei, "Education and HIV/AIDS Prevention: Evidence from a Randomized Evaluation in Western Kenya," World Bank Policy Research Working Paper 4024 (2006).

20. *The Millennium Development Goals Report, 2010,* United Nations.

21. Mark Pitt, Mark Rosenzweig, and Donna Gibbons, "The Determinants and Consequences of the Placement of Government Programs in Indonesia," *World Bank Economic Review* 7 (3) (1993): 319–348.

22. Lant H. Pritchett, "Desired Fertility and the Impact of Population Policies," *Population and Development Review* 20 (1) (1994): 1–55.

23. Mizanur Rahman, Julie DaVanzo, and Abdur Razzaque, "When Will Bangladesh Reach Replacement-Level Fertility? The Role of Education and Family Planning Services," working paper, Department of Economic and Social Affairs, Population Division, United Nations, available at http://www.un.org/esa/population/.

24. Available at http://apps.who.int/ghodata/ under the heading MDG 5, adolescent fertility.

25. Esther Duflo, Pascaline Dupas, Michael Kremer, and Samuel Sinei, "Education and HIV/AIDS Prevention: Evidence from a Randomized Evaluation in Western Kenya," World Bank Policy Research Working Paper 4024 (2006).

26. See the description in Kristof and WuDunn, *Half the Sky*, p. 137.

27. Pascaline Dupas, "Do Teenagers Respond to HIV Risk Information? Evidence from a Field Experiment in Kenya," *American Economic Journal: Applied Economics* 3 (1) (January 2011): 1–36.

28. Erica Field, "Fertility Responses to Urban Land Titling Programs: The Roles of Ownership Security and the Distribution of Household Assets," Harvard University (2004), mimeo.

29. Nava Ashraf, Erica Field, and Jean Lee, "Household Bargaining and Excess Fertility: An Experimental Study in Zambia," Harvard University (2009), mimeo.

30. Kaivan Munshi and Jacques Myaux, "Social Norms and the Fertility Transition," *Journal of Development Economics* 80 (1) (2005): 1–38.

31. Eliana La Ferrara, Alberto Chong, and Suzanne Duryea, "Soap Operas and Fertility: Evidence from Brazil," BREAD Working Paper 172 (2008).

32. Abhijit Banerjee, Xin Meng, and Nancy Qian, "Fertility and Savings: Micro-Evidence for the Life-Cycle Hypothesis from Family Planning in China," working paper (2010).

33. Ibid.

34. Ummul Ruthbah, "Are Children Substitutes for Assets: Evidence from Rural Bangladesh," MIT Ph.D. dissertation (2007).

35. Seema Jayachandran and Ilyana Kuziemko, "Why Do Mothers Breastfeed Girls Less Than Boys? Evidence and Implications for Child Health in India," NBER Working Paper W15041 (2009).

36. Amartya Sen, "More Than 100 Million Women Are Missing," *New York Review of Books* 37 (20) (1990).

37. Fred Arnold, Sunita Kishor, and T. K. Roy, "Sex-Selective Abortions in India," *Population and Development Review* 28 (4) (December 2002): 759–784.

38. Andrew Foster and Mark Rosenzweig, "Missing Women, the Marriage Market and Economic Growth," working paper (1999).

39. Nancy Qian, "Missing Women and the Price of Tea in China: The Effect of Sex-Specific Income on Sex Imbalance," *Quarterly Journal of Economics* 122 (3) (2008): 1251–1285.

40. Some of the key research in this area was conducted by François Bourguignon, Pierre-André Chiapori, Marjorie McElroy, and Duncan Thomas.

41. Christopher Udry, "Gender, Agricultural Production and the Theory of the Household," *Journal of Political Economy* 104 (5) (1996): 1010–1046.

42. Esther Duflo and Christopher Udry, "Intrahousehold Resource Allocation in Côte d'Ivoire: Social Norms, Separate Accounts and Consumption Choices," NBER Working Paper W10489 (2004).

43. Franque Grimard, "Household Consumption Smoothing Through Ethnicities: Evidence from Côte d'Ivoire," *Journal of Development Economics* 53 (1997): 391–422.

44. Claude Meillassoux, *Anthropologie économique des Gouros de Côte d'Ivoire* (Paris: F. Maspero, 1965).

45. Esther Duflo, "Grandmothers and Granddaughters: Old Age Pension and Intra-Household Allocation in South Africa," *World Bank Economic Review* 17 (1) (2003): 1–25.

Chapter 6

1. Jeemol Unni and Uma Rani, "Social Protection for Informal Workers in India: Insecurities, Instruments and Institutional Mechanisms," *Development and Change* 34 (1) (2003): 127–161.

2. Mohiuddin Alamgir, *Famine in South Asia: Political Economy of Mass Starvation* (Cambridge, MA: Oelgeschlager, Gunn and Hain, 1980).

3. Martin Ravallion, *Markets and Famines* (Oxford: Clarendon, 1987).

4. Seema Jayachandran, "Selling Labor Low: Wage Responses to Productivity Shocks in Developing Countries," *Journal of Political Economy* 114 (3) (2006): 538–575.

5. "Crisis Hitting Poor Hard in Developing World, World Bank Says," World Bank Press Release, 2009/220/EXC, February 12, 2009.

6. Daniel Chen, "Club Goods and Group Identity: Evidence from Islamic Resurgence During the Indonesian Financial Crisis," *Journal of Political Economy* 118 (2) (2010): 300–354.

7. Mauro Alem and Robert Townsend, "An Evaluation of Financial Institutions: Impact on Consumption and Investment Using Panel Data and the Theory of Risk-Bearing," working paper (2010).

8. B. P. Ramos and A. F. T. Arnsten, "Adrenergic Pharmacology and Cognition: Focus on the Prefrontal Cortex," *Pharmacology and Therapeutics* 113 (2007): 523–536; D. Knoch, A. Pascual-Leone, K. Meyer, V. Treyer, and E. Fehr, "Diminishing Reciprocal Fairness by Disrupting the Right Prefrontal Cortex," *Science* 314 (2006): 829–832; T. A. Hare, C. F. Camerer, and A. Rangel, "Self-Control in Decision-Making Involves Modulation of the vmPFC Valuation System," *Science* 324 (2009): 646–648; A. J. Porcelli and M. R. Delgado, "Acute Stress Modulates Risk Taking in Financial Decision Making," *Psychological Science: A Journal of the American Psychological Society/APS* 20 (2009): 278–283; and R. van den Bos, M. Harteveld, and H. Stoop, "Stress and Decision-Making in Humans: Performance Is Related to Cortisol Reactivity, Albeit Differently in Men and Women," *Psychoneuroendocrinology* 34 (2009): 1449–1458.

9. Seema Jayachandran, "Selling Labor Low: Wage Responses to Productivity Shocks in Developing Countries," *Journal of Political Economy* 114 (3) (2006): 538–575.

10. Nirmala Banerjee, "A Survey of Occupations and Livelihoods of Households in West Bengal," Sachetana, Kolkata (2006), mimeo.

11. Mark Rosenzweig and Oded Stark, "Consumption Smoothing, Migration, and Marriage: Evidence from Rural India," *Journal of Political Economy* 97 (4) (1989): 905–926.

12. Hans Binswanger and Mark Rosenzweig, "Wealth, Weather Risk and the Composition and Profitability of Agricultural Investments," *Economic Journal* 103 (416) (1993): 56–78.

13. Radwan Shaban, "Testing Between Competing Models of Sharecropping," *Journal of Political Economy* 95 (5) (1987): 893–920.

14. Christopher Udry, "Risk and Insurance in a Rural Credit Market: An Empirical Investigation in Northern Nigeria," *Review of Economic Studies* 61 (3) (1994): 495–526.

15. Paul Gertler and Jonathan Gruber, "Insuring Consumption Against Illness," *American Economic Review* 92 (1) (March 2002): 51–70.

16. Marcel Fafchamps and Susan Lund: "Risk-Sharing Networks in Rural Philippines," *Journal of Development Economics* 71 (2) (2003): 261–287.

17. Betsy Hartman and James Boyce, *Quiet Violence: View from a Bangladesh Village* (San Francisco: Food First Books, 1985).

18. Andrew Kuper, "From Microfinance into Microinsurance," *Forbes,* November 26, 2008.

19. Shawn Cole, Xavier Gine, Jeremy Tobacman, Petia Topalova, Robert Townsend, and James Vickery, "Barriers to Household Risk Management: Evidence from India," Harvard Business School Working Paper 09-116 (2009).

20. Ibid.

21. Alix Zwane, Jonathan Zinman, Eric Van Dusen, William Pariente, Clair Null, Edward Miguel, Michael Kremer, Dean S. Karlan, Richard Hornbeck, Xavier Giné, Esther Duflo, Florencia Devoto, Bruno Crepon, and Abhijit Banerjee, "The Risk of Asking: Being Surveyed Can Affect Later Behavior," *Proceedings of the National Academy of Sciences,* forthcoming (2010).

22. Dean Karlan, Isaac Osei-Akoto, Robert Osei, and Christopher Udry, "Examining Underinvestment in Agriculture: Measuring Returns to Capital and Insurance," Yale University (2010), mimeo.

Chapter 7

1. Dean Karlan and Sendhil Mullainathan, "Debt Cycles," work in progress (2011).

2. Robin Burgess and Rohini Pande, "Do Rural Banks Matter? Evidence from the Indian Social Banking Experiment," *American Economic Review* 95 (3) (2005): 780–795.

3. Shawn Cole, "Fixing Market Failures or Fixing Elections? Agricultural Credit in India," *American Economic Journal: Applied Economics* 1 (1) (2009): 219–250.

4. Scott Fulford, "Financial Access, Precaution, and Development: Theory and Evidence from India," Boston College Working Paper 741 (2010).

5. Irfan Aleem, "Imperfect Information, Screening, and the Costs of Informal Lending: A Study of a Rural Credit Market in Pakistan," *World Bank Economic Review* 4 (3) (1990): 329–349.

6. Julian West, "Pay Up—or We'll Send the Eunuchs to See You: Debt Collectors in India Have Found an Effective New Way to Get Their Money," *Sunday Telegraph*, August 22, 1999.

7. The Law Commission of India, Report Number 124, "The High Court Arrears—a Fresh Look" (1988), available at http://bombayhighcourt.nic.in/libweb/commission/Law_Commission_Of_India_Reports.html#11.

8. Benjamin Feigenberg, Erica Field, and Rohini Pande, "Building Social Capital Through Microfinance," NBER Working Paper W16018 (2010).

9. Yet the physical threat may not be entirely absent. A credit officer of a particular MFI once complained to one of our research assistants that he would never be promoted: The men with the high titles all had larger, burlier, more intimidating physiques.

10. Microfinance Information eXchange, data available at http://www.mixmarket.org.

11. "What Do We Know About the Impact of Microfinance?" CGAP, World Bank, available at http://www.cgap.org/p/site/c/template.rc/1.26.1306/.

12. Abhijit Banerjee, Esther Duflo, Rachel Glennerster, and Cynthia Kinnan, "The Miracle of Microfinance?: Evidence from a Randomized Evaluation," MIT, May 30, 2009, mimeo.

13. Dean Karlan and Jonathan Zinman, "Expanding Microenterprise Credit Access: Using Randomized Supply Decisions to Estimate the Impacts in Manila," Yale, manuscript (2010).

14. Brigit Helms, "Microfinancing Changes Lives Around the World—Measurably," *Seattle Times,* April 7, 2010.

15. Erica Field and Rohini Pande, "Repayment Frequency and Default in Microfinance: Evidence from India," *Journal of the European Economic Association* 6 (2–3) (2008): 501–509; Erica Field, Rohini Pande, and John Papp, "Does Microfinance Repayment Flexibility Affect Entrepreneurial Behavior and Loan Default?" Centre for Micro Finance Working Paper 34 (2009); and Feigenberg et al., ibid.

16. Xavier Giné and Dean Karlan, "Group Versus Individual Liability: A Field Experiment in the Philippines," World Bank Policy Research Working Paper 4008 (2006); and Xavier Giné and Dean Karlan, "Group Versus Individual Liability: Long Term Evidence from Philippine Microcredit Lending Groups," working paper (2010).

17. Emily Breza, "Peer Pressure and Loan Repayment: Evidence from a Natural Experiment," working paper (2010).

18. Abhijit Banerjee and Kaivan Munshi, "How Efficiently Is Capital Allocated? Evidence from the Knitted Garment Industry in Tirupur," *Review of Economic Studies* 71 (2004): 19–42.

19. Abhijit Banerjee and Esther Duflo, "Do Firms Want to Borrow More? Testing Credit Constraints Using a Directed Lending Program," working paper (2004).

20. Dilip Mookherjee, Sujata Visaria, and Ulf von Lilienfeld-Toal, "The Distributive Impact of Reforms in Credit Enforcement: Evidence from Indian Debt Recovery Tribunals," BREAD Working Paper 254 (2010).

Chapter 8

1. Gary Becker and Casey Mulligan, "The Endogenous Determination of Time Preference," *Quarterly Journal of Economics* 112 (3) (1997): 729–758.

2. Stuart Rutherford, *The Poor and Their Money: Microfinance from a Twenty-First-Century Consumer's Perspective* (New York: Oxford University Press, 2001); and Daryl Collins,

Jonathan Morduch, Stuart Rutherford, and Orlanda Ruthven, *Portfolios of the Poor: How the World's Poor Live on $2 a Day* (Princeton and Oxford: Princeton University Press, 2009).

3. Pascaline Dupas and Jonathan Robinson, "Saving Constraints and Microenterprise Development: Evidence from a Field Experiment in Kenya," NBER Working Paper 14693, revised November 2010.

4. Simone Schaner, "Cost and Convenience: The Impact of ATM Card Provision on Formal Savings Account Use in Kenya," working paper (2010).

5. Esther Duflo, Michael Kremer, and Jonathan Robinson, "Why Don't Farmers Use Fertilizer? Experimental Evidence from Kenya," unpublished (2007); and Esther Duflo, Michael Kremer, and Jonathan Robinson, "How High Are Rates of Return to Fertilizer? Evidence from Field Experiments in Kenya," *American Economic Review* 98 (2) (2008): 482–488.

6. Esther Duflo, Michael Kremer, and Jonathan Robinson, "Nudging Farmers to Use Fertilizer: Theory and Experimental Evidence," forthcoming in *American Economic Review,* NBER Working Paper W15131 (2009).

7. Samuel M. McClure, David I. Laibson, George Loewenstein, and Jonathan D. Cohen, "Separate Neural Systems Value Immediate and Delayed Monetary Rewards," *Science* 306 (5695) (2004): 421–423.

8. Nava Ashraf, Dean Karlan, and Wesley Yin, "Tying Odysseus to the Mast: Evidence from a Commitment Savings Product in the Philippines," *Quarterly Journal of Economics* 121 (2) (2006): 635–672.

9. Pascaline Dupas and Jonathan Robinson, "Savings Constraints and Preventive Health Investments in Kenya," UCLA (2010), mimeo.

10. Abhijit Banerjee and Sendhil Mullainathan, "The Shape of Temptation: Implications for the Economic Lives of the Poor," MIT (April 2010), mimeo.

11. See, for example, Kathleen D. Vohs and Ronald J. Faber, "Spent Resources: Self-Regulatory Resource Availability Affects Impulse Buying," *Journal of Consumer Research* 33 (March 2007): 537–548. In one experiment reported in this paper, college students were instructed to spend a few minutes writing down their thoughts, without thinking of a white bear. Given $10 afterward to save or spend on a small assortment of products, they spent much more money than students who had free-associated without having to avoid thoughts of bears.

12. For a description of the Townsend Thai data and detailed accounting conventions used there, see Krislert Samphantharak and Robert Townsend, *Households as Corporate Firms: Constructing Financial Statements from Integrated Household Surveys*, Cambridge University Press Econometric Society Monograph No. 46 (2010). We define household resources as average net assets from the household balance sheet. Net assets include all savings, capital, and household assets net of borrowing.

13. Dean Karlan and Sendhil Mullainathan, "Debt Cycles," work in progress (2011).

14. Abhijit Banerjee, Esther Duflo, Rachel Glennerster, and Cynthia Kinnan, "The Miracle of Microfinance?," MIT, manuscript (2010). Bruno Crépon, Florencia Devoto, Esther Duflo, and William Parienté, "Evaluation d'impact du microcrédit en zone rural: Enseignement d'une expérimentation randomisée au Maroc," MIT, mimeo.

Chapter 9

1. C. K. Prahalad, *The Fortune at the Bottom of the Pyramid* (Philadelphia: Wharton School Publishing, 2004).

2. Tarun Khanna, *Billions of Entrepreneurs: How China and India Are Reshaping Their Futures—and Yours* (Boston: Harvard Business School Publishing, 2007).

3. Suresh de Mel, David McKenzie, and Christopher Woodruff, "Returns to Capital in Microenterprises: Evidence from a Field Experiment," *Quarterly Journal of Economics* 123 (4) (2008): 1329–1372.

4. David McKenzie and Christopher Woodruff, "Experimental Evidence on Returns to Capital and Access to Finance in Mexico," *World Bank Economic Review* 22 (3) (2008): 457–482.

5. Abhijit Banerjee, Raghabendra Chattopadhyay, Esther Duflo, and Jeremy Shapiro, "Targeting the Hard-Core Poor: An Impact Assessment," MIT (2010), mimeo.

6. For a description of the Townsend data, see Krislert Samphantharak and Robert Townsend, "Households as Corporate Firms: Constructing Financial Statements from Integrated Household Surveys," University of California at San Diego and University of Chicago (2006), mimeo.

7. The study in Peru is Dean Karlan and Martin Valdivia, "Teaching Entrepreneurship: Impact of Business Training on Microfinance Clients and Institutions," *Review of Economics and Statistics*, forthcoming. The study in India is Erica Field, Seema Jayachandran, and Rohini Pande, "Do Traditional Institutions Constrain Female Entrepreneurship? A Field Experiment on Business Training in India," *American Economic Review Papers and Proceedings* 100 (2) (May 2010): 125–129.

8. Alejandro Drexler, Greg Fischer, and Antoinette Schoar, "Keeping It Simple: Financial Literacy and Rules of Thumb," London School of Economics, mimeo.

9. Suresh de Mel, David McKenzie, and Christopher Woodruff, "Are Women More Credit Constrained? Experimental Evidence on Gender and Microenterprise Returns," *American Economic Journal: Applied Economics* 1 (3) (July 2009): 1–32.

10. Andrew Foster and Mark Rosenzweig, "Economic Development and the Decline of Agricultural Employment," *Handbook of Development Economics* 4 (2007): 3051–3083.

11. David Atkin, "Working for the Future: Female Factory Work and Child Height in Mexico," working paper (2009).

12. Kaivan Munshi, "Networks in the Modern Economy: Mexican Migrants in the U.S. Labor Market," *Quarterly Journal of Economics* 118 (2) (2003): 549–599.

13. Cally Ardington, Anne Case, and Victoria Hosegood, "Labor Supply Responses to Large Social Transfers: Longitudinal Evidence from South Africa," *American Economic Journal* 1 (1) (January 2009): 22–48.

Chapter 10

1. The argument was made in the 1970s by Peter Bauer; see e.g., Peter Thomas Bauer, *Dissent on Development* (Cambridge: Harvard University Press, 1972).

2. Ritva Reinikka and Jakob Svensson, "The Power of Information: Evidence from a Newspaper Campaign to Reduce Capture," working paper, IIES, Stockholm University (2004).

3. See, for example, Easterly's post on randomized control trials, available at http:// aidwatchers.com/2009/07/development-experiments-ethical-feasible-useful/.

4. See, for example, Jeffrey Sachs, "Who Beats Corruption," available at http://www .project-syndicate.org/commentary/sachs106/English.

5. Daron Acemoglu and James Robinson, *Economic Origins of Dictatorship and Democracy* (New York: Cambridge University Press, 2005).

6. Daron Acemoglu and James Robinson, *Why Nations Fail* (forthcoming, Crown, 2012).

7. See, for example, Tim Besley and Torsten Persson, "Fragile States and Development Policy" (manuscript, November 2010), which argues that fragile states are a key symptom of

underdevelopment in the world and that such states are incapable of delivering basic services to their citizens.

8. Daron Acemoglu, Simon Johnson, and James Robinson, "The Colonial Origins of Comparative Development: An Empirical Investigation," *American Economic Review* 91 (5) (2001): 1369–1401.

9. Abhijit Banerjee and Lakshmi Iyer, "History, Institutions, and Economic Performance: The Legacy of Colonial Land Tenure Systems in India," *American Economic Review* 95 (4) (2005): 1190–1213.

10. Dwyer Gunn, "Can 'Charter Cities' Change the World? A Q&A with Paul Romer," *New York Times,* September 29, 2009; and see "Charter Cities," available at http://www.chartercities.org.

11. Paul Collier, *The Bottom Billion: Why the Poorest Countries Are Failing and What Can Be Done About It* (New York: Oxford University Press, 2007); and Paul Collier, *Wars, Guns, and Votes: Democracy in Dangerous Places* (New York: HarperCollins, 2009).

12. William Easterly, "The Burden of Proof Should Be on Interventionists—Doubt Is a Superb Reason for Inaction," *Boston Review* (July–August 2009).

13. See Rajiv Chandrasekaram, *Imperial Life in the Emerald City: Inside Iraq's Green Zone* (New York: Knopf, 2006), as well as Easterly's insightful critique of the army operation manual, available at http://www.huffingtonpost.com/william-easterly/will-us-armys-development_b_217488.html.

14. William Easterly, "Institutions: Top Down or Botton Up," *American Economic Review: Papers and Proceedings* 98 (2) (2008): 95–99.

15. See *The White Man's Burden,* p. 133.

16. Ibid., p. 72.

17. William Easterly, "Trust the Development Experts—All 7 Billion," *Financial Times,* May 28, 2008.

18. *The White Man's Burden,* p. 73.

19. Marianne Bertrand, Simeon Djankov, Rema Hanna, and Sendhil Mullainathan, "Obtaining a Driving License in India: An Experimental Approach to Studying Corruption," *Quarterly Journal of Economics* (November 2007): 1639–1676.

20. See his presentation on the subject, available at http://dri.fas.nyu.edu/object/withoutknowinghow.html.

21. Rohini Pande and Christopher Udry, "Institutions and Development: A View from Below," Yale Economic Growth Center Discussion Paper 928 (2005).

22. Monica Martinez-Bravo, Gerard Padro-i-Miquel, Nancy Qian, and Yang Yao, "Accountability in an Authoritarian Regime: The Impact of Local Electoral Reforms in Rural China," Yale University (2010), manuscript.

23. Benjamin Olken, "Monitoring Corruption: Evidence from a Field Experiment in Indonesia," *Journal of Political Economy* 115 (2) (April 2007): 200–249.

24. Abhijit Banerjee, Esther Duflo, Daniel Keniston, and Nina Singh, "Making Police Reform Real: The Rajasthan Experiment," draft paper, MIT (2010).

25. Thomas Fujiwara, "Voting Technology, Political Responsiveness, and Infant Health: Evidence from Brazil," University of British Columbia, mimeo (2010).

26. World Bank, *World Development Report 2004: Making Services Work for Poor People* (2003).

27. Raghabendra Chattopadhyay and Esther Duflo, "Women as Policy Makers: Evidence from a Randomized Policy Experiment in India," *Econometrica* 72 (5) (2004): 1409–1443.

28. Leonard Wantchekon, "Clientelism and Voting Behavior: Evidence from a Field Experiment in Benin," *World Politics* 55 (3) (2003): 399–422.

29. Abhijit Banerjee and Rohini Pande, "Ethnic Preferences and Politician Corruption," KSG Working Paper RWP07-031 (2007).

30. Nicholas Van de Walle, "Presidentialism and Clientelism in Africa's Emerging Party Systems," *Journal of Modern African Studies* 41 (2) (June 2003): 297–321.

31. Abhijit Banerjee, Donald Green, Jennifer Green, and Rohini Pande, "Can Voters Be Primed to Choose Better Legislators? Experimental Evidence from Rural India," working paper (2009).

32. Abhijit Banerjee, Selvan Kumar, Rohini Pande, and Felix Su, "Do Informed Voters Make Better Choices? Experimental Evidence from Urban India," working paper (2010).

33. Raymond Fisman, "Estimating the Value of Political Connections," *American Economic Review* 91 (4) (September 2001): 1095–1102.

34. Abhijit Banerjee, Esther Duflo, and Rachel Glennerster, "Putting a Band-Aid on a Corpse: Incentives for Nurses in the Indian Public Health Care System," *Journal of the European Economics Association* 6 (2–3) (2009): 487–500.

35. Abhijit Banerjee, Rukmini Banerji, Esther Duflo, Rachel Glennerster, and Stuti Khemani, "Pitfalls of Participatory Programs: Evidence from a Randomized Evaluation in Education in India," *American Economic Journal: Economic Policy* 2 (1) (2010): 1–20.

36. Esther Duflo, Pascaline Dupas, and Michael Kremer, "Pupil-Teacher Ratio, Teacher Management and Education Quality" (June 2010), mimeo.

37. Rikhil Bhavani, "Do Electoral Quotas Work After They Are Withdrawn? Evidence from a Natural Experiment in India," *American Political Science Review* 103 (1) (2009): 23–35.

38. Lori Beaman, Raghabendra Chattopadhyay, Esther Duflo, Rohini Pande, and Petia Topalova, "Powerful Women: Does Exposure Reduce Bias?" *Quarterly Journal of Economics* 124 (4) (2009): 1497–1540.

39. Ana Lorena De La O, "Do Poverty Relief Funds Affect Electoral Behavior? Evidence from a Randomized Experiment in Mexico," Yale University (2006), manuscript.

40. Leonard Wantchekon, "Can Informed Public Deliberation Overcome Clientelism? Experimental Evidence from Benin," New York University (2009), manuscript.

Index

Abhijit Vinayak Banerjee was educated at the University of Calcutta, Jawaharlal Nehru University, and Harvard University. He is currently the Ford Foundation International Professor of Economics at the Massachusetts Institute of Technology. Banerjee is a past president of the Bureau for Research in the Economic Analysis of Development, a Research Associate of the NBER, a CEPR research fellow, International Research Fellow of the Kiel Institute, a fellow of the American Academy of Arts and Sciences and the Econometric Society, and has been a Guggenheim Fellow and an Alfred P. Sloan Fellow. He is the recipient of many awards, including most recently the inaugural Infosys Prize in 2009, and has been an honorary advisor to many organizations, including the World Bank and the Government of India.

Esther Duflo is Abdul Latif Jameel Professor of Poverty Alleviation and Development Economics in the Department of Economics at MIT. She was educated at the École Normale Supérieure, in Paris, and at MIT. Upon completing her PhD she was appointed assistant professor of economics at MIT, and has been there ever since. She is a fellow of the American Academy for Arts and Science and the Econometric Society. She has received numerous honors and prizes, including a John Bates Clark Medal for the best American economist under 40 in 2010, a MacArthur "genius" Fellowship in 2009, and the inaugural Calvo-Armengol International prize in 2010. She was recognized as one of the best eight young economists by *The Economist* magazine, one of the 100 most influential thinkers by *Foreign Policy* since the list has existed (2008, 2009 and 2010), and one of the "forty under forty" most influential business leaders by *Fortune* magazine in 2010.

In 2003, Banerjee and Duflo cofounded the Abdul Latif Jameel Poverty Action Lab (J-PAL), which they have been directing together ever since. J-PAL is a network of affiliated professors in five offices around the world who are united by their use of randomized control trials to answer questions critical to poverty alleviation. J-PAL's mission is to reduce poverty by ensuring that policy is based on scientific evidence. In 2009 J-PAL won the BBVA "Frontier of Knowledge" Award in the development cooperation category.

PublicAffairs is a publishing house founded in 1997. It is a tribute to the standards, values, and flair of three persons who have served as mentors to countless reporters, writers, editors, and book people of all kinds, including me.

I. F. STONE, proprietor of *I. F. Stone's Weekly*, combined a commitment to the First Amendment with entrepreneurial zeal and reporting skill and became one of the great independent journalists in American history. At the age of eighty, Izzy published *The Trial of Socrates*, which was a national bestseller. He wrote the book after he taught himself ancient Greek.

BENJAMIN C. BRADLEE was for nearly thirty years the charismatic editorial leader of *The Washington Post*. It was Ben who gave the *Post* the range and courage to pursue such historic issues as Watergate. He supported his reporters with a tenacity that made them fearless and it is no accident that so many became authors of influential, best-selling books.

ROBERT L. BERNSTEIN, the chief executive of Random House for more than a quarter century, guided one of the nation's premier publishing houses. Bob was personally responsible for many books of political dissent and argument that challenged tyranny around the globe. He is also the founder and longtime chair of Human Rights Watch, one of the most respected human rights organizations in the world.

·   ·   ·

For fifty years, the banner of Public Affairs Press was carried by its owner Morris B. Schnapper, who published Gandhi, Nasser, Toynbee, Truman, and about 1,500 other authors. In 1983, Schnapper was described by *The Washington Post* as "a redoubtable gadfly." His legacy will endure in the books to come.

Peter Osnos, *Founder and Editor-at-Large*